Java Servlets

Java
Servlets

Karl Moss

McGraw-Hill
New York • San Francisco • Washington, D.C. • Auckland • Bogotá
Caracas • Lisbon • London • Madrid • Mexico City • Milan
Montreal • New Delhi • San Juan • Singapore
Sydney • Tokyo • Toronto

McGraw-Hill

A Division of The McGraw·Hill Companies

2 3 4 5 6 7 8 9 0 AGM/AGM 9 0 3 2 1 0 9 8

P/N 043483-2
PART OF
ISBN 0-07-913779-2

The sponsoring editor for this book was Simon Yates and the production supervisor was Claire Stanley. It was set in Vendome by Multiscience Press, Inc.

Printed and bound by Quebecor/Martinsburg.

McGraw-Hill books are available at special quantity discounts to use as premiums and sales promotions, or for use in corporate training programs. For more information, please write to the Director of Special Sales, McGraw-Hill, 11 West 19th Street, New York, NY 10011. Or contact your local bookstore.

 This book is printed on recycled, acid-free paper containing a minimum of 50% recycled de-inked fiber.

All brand names and product names are the trademarks, registered trademarks, or trade names of their respective holders.

CONTENTS

	Acknowledgments	ix
	Introduction	xi
Chapter 1	Servlet Overview	1
	What Are Servlets?	2
	Why Use Servlets?	3
	What Do You Need to Write Servlets?	4
	What Do You Need to Run Servlets?	4
	Summary	6
Chapter 2	The Java Web Server	7
	The JavaServer Architecture	8
	Administration	10
	Internal Servlets	28
	Accessing the Java Web Server	30
	Summary	31
Chapter 3	Your First Servlet	33
	The Basic Flow	34
	Servlet Example: Properties	36
	Summary	42
Chapter 4	Web Server Alternatives: JRun	43
	What Is JRun?	44
	Administration	45
	More Free Stuff	51
	Summary	51
Chapter 5	Servlet Chaining	53
	What Is Servlet Chaining?	54
	Chaining Example: Table Filter	54
	Triggering a Servlet Chain	58
	Summary	68

Chapter 6   Server-Side Includes   69

What Are Server-Side Includes?   70
The Servlet Tag Syntax   71
Server-Side Includes Example: Echo Servlet Tag   72
Server-Side Includes Example: Standard Header
and Standard Footer   76
Summary   81

Chapter 7   HTML Forms   83

HTML Forms or Java Applets?   84
Form Basics   84
The EchoSurvey Servlet   108
Summary   111

Chapter 8   Using JDBC in Servlets   113

JDBC Overview   114
JDBC Servlet: EmployeeList   130
Connection Pooling   140
Working with Images   153
Summary   158

Chapter 9   Putting It All Together:
The Servlet Connection   159

The Challenge   160
The Servlet Connection   160
Summary   179

Chapter 10   HTTP Tunneling   181

HTTP   182
What Is Tunneling?   183
The Basic Flow   183
Tunneling for Java 1.0.2   184
New for Java 1.1: Serialization   207
Summary   227

Chapter 11   Automating Servlet Programming   229

Writing the Client Is Always the Same   230
Writing the Server Is Always the Same   232

Let Java Write the Client and Server for You   234
Summary   269

Chapter 12   Easing the Distribution Process:
                 Automatic JAR File Creation   271

Discovering Class File Dependencies   272
Opening and Reading a Class File   281
Reading the Number of Entries in the
Constant Pool   285
Putting It All Together:
The CreateArchive Application   289
Distributing an Applet   291
A Few Pitfalls   294
Summary   295

Chapter 13   Three-Tier JDBC Driver   297

JDBC Driver Types   298
The Challenge: A Lightweight JDBC Driver   299
JDBC Hurdles   301
Writing SQLServlet   302
SQLServlet Example: SimpleQueryApplet   336
Summary   346

Chapter 14   Using Servlets and RMI   347

The Challenge: Accessing Other Java Servers   348
RMI Overview   349
RMI Example: CustomerInfo   350
Converting a Servlet into an RMI Server   361
Making RMI Even Easier   361
Summary   361

Appendix   363

Index   435

ACKNOWLEDGMENTS

First and foremost I would like to thank Shanna, my wife and friend, for all her support; I appreciate that you took up the slack for the last few months. I would also like to thank Vallory, Jillian, and Austin for not complaining (too much) about their dad being attached to the computer and being in a Java-induced trance most of the time.

Thanks also to the great folks at McGraw-Hill, especially Simon Yates, for making the writing of this book as painless as possible.

A final tip of the hat goes to Deva Kumar, who went to bat for me and made this book a reality.

INTRODUCTION

Purpose and Objective

As the popularity of Java continues to soar, more and more people are taking a serious look at how to leverage this powerful language to perform useful tasks. The main focus of Java in the past has been on the client (or browser) side, specifically applets, which is only half of the picture. Until now, the server has traditionally been reserved for complex Common Gateway Interface (CGI) scripts written in C or Perl. JavaSoft has introduced the Java servlet API, which not only serves as a CGI replacement but has all the advantages of Java.

This book is designed to provide you with an in-depth understanding of the servlet API and how to design and build real-world server applications. Throughout this book we'll be developing servlets (Java applications that utilize the servlet API) and integrating other Java technologies such as JDBC and RMI.

Who Should Read This Book

This book is for developers and programmers interested in exploiting the power of Java on a Web server. The focus of this book is on using the servlet API and solving real-world problems using Java in a client/server environment.

This book assumes you are familiar with object-oriented programming and the Java programming language.

What's on the CD-ROM?

The accompanying CD-ROM contains the following.

- JRun servlet runner from Live Software (http://www.livesoftware.com) for the following Web servers and operating systems.
  — Apache for UNIX (JRun212Apache.tar.gz)

- — Apache for Win95/NT (JRun212Apache.zip)
- — Microsoft IIS/PWS (JRun212IIS.zip)
- — Netscape Enterprise 3.x for UNIX (JRun212nes.tar.gz)
- — Netscape Enterprise 3.x for Win95/NT (JRun212nes.zip)

Please visit Live Software's Web site for up-to-date versions and information.

- ■ ServletExec servlet runner from New Atlanta Communications (http://www.newatlanta.com) for the following Web servers and operating systems.
  - — Web servers for MacOS: WebSTAR, Quid Pro Quo, AppleShare IP, WebTen (ServletExec_MacOS_1_1_1.hqx)
  - — Microsoft IIS/PWS (ServletExec_ISAPI_1_1_1.exe)
  - — Netscape FastTrack and Enterprise 3.x for UNIX (ServletExec_NSAPI_1_1_1.bin)
  - — Netscape FastTrack and Enterprise 3.x for Win95/NT (ServletExec_NSAPI_1_1_1.EXE)

Please visit New Atlanta's Web site for up-to-date versions and information.

- ■ JBuilder Integrated Development Environment from Inprise (formerly known as Borland)
- ■ Source code for all the applications developed in this book

Java Servlets

Servlet
Overview

The Internet has brought about the invention of many new technologies in client/server computing—the most notable of which is Java. Java not only specifies a computer language but serves also as a complete client/server solution where programs are automatically downloaded to the client and executed. Much of the focus in the past has been on the client-side development of applets and Graphical User Interface (GUI) components. Applets are an important part of client/server computing, but they are only half of the picture. We're going to take an in-depth look at the other half of the picture—servlets.

What Are Servlets?

A servlet can be thought of as a server-side applet. Servlets are loaded and executed by a Web server in the same manner that applets are loaded and executed by a Web browser. As shown in Figure 1.1, a servlet accepts requests from a client (via the Web server), performs some task, and returns the results.

The following list describes the basic flow when using servlets.

- The client (most likely a Web browser) makes a request via HTTP.
- The Web server receives the request and forwards it to the servlet. If the servlet has not yet been loaded, the Web server will load it into the Java virtual machine and execute it.
- The servlet will receive the HTTP request and perform some type of process.
- The servlet will return a response back to the Web server.
- The Web server will forward the response to the client.

Because the servlet is executing on the server, the security issues usually associated with applets do not apply. This opens up a tremendous number of opportunities that are not possible, or at least are very difficult, when working with applets. Communicating with legacy systems via CORBA, RMI, sockets, and native calls are just a few examples. Also keep in mind that the Web browser does not communicate directly with a servlet; the servlet is loaded and executed by the Web server. This means that if your Web server is secure behind a firewall, then your servlet is secure as well.

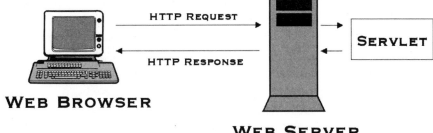

Figure 1.1
Basic servlet flow.

Why Use Servlets?

In their most basic form, servlets are a great replacement for Common Gateway Interface (CGI) scripts. CGI scripts are typically written in Perl or C and are usually tied to a particular server platform. Since servlets are written in Java, they are immediately platform independent. Java's promise of write once, run anywhere can now be realized on the server as well. Servlets have other distinct advantages over CGI scripts.

- Servlets are persistent. Servlets are loaded only once by the Web server and can maintain services (such as a database connection) between requests. CGI scripts, on the other hand, are transient. Each time a request is made to a CGI script, it must be loaded and executed by the Web server. When the CGI script is complete, it is removed from memory and the results are returned to the client. All program initialization (such as connecting to a database) must be repeated each time a CGI script is used.

- Servlets are fast. Since servlets only need to be loaded once, they offer much better performance over their CGI counterparts.

- Servlets are platform independent. As mentioned before, servlets are written in Java, which inherently brings platform independence to your development effort.

- Servlets are extensible. Since servlets are written in Java, this brings all of the other benefits of Java to your servlet. Java is a robust, object-oriented programming language, which easily can be extended to suit your needs.

- Servlets are secure. The only way to invoke a servlet from the outside world is through a Web server. This brings a high level of security, especially if your Web server is protected behind a firewall.

- Servlets can be used with a variety of clients. While servlets are written in Java, we'll see throughout this book that you can use them just as easily from Java applets as from HTML.

The number of ways to use servlets is limited only by your imagination. If you think about all of the services available on the server that you have access to, such as database servers and legacy systems, the possibilities are virtually endless.

What Do You Need to Write Servlets?

JavaSoft has done its best to make servlet development quick and easy. The result of this effort is the Java Servlets Development Kit (JSDK), which can be downloaded from the JavaSoft home page (http://java.sun.com). The JSDK is included as part of the Java Development Kit starting with version 1.2. If you are still using JDK version 1.1, you'll have to download the JSDK version 1.0.1 separately. Included in the JSDK is the Java servlet API, which is a standard Java extension API. This means that while it is not part of the core Java framework (which must always be part of all products bearing the Java brand), it will be made available by vendors as add-on packages. The servlet API is found in the javax.servlet package.

What Do You Need to Run Servlets?

As previously mentioned, all that is required to run servlets is a Web server that supports the servlet API. The grandfather of them all is the Java Web server from JavaSoft. Chapter 2 is devoted to the configuration and special features of the Java Web server. Tables 1.1 and 1.2 give partial listings of server implementations and server add-ons provided

TABLE 1.1

Third-Party
Server
Products
Supporting
Java Servlets

Vendor	Product
Apache	Apache JServ
ATG	Dynamo Application Server
Cybotics	Cybotics Search Engine
IBM	Internet Connection Server
KonaSoft	KonaSoft Enterprise Server
Lotus	Domino Go Webserver
Novocode	NetForge Web Server
O'Reilly	WebSite Professional
Tandem	iTP WebServer
W3C	Jigsaw HTTP Server
WebLogic	Tengah Application Server

by third-party vendors. We'll take a closer look at one server add-on in Chapter 4, when we explore JRun from Live Software.

You also need to remember that in order to use servlets, you'll definitely need some type of client application that invokes the servlet. The most basic form of client application we'll be looking at is HTML. HTML is very lightweight and is universally supported by all Web browsers. We'll also be exploring how to leverage the power of servlets from within applets. While you will need to use a Java-enabled Web browser (and be aware of the version of Java supported), using applets can be tremendously beneficial; not only do you solve distribution and portability problems by using applets, but they are a great way to develop interactive client/server systems.

TABLE 1.2

Third-Party
Add-On
Products
Supporting
Java Servlets

Vendor	Product
IBM	Servlet Express
Live Software	JRun
New Atlanta	ServletExec
Unicom	Servlet CGI Development Kit

Summary

We've just taken a very quick look at Java servlets—what they are, why you should use them, and what you need to write and run servlets.

In the next chapter, we're going to take a look at the Java Web server from JavaSoft. The Java Web server was the first to support servlets and is an excellent example of an industrial-strength Java application.

# CHAPTER 2

The Java
Web Server

In this chapter, we will explore the Java Web server provided by JavaSoft. The Java Web server is an implementation of the Java-Server architecture, which defines a generic server and service framework. Before looking at the Java Web server, let's take a look at the JavaServer architecture and the framework that it defines.

The JavaServer Architecture

Since the summer of 1996, JavaSoft has been busy defining a framework for extending Java into the world of the server. This framework, known as the JavaServer architecture, defines services, the server process, and the servlet API. The Java Web server was the first to implement these frameworks completely in Java.

The Service Framework

The service framework defines a set of interfaces for implementing services that interact with clients using multiple handler threads. A service is defined as an implementation of an individual protocol, such as HTTP or FTP. Note that only connection-based protocols are currently defined; datagram-based support will be added in the future. The core service classes provided by the JavaServer architecture include administration, thread management, connection management, session management, and security.

When a service is initiated, it will acquire a specific server socket. After acquiring a server socket, the service will create a pool of handler threads (see Figure 2.1); each thread will sit idle waiting for a connection request. Once a connection request has been received, a handler thread will perform all protocol interactions on that connection.

The size of the handler thread pool is dynamic and has both upper and lower size bounds. The size of the thread pool can also be changed while a service is running via an administration tool, as we'll see later.

The Server Framework

A server is one instance of a Java virtual machine. One server can support multiple concurrent services, which are configured to start when

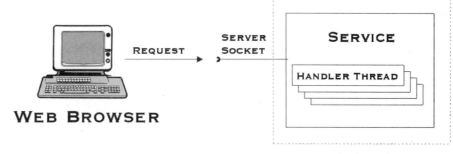

Figure 2.1

JavaServer service handler threads.

the server process is initiated. A server, such as the Java Web server, will most likely start an administrative service, an HTTP service, and perhaps a Web proxy service, as illustrated in Figure 2.2. Services can be added, removed, or configured while the server is running.

The Servlet Framework

A servlet is a Java object that conforms to a specific interface, as defined by the JavaServer architecture. Servlets are loaded and invoked by services, and a service can utilize multiple servlets (see Figure 2.3). You can think of servlets as an easy way to extend the functionality of a server—either with internal servlets, which are provided with the server, or with user-written servlets, which function as add-ons. We'll be taking a closer look at some of the internal servlets used by the Java Web server later

Figure 2.2

JavaServer example services.

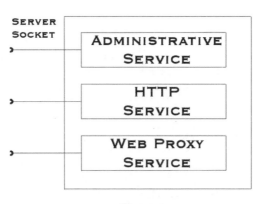

Figure 2.3

JavaServer example services using servlets.

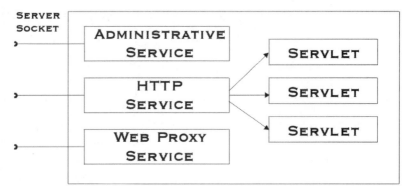

in this chapter. As with services, servlets can be added, removed, or configured while the server is running.

Administration

As mentioned previously, one of the aspects of the JavaServer architecture is the definition of administration interfaces for the server, services, and servlets. The Java Web server administration tool is a great example of a Java applet utilizing these interfaces to interact with the server.

By default the Java Web server administration tool is installed on port 9090; this is a configurable option that can easily be changed from within the administration tool. To invoke the administration tool, you need to access the administration port of the server with a Java-enabled Web browser. Throughout this book, I'll be using both Microsoft Internet Explorer (version 4.0) and Netscape Navigator (version 4.0). Figure 2.4 shows the login screen of the Java Web server administration tool for server "larryboy" on the default port of 9090.

The default user name and password are both "admin." As we'll see, configuring additional users is quite simple through the administration tool. Figure 2.5 shows the main administration screen after successfully logging in.

This screen is also known as the "Manage Server and Services" page; it shows the current state of the Java Web server and the services that are

Figure 2.4

Java Web server
administration login.

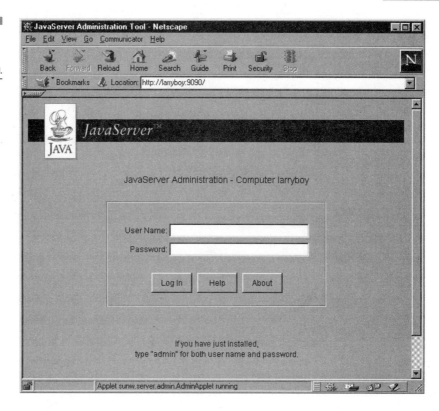

installed and currently running. Remember that a JavaServer (in this case the Java Web server) is made up of one server process and one or more services. The "Manage Server and Services" page shows the services that make up the Java Web server.

- Web service—A standard HTTP protocol service, which, by default, is installed on port 8080.

- Secure Web service—A secure HTTP protocol service (known as SHTTP), which, by default, is installed on port 7070. The SHTTP service is available only for licensed copies of the Java Web server.

- Proxy service—A Web proxy, which, by default, is installed on port 6060. A Web proxy can be installed to improve Web server performance through advanced caching.

To manage a service, you can either click on the service and press the Manage button or double-click on the service. To start or stop a service, use the Restart and Stop buttons, respectively. All of the Java Web server

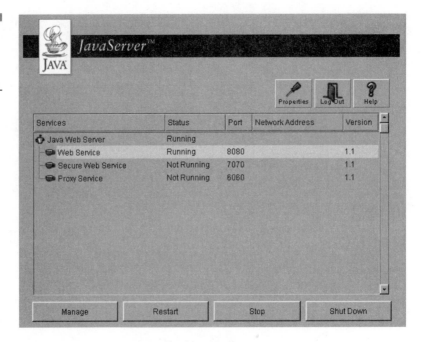

services are very similar in their administration; let's take a closer look at the Web service administration.

Web Service Administration

Administering the Web service allows you to control how the HTTP Web service behaves. Figure 2.6 shows the main page for managing the HTTP Web service.

Notice the icons across the top of the page. These icons define the administration controls available for the service. Along the left side of the page is a tree showing the different areas for the current control. Let's take a closer look at the administration controls available for the HTTP Web service: setup, monitor, security, and servlets.

Setup Control   The setup control allows for the general configuration of the Web service. The setup control is grouped into several different areas (as shown in the tree on the left side of the screen in Figure 2.6).

Figure 2.6

Java Web server
main HTTP Web
service page.

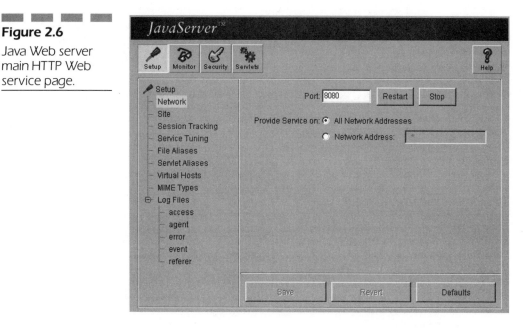

Network Setup   The network setup area allows you to define and modify basic network settings for the Web service (shown in Figure 2.7).
These options are as follows.

- Port—This defines the port number that the HTTP Web service
  will listen on for client requests. The default is 8080, but you can
  change the port to be any number between 1 and 65535. If you
  change the port number, you must stop and restart the Web service before the change takes effect.

- Provide service on—If your service is set up for multihoming, you
  can accept connections from more than one network address.

Figure 2.7

Java Web server
network settings
page.

Figure 2.8

Java Web server site contents settings page.

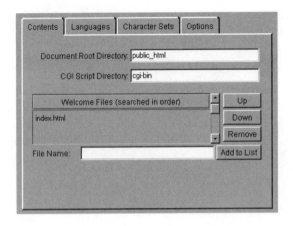

Site Setup   The site setup area allows you to define and modify basic settings for the Web service. The site setup is split into four tabs: Contents, languages, character sets, and options. Figure 2.8 shows the contents tab. These options are as follows.

- Document root directory—This is the name of the directory on the server where HTML files are placed. The default value is "public_html"—for example, if the Java Web server were installed in the "/JavaWebServer" directory, the default location for HTML files would be "/JavaWebServer/default_html."

- CGI script directory—This is the name of the relative directory where CGI scripts can be found—that is, the subdirectory beneath the Java Web server home directory.

- Welcome files—This is a list of welcome documents that will be searched for and displayed when a user enters your Web site. If a user enters the site without specifying a document, the Web server will search for a welcome file (in the order specified) and display the first one found.

The languages tab for the site setup defines the language used for the Web site's documents.

The character sets tab for the site setup defines character sets used by the Web server.

The options tab for the site setup (shown in Figure 2.9) allows you to set basic options within the Web server. These options are as follows.

Figure 2.9

Java Web server site options settings page.

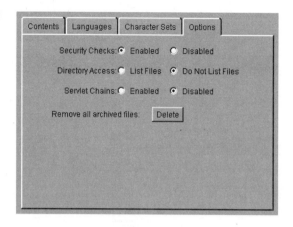

- Security checks—This setting controls whether the server should check access control lists before allowing connections. The default is enabled.

- Directory access—This setting controls whether files will be listed if a client attempts to access a directory in the server. If an Index.html file is given in the general settings tab, then it will always be displayed if a directory is accessed. If an Index.html file is not given, and the directory access is "List Files," a list of all the files in the directory is returned to the client; if the directory access is "Do Not List Files," the client is refused access to the server. The default is "Do Not List Files."

- Servlet chains—This setting controls whether servlets can be chained. We'll explore servlet chaining in Chapter 5. The default is disabled.

Session Tracking Setup   The session tracking setup (shown in Figure 2.10) allows you to control whether the Web service will utilize session tracking. Session tracking allows clients to establish a session with the Web service and can maintain state information that spans multiple connections and requests.

Service Tuning Setup   The service tuning area allows you to modify performance settings for the Web service. The service tuning area is split into three tabs: general, handler threads, and connection persistence.

Figure 2.10

Java Web server
session tracking
settings page.

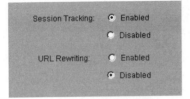

Figure 2.11 shows the fields for the general service tuning tab. These fields are as follows.

- Capacity—This is the maximum number of simultaneous client connections that are allowed for the Web service. The default is 50.

- Memory cache—This field defines the number of megabytes used by the server cache. A value of 0 disables the cache; otherwise, the value must be between 1 and 8. The default value is 1 megabyte.

Figure 2.12 shows the fields for the handler threads tab. Remember from the JavaServer architecture overview that a pool of handler threads is created when the service is started. A handler thread sits idle until a client request is made on the service socket; when a request is made, the handler thread services the request. The fields are as follows.

- Minimum—This is the minimum number of handlers in the pool. The default is 10.

- Maximum—This is the maximum number of handlers in the pool. The default is 50.

Figure 2.11

Java Web server
general service
tuning page.

Figure 2.12

Java Web server
handler threads
tuning page.

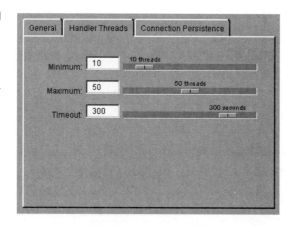

Figure 2.12

Java Web server
handler threads
tuning page.

- Timeout—This is the timeout value for an idle handler in seconds. If a handler is idle for more than the given timeout value, it is removed from the pool (unless it would bring the pool size below the minimum). The default is 300 seconds.

Figure 2.13 shows the fields for the connection persistence tab. These fileds are as follows.

- Keep alive—This sets the number of HTTP requests allowed on a single TCP/IP connection before connection is terminated. The default is 5.

- Timeout—This is the timeout value for a connection in seconds. The default is 30 seconds.

Figure 2.13

Java Web server
connection
persistence tuning
page.

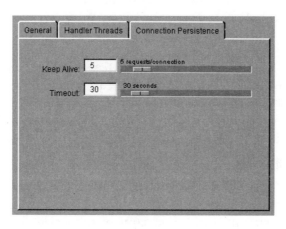

Figure 2.14

Java Web server file alias page.

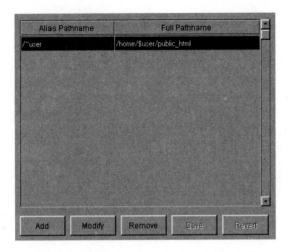

File Alias Setup   The file alias area allows you to create aliases, or short-cuts, to commonly used files or to create a nickname for a lengthy file path. Figure 2.14 shows the fields for the file alias area. These fields are as follows.

- Alias pathname—Defines the alias, or shortcut, for the pathname.
- Full pathname—Defines the full pathname.

Consider a scenario where you have an HTML file named "Stats.html" located at "cars/ford/mustang/1965." Normally, a client would access this file on the server "larryboy" by using the address "http://larryboy/cars/ford/mustang/1965/Stats.html." You could set up an alias pathname of "65Stang" for the full pathname of "cars/ford/mustand/1965," thus allowing the client to access the file by using the address "http://larryboy/65Stang/Stats.html."

Servlet Alias Setup   The servlet alias area allows you to create aliases for commonly used servlets, to create a nickname for a servlet with a lengthy name, or to force the invocation of servlets when a certain file name pattern is encountered. Figure 2.15 shows the fields for the servlet alias area. These fields are as follows.

- Alias—Defines the alias, or shortcut, for the servlet. You can also define file name patterns, such as "*.shtml"; server-side includes are invoked in this manner, as we'll see in Chapter 6.
- Servlet invoked—The name of the servlet to be invoked by the Web service. You can also specify multiple servlets that will be in-

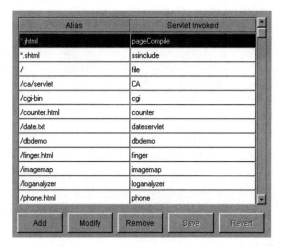

Figure 2.15

Java Web server
servlet alias page.

voked one after another (or chained); we'll be taking a closer look at servlet chaining in Chapter 5.

Virtual Host Setup   The virtual host area allows you to specify multiple host names to be serviced. This can occur in two ways.

1. A server with only one interface card and IP address—if you have configured multiple DNS host maps for a single IP address, you can register those DNS names with the Web service via the virtual host area.

2. A server with multiple interface cards and multiple IP addresses— you can register each DNS name with the Web service via the virtual host area.

Figure 2.16 shows the fields for the virtual host area. The fields are as follows.

■ Host—This is the host (or DNS) name.

■ Document root—This is the relative directory that will be used as the root for this host—for example, if the Java Web server were installed in the "/JavaWebServer" directory and its document root directory were "public_html" and the document root for the virtual host were "Alfred_Root," then the default location for HTML files on the virtual host would be "/JavaWebServer/public_html/Alfred_Root."

Figure 2.16

Java Web server virtual host page.

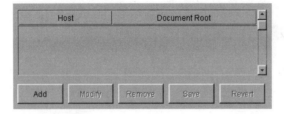

Mime Type Setup The mime type area allows you to manage the list of suffix-to-mime type mappings for the Web service. A mime type is a way to determine the contents of a file; thus, you can map an extension (such as ".wav") to a particular mime type (such as "audio/x-wav") so that the Web service knows what type of file is being handled. Figure 2.17 shows the fields for the mime type area. These fields are as follows.

- Extension—This is the file extension being mapped.
- Type/subtype—This is the mime type/subtype that the file extension is mapped to. The type defines the generic file category (such as "audio") and the subtype defines the exact type within the generic type (such as "x-wav").

Log File Setup The log file area allows you to configure the log files used by the Web services. There are five different log files.

1. Access log—This is a log containing information about incoming requests; it provides details such as remote user, remote host, and description.

2. Agent log—This is a log containing information about the client browser types.

3. Error log—This is a log containing information about service errors.

4. Event log—This is a log containing information about service events such as startup, shutdown, and servlet invocation.

5. Referrer log—This is a log containing information about file requests.

Figure 2.18 shows the fields for the log file area. Note that all the different log files use the same fields. These fields are as follows.

- Log name—This read-only field indicates which log type is currently being viewed.

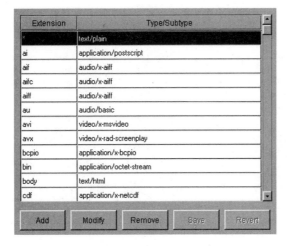

Figure 2.17

Java Web server
mime type page.

- Description—This gives a short description of the log.
- Which messages—This combo box allows you to filter which messages get logged.
- Log to—This combo box allows you to specify how the messages are to be logged. Table 2.1 shows the valid selections. Depending upon the target log type, you will be prompted for additional information such as the file name and maximum size.

Monitor Control The monitor control allows you to monitor, display, and chart log data for the Web service in a variety of ways. You can also specify how to sort and filter data by day, week, and month.

Figure 2.18

Java Web server log
file page.

TABLE 2.1

Log File
Destination
Types

Type	Description
Rolling File	Collects messages until a given threshold is reached. At that point the file is renamed and a new (empty) log file is created. The previous log file is named "logfile.1." If "logfile.1" already exists, it is renamed "logfile.2"; if "logfile.2" exists, it is renamed "logfile.3," etc.
Single File	Collects messages until a given threshold is reached. At that point messages are written starting at the beginning of the file, overwriting the previous contents.
Standard Output	Messages are written to the standard output device of the Web service, most likely the screen owned by the process.
Standard Error	Messages are written to the standard error log of the Web service.

The monitor control also allows you to view resource consumption by the Web service. Figure 2.19 shows an example resource usage screen.

Figure 2.19

Java Web server
resource usage
page.

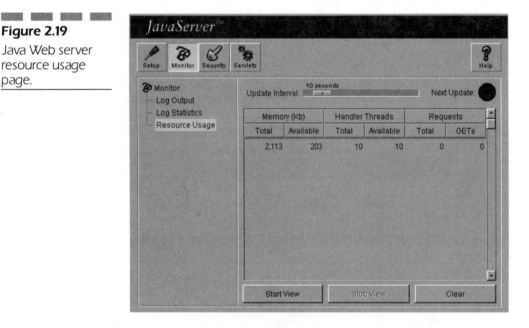

Security Control   The security control allows you to administer security for the Web service. The security control is grouped into four different areas: users, groups, access control lists, and resources.

Users Setup   The users area allows you to manage users who have access to the Web service, including the type of file and servlet access they are permitted. Each user account contains a user name, password, and security realm. Security realms are used to control the resources users have permission to access. Figure 2.20 shows the fields in the users area. Once a user has been added to a particular realm, he or she can then be granted access to certain areas by adding the user to an Access Control List (ACL); we'll see this a bit later. The fields in the users area are as follows.

- Realm—As mentioned before, a realm is used to control the resources users have permission to access.
- Name—This list contains the name of each user belonging to the security realm.

In order to change the user name or password, press the Password button and a dialog will be shown that will allow editing of these fields.

Figure 2.20

Java Web server users administration.

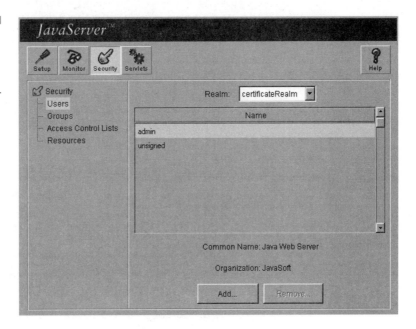

Figure 2.21

Java Web
server groups
administration.

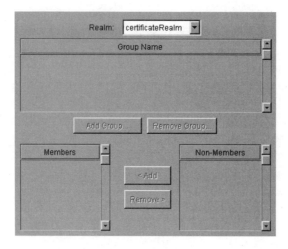

Figure 2.21

Java Web
server groups
administration.

Groups Setup   Each security realm consists of any number of security groups. The groups area allows you to manage each security group. Figure 2.21 shows the fields in the groups area. A user must belong to the realm before he or she can be added to a group. The fields are as follows.

- Realm—This is the security realm you are managing.
- Group name—This is a list of groups in the security realm. You can add a new group by pressing the Add Group... button.
- Members—This is a list of users belonging to the group currently selected in the group list.
- Nonmembers—This is a list of users belonging to the security realm but not belonging to the currently selected group.

Use the Add and Remove buttons to move users from nonmembers to members and vice versa.

Access Control Lists Setup   The access control list area allows you to administer ACLs for a particular security realm. ACLs are used to control the resources users have access to, including files and servlets. Figure 2.22 shows the fields in the ACL area. These fields are as follows.

- Realm—This is the security realm you are managing.
- Access control lists—This is a list of ACLs in the security realm. You can add a new ACL by pressing the Add ACL... button.
- Principal/permissions—This is a list of users, groups, and computers having permissions set up for the ACL currently selected in the

Figure 2.22

Java Web server
access control lists
administration.

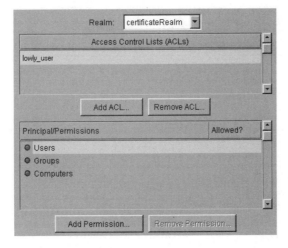

Figure 2.22

Java Web server
access control lists
administration.

ACL list. This is a tree that you can expand and collapse to
show the permissions assigned to particular users, groups, and
computers.

To add a permission for a user, group, or computer press the Add Permission... button. This dialog, shown in Figure 2.23, allows you to specify
the permissions allowed for files, folders, and servlets.

Figure 2.23

Java Web server
permissions
administration.

TABLE 2.2

File and Folder
Permissions

Type	Description
GET	Permission to retrieve information from the server
PUT	Permission to put a new copy of existing data on the server
POST	Permission to put new data on the server
DELETE	Permission to delete data from the server

TABLE 2.3

Servlet
Permissions

Type	Description
Load Servlet	Permission to load a named servlet from the server
Read Files	Permission to read any file on the server where the servlet is being executed
Write Files	Permission to write to any file on the server where the servlet is being executed
Listen to Socket	Permission to use sockets on the server where the servlet is being executed
Open Remote Socket	Permission to open a socket from within the servlet being executed
Link Libraries	Permission to use libraries loaded by `System.loadLibrary()` from within the servlet being executed
Execute Programs	Permission to execute programs from within the servlet being executed
Access System Properties	Permission to access system properties from within the servlet being executed

Table 2.2 shows the types of access you can control for files and folders, and Table 2.3 shows the types of access you can control for servlets.

Resources Setup   The resources area allows you to control access to particular server resources such as files, folders, and servlets. You control access to these resources by assigning them to an ACL. Figure 2.24 shows the fields for the resources area. These fields are as follows.

- Realm—This is the security realm you are managing.
- Resource—This is the name of the resource that is being controlled. This can be a particular file, a directory name, or a servlet.

Figure 2.24

Java Web server
resource
permissions
administration.

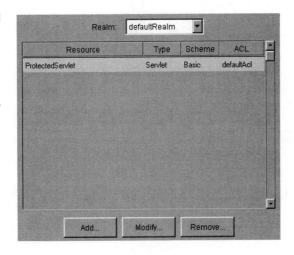

- Type—Defines the permission group of the resource: file or servlet.
- Scheme—Defines the authentication method used to protect the resource. Table 2.4 shows types of schemes for the Web service.
- ACL—The name of the access control list that controls the permissions of the resource.

Servlets Control   The servlets control allows you to manage servlet loading information. Figure 2.25 shows the fields for the servlets control page. These fields are as follows.

- Name—The unique name assigned to the servlet. Note that this does not have to be the name of the servlet class; you can assign any external name to the servlet.
- Description—A brief description of the servlet. This is only used from within the Web service.

TABLE 2.4

Authentication
Schemes

Type	Description
Basic	Sends plain-text passwords over the network.
Digest	Sends password functions over the network; not the actual text of the password. At the time of this writing very few browsers support digest authentication.

Figure 2.25

Java Web server
servlets
administration.

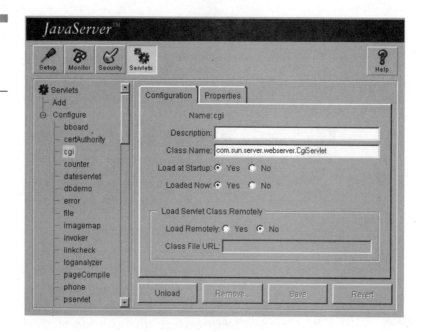

- Class name—This is the Java class name of the servlet, including the package name (if one exists).
- Arguments—A list of arguments to be passed to the servlet. Arguments are given in "key=value" pairs.
- Load at startup—Controls whether the Web service should load the servlet when the service is started.
- Loaded now—Shows whether the servlet is currently loaded. You can also load and unload the applet by changing this field.
- Load remotely—Controls whether the Web service should load the servlet from a remote location.
- Class file URL—If the servlet is being loaded from a remote location, this field contains the URL of the remote servlet class.

Internal Servlets

The JavaServer architecture was designed to allow for user extensions to the services the server provides; these types of extensions are, of course, servlets. The Java Web server capitalizes on this design by utilizing various internal servlets.

Admin Servlet

The admin servlet services requests made by the Java Web server administration tool.

CGI Servlet

The CGI servlet serves as a direct replacement for the Common Gateway Interface (CGI). The CGI servlet allows any client using CGI 1.1 functionality to utilize the Java Web server.

File Servlet

The file servlet is responsible for serving document files for the Java Web server. It includes a smart caching algorithm to increase response time for frequently accessed documents. The file servlet also examines documents for server-side includes and passes them to the server-side include servlet for further processing.

Imagemap Servlet

The imagemap servlet handles server-side imagemaps.

Invoker Servlet

The invoker servlet is responsible for invoking user-written servlets.

Server-Side Include Servlet

The server-side include servlet processes server-side includes. Server-side includes are used for embedding servlets within documents. When the file servlet recognizes that a document contains a server-side include, the document is forwarded to the Server-Side Include (SSI) servlet for processing. The SSI servlet will parse the document for the servlet tag. Once a servlet tag is found, the corresponding servlet is invoked (utilizing the invoker servlet). The output from the servlet is then merged with the original document. We'll be taking a more in-depth look at server-side includes in Chapter 5.

Accessing the Java Web Server

By default, the HTTP Web service of the Java Web server is installed on port 8080. The Web service port number is easily changed using the administration applet, as we have already seen (refer to Figure 2.7). Figure 2.26 shows the default Index.html file supplied by the Java Web server on port 8080 of server "larryboy."

Figure 2.26

Java Web server default home page.

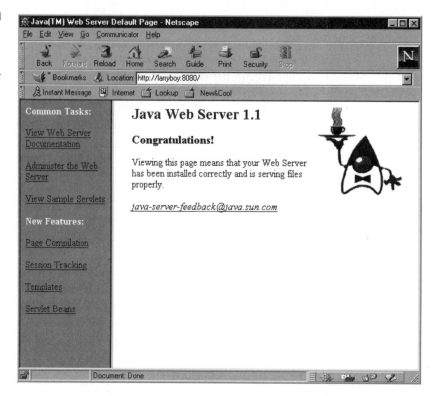

Summary

In this chapter, we've covered the foundation of the Java Web server: the JavaServer architecture. This architecture defines and implements the basic frameworks by which servers can be built. We took a closer look at the services that make up the Java Web server—specifically, the HTTP, proxy, and administration services—and the various internal servlets the Web server utilizes for specific client requests. We also focused on the Java Web server administration applet and the various configuraton and administration options available within the HTTP service.

In the next chapter, we'll be writing our first simple servlet. As you'll discover, the JavaServer architecture makes it easy for you to extend the functionality of the server by creating servlets of your very own.

Your First Servlet

N ow that we've covered the internals of the JavaServer architecture, let's actually see it in action. In this chapter, we will write a very simple servlet, which will receive an HTML POST request, process parameters, and format the HTML that will be sent back to the client (or the Web browser). If you've ever done this before with a CGI script, I'm sure you will agree that working with servlets is much easier.

The Basic Flow

Before looking at the basic flow of a servlet, let's take another look at the JavaServer architecture and how an HTTP request winds up invoking a servlet.

As Figure 3.1 illustrates, the client (Web browser) will make a request to the server to load an HTML page. The HTTP Web service within the server will receive the request, recognize that it is an HTML file read request, and invoke the file servlet to actually perform the file I/O. The HTML page will then be returned to the client and displayed within the Web browser. If the Web browser makes an HTML POST request, the HTTP Web service will again receive the request. If the POST requires that a servlet be loaded, the request is forwarded to the invoker servlet, which will then invoke the servlet. The servlet then does some type of processing and returns data back to the client via HTTP.

Figure 3.1

JavaServer HTTP request flow.

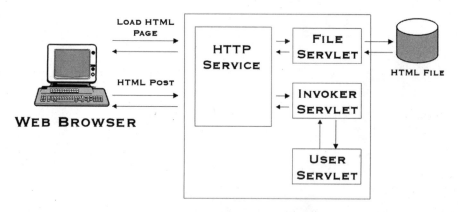

How exactly does the HTTP Web service know if a servlet should be invoked? On the client-side you need to specify a URL that names the specific servlet you want to invoke.

```
http://some.server.com/servlet/my_servlet?arguments
```

Since this URL is using HTTP, the HTTP Web service will receive the request. Let's look at how the Java Web service would resolve this URL into a servlet that needs invoking. If you think back to Chapter 2, where we discussed the administration of the server, you might remember the servlet alias setup within the Web service (refer to Figure 2.15). It is through this administration page that the alias "/servlet" is assigned to the servlet "invoker." Whenever the Web service finds "/servlet" in a URL, the invoker servlet will be called to service the request.

The basic flow within the servlet is as follows.

1. The servlet is loaded. If the servlet has not already been loaded, it will be resolved and loaded by the invoker servlet. Note that the servlet may reside locally or it may be loaded from a remote host: This is done via the servlets control page in the HTTP Web service for the Java Web server (refer to Figure 2.25). The servlet is loaded only once; multiple threads of the same servlet will handle multiple client requests.

2. The servlet is initialized. The `init()` method on the servlet is called to allow the servlet to perform some type of initialization (such as connecting to a database). The `init()` method is called only once after a servlet is loaded, and it is guaranteed to finish before any requests are made to the servlet.

3. For an HTML POST request, the `doPost()` method is called on the servlet.

4. The servlet performs some type of processing and returns the response via an output stream.

5. The response is initially received by the HTTP Web service. The Web service may perform some other type of processing, such as servlet chaining or server-side includes. We'll take a closer look at these in Chapters 5 and 6, respectively.

The JavaServer architecture has made it very easy to focus on writing just the servlet pieces that are needed to perform work; you don't need to be concerned about loading and unloading a servlet, handling the

HTTP protocol, performing chaining, invoking server-side includes, and so on. The servlet API does a great job of compartmentalizing the areas of work that need to be done.

Servlet Example: Properties

To illustrate how easy it is to write a servlet, let's take a look at one that will simply return an HTML page back to the client, containing information about the client, any parameters that were passed, and all the system properties of the server.

Writing the Servlet

There are only two basic steps in writing a servlet for use with an HTTP request.

1. Create a new servlet class that extends javax.servlet.http.HttpServlet. This class extends javax.servlet.GenericServlet and contains specialized code to parse the HTTP header and package client information into the javax.servlet.http.HttpServletRequest class. Refer to the appendix for a complete description of the API.

2. Override one or both of the doGet and doPost methods. This is where the real work of the servlet will take place.

A servlet can also optionally override the init and destroy methods to perform some type of initialization and destruction for the servlet. A good example of this would be to initialize a database connection in the init method and close the connection in the destroy method.

Our properties servlet (see Figure 3.2) is a good example of these steps. While the init and destroy methods do not perform any work, they illustrate how they are overridden. Remember that the source code for all the examples in this book can be found on the accompanying CD-ROM.

```java
package javaservlets.samples;

import javax.servlet.*;
import javax.servlet.http.*;

/**
 * <p>This is a simple servlet that will echo information about
 * the client and also provide a listing of all of the
 * system properties on the server.
 */

public class Properties extends HttpServlet
{
  /**
    * <p>Performs the HTTP POST operation
    *
    * @param req The request from the client
    * @param resp The response from the servlet
    */

  public void doPost(HttpServletRequest req,
                     HttpServletResponse resp)
    throws ServletException, java.io.IOException
    {
      // Set the content type of the response
      resp.setContentType("text/html");

      // Create a PrintWriter to write the response
      java.io.PrintWriter out =
        new java.io.PrintWriter(resp.getOutputStream());

      // Print the HTML header
      out.println("<html>");
      out.println("<head>");
      out.println("<title>Java Servlets Sample - Properties</title>");
      out.println("</head>");
      out.println("<h2><center>");
      out.println("Information About You</center></h2>");
      out.println("<br>");

      // Create a table with information about the client
      out.println("<center><table border>");

      out.println("<tr>");
      out.println("<td>Method</td>");
      out.println("<td>" + req.getMethod() + "</td>");
      out.println("</tr>");

      out.println("<tr>");
      out.println("<td>User</td>");
      out.println("<td>" + req.getRemoteUser() + "</td>");
      out.println("</tr>");
```

```
      out.println("<tr>");
      out.println("<td>Client</td>");
      out.println("<td>" + req.getRemoteHost() + "</td>");
      out.println("</tr>");

      out.println("<tr>");
      out.println("<td>Protocol</td>");
      out.println("<td>" + req.getProtocol() + "</td>");
      out.println("</tr>");

      java.util.Enumeration enum = req.getParameterNames();
      while (enum.hasMoreElements()) {
        String name = (String) enum.nextElement();
        out.println("<tr>");
        out.println("<td>Parameter '" + name + "'</td>");
        out.println("<td>" + req.getParameter(name) + "</td>");
        out.println("</tr>");
      }

      out.println("</table></center><br><hr><br>");

      // Create a table with information about the server

      out.println("<h2><center>");
      out.println("Server Properties</center></h2>");
      out.println("<br>");

      out.println("<center><table border width=80%>");

      java.util.Properties props = System.getProperties();
      enum = props.propertyNames();

      while (enum.hasMoreElements()) {
        String name = (String) enum.nextElement();
        out.println("<tr>");
        out.println("<td>" + name + "</td>");
        out.println("<td>" + props.getProperty(name) + "</td>");
        out.println("</tr>");
      }
      out.println("</table></center>");

      // Wrap up
      out.println("</html>");
      out.flush();
    }

  /**
   * <p>Initialize the servlet. This is called once when the
   * servlet is loaded. It is guaranteed to complete before any
   * requests are made to the servlet
   *
   * @param cfg Servlet configuration information
   */

  public void init(ServletConfig cfg)
    throws ServletException
    {
      super.init(cfg);
    }
```

```
/**
 * <p>Destroy the servlet. This is called once when the servlet
 * is unloaded.
 */

public void destroy()
   {
     super.destroy();
   }
}
```

Notice how you can use the HttpServletRequest object to gather information about the client. Also notice that you send the formatted HTML back to the client via an output stream, which was retrieved through the HttpServletResponse object; creating a PrintWriter object using this output stream makes sending HTML back to the client a breeze.

Note that in order to compile the servlet you will need to have the servlet API classes on your CLASSPATH. If you have installed the Java Web server, these classes can be found in the "lib/classes.jar" file in the Java Web server home directory.

Configuring the Server

Before our new properties servlet can be used, we need to configure the server. Let's take a look at configuring the Java Web server to use the properties servlet. As was covered in Chapter 2, we'll need to use the administration tool to configure the servlet properties. Figure 3.3 shows the servlet control page of the Web service.

We'll call the servlet "properties," but you can name it anything you wish; the name of the servlet is not tied to the name of the class.

Next the class file of the servlet needs to be placed on the CLASSPATH of the Java Web server. You may be surprised to discover that the Java Web server sets its own CLASSPATH; it does not use the CLASSPATH of the server. See the documentation with the Java Web server for details on how to modify the CLASSPATH. However, you will always be safe in placing the class file in the "/servlets" directory in the Java Web server home directory. In our case, the properties servlet is in the "javaservlets.samples" package, so "Properties.class" should be placed in "/JavaWebServer/servlets/javaservlets/samples."

Figure 3.3

Servlet control for
properties servlet.

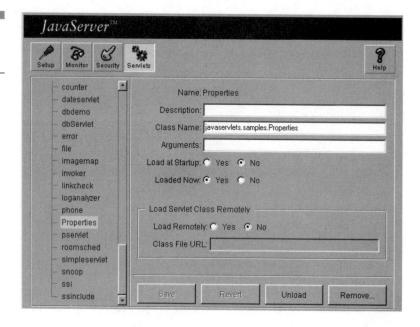

Writing the HTML to Invoke the Servlet

In order to invoke the servlet we need to create an HTML page that will POST an HTML request using the servlet URL. Figure 3.4 shows the HTML that will wait for the user to press a button and then submit the POST request.

Don't forget to move the HTML file to a place where it can be accessed by the client. This will be somewhere under the public HTML directory of your Web server. For the Java Web server this would be the "/public_html" directory in the Java Web server home directory.

See It in Action

OK, we've written the servlet, configured the Java Web server, written the HTML to invoke the servlet, and placed all the files in the appropriate places. Figure 3.5 shows the loaded HTML page, and Figure 3.6 shows the HTML page returned by the properties servlet.

Figure 3.4

Properties HTML
listing.

```html
<html>
<head>
<title>Java Servlets Sample - Properties</title>
</head>
<body>

<form METHOD="POST"
ACTION="/servlet/Properties"
ENCTYPE="x-www-form-encoded">
<h2><center>Java Servlets Sample - Properties</center></h2>
<hr>
<p>Press the button below to call a sample servlet that will
return information about you, and also list the system properties
on the server. This is done via a simple servlet.
<br><br>
<center>
<INPUT NAME="Test" TYPE="submit" VALUE="Test Properties servlet">
</center>
<br>
<hr>

</body>
</html>
```

Figure 3.5

Properties HTML
page.

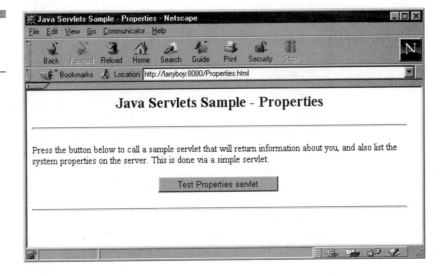

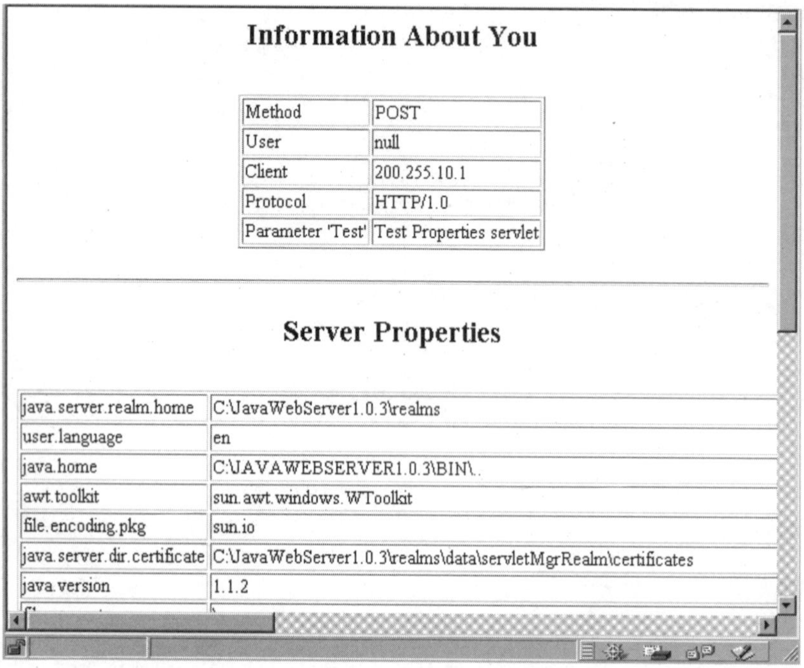

Figure 3.6

Properties HTML
response page.

Summary

In this chapter, we saw how to write a simple servlet, which accepted an HTML POST request and formatted the response as an HTML page. We outlined the basic flow of a servlet, as well as the flow of an HTTP request through the JavaServer architecture. We also covered how to configure the Java Web server to use a servlet and how to write the HTML to invoke it.

Coming up next, we'll take a look at JRun from Live Software. JRun is a free servlet runner that can be used with leading Web servers.

Web Server Alternatives: JRun

W e've already taken a look at the JavaServer architecture and the Java Web server from JavaSoft. In this chapter, we'll explore a great alternative to using the Java Web server: JRun from Live Software (www.livesoftware.com). Not only is it a great product, but it's absolutely free!

What Is JRun?

JRun is a Web server extension that allows many industry-leading servers to become 100 percent servlet API-compatible and, most importantly, invoke servlets. JRun consists of native code, which is called by the Web server directly, and Java code, which provides an interface between the Web server and the servlets being invoked. JRun adheres to the JavaServer architecture and implements the Java servlet API. This allows you to write servlets and not know (or care) in which environment they will be invoked—this fulfills the "write once, run anywhere" promise of Java.

As mentioned earlier, the great folks at Live Software are giving JRun away for free. Why would anyone give away a super product such as JRun? Here's what Live Software has to say.

> Live Software's mission is to develop products that allow for the user of Java servlets and other Java component technologies as the fundamental building block for all server-side applications. One of the major obstacles to getting our high-quality servlets in your hands is your ability to run them. JRun exists to break this barrier between our products and our customers. By providing JRun to all users at no cost, we ensure that a high-quality environment is available to anyone.

In essence, Live Software has opened the door for developers to create and deploy servlets using Web servers already in use. The implications are tremendous; if you work in a large corporation, you don't have to convince anyone to change Web servers (which would be very difficult). If you have your own personal Web server, you don't have to purchase a new server. With JRun you just need to install a no-cost, add-on extension to your Web server, which I have found to have no effect on the

TABLE 4.1

JRun Server and
Platform
Availability

Server	Platform	Bundled with Server?
Apache	Windows/95, NT/Intel, Solaris, AIX, IRIX, HPUX, Linus	
Apple's AppleShare IP	MacOS 8.x	
Microsoft Active Server Pages (ASP)	Windows 95, NT/Intel	
Microsoft Internet Information Server (IIS)	Windows NT/Intel, NT/Alpha	
Microsoft Personal Web Server (PWS)	Windows 95	
Netscape FastTrack & Enterprise Servers	Windows 95, NT/Intel, NT/Alpha, Solaris, AIX, IRIX, HPUX	
O'Reilly & Associates' WebSite	Windows 95, NT/Intel	Yes
StarNine's WebSTAR	MacOS 8.x	Yes

server other than enabling the use of servlets. In addition, JRun is also
being bundled as a standard part of several Web servers (see Table 4.1).
For the most current list, please visit Live Software's Web page
(www.livesoftware.com).

Don't be fooled into thinking that just because it's free Live Software
doesn't support it. JRun is a supported product and Live Software is
highly committed to its quality and continued support.

Administration

Since JRun adheres to the JavaServer architecture, it has many similari-
ties to the Java Web server (which we explored in Chapter 2). Let's examine JRun's features by looking at its administration.

Figure 4.1

JRun administration
tool.

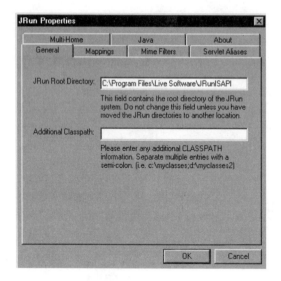

General Settings

The initial screen after starting the JRun administration program is
shown in Figure 4.1. The administration is grouped into two tabbed
dialogs.

1. JRun root directory—This is the directory in which JRun was installed. This should not be changed unless JRun has been moved
to a different location.

2. Additional CLASSPATH—This field contains any additional
CLASSPATH settings for the JRun environment. Directory entries, JAR files, and ZIP files should be separated by semicolons.

Servlet Mappings

As shown in Figure 4.2, the servlet mappings tab allows you to define
prefix and suffix mappings for your servlets.

Prefix mappings allow you to specify that a given servlet be invoked
whenever a request contains a particular prefix; for example, if a browser made a request—http://www.domain.com/foobar—and you have a
prefix mapping of "/foobar" set up to invoke the foobar servlet, then the
foobar servlet would be invoked. Any information after the prefix will
be passed on to the servlet.

Figure 4.2

JRun servlet
mappings.

Figure 4.2

JRun servlet
mappings.

The mapping of a prefix to "/" is a special case that causes the name after the prefix to be invoked as a servlet. The default is "/servlet," but you can add additional prefixes that will cause a servlet to be invoked.

Suffix mappings allow you to specify that a given servlet be invoked whenever a request contains a particular file extension. This is how server-side includes are invoked, which we'll examine in Chapter 6.

You can also set up a chain of servlets to invoke by specifying multiple servlet class names, each separated by a comma. This is a powerful way to redirect the output from one servlet to the input of another. If you have ever used UNIX piping before, you will understand the endless possibilities of servlet chaining.

Mime Filters

The mime filters tab allows you to manage the list of servlet-to-mime type mappings. A mime type is a way to determine the contents of a file; thus, you can map a particular servlet (such as uppercase servlet) to a particular mime type (such as text/html). Whenever a servlet outputs a mime type that exists in this table, the corresponding servlet will be invoked (see Figure 4.3). This, along with servlet mapping, allows you to chain servlets together. You can also specify multiple servlets to invoke, thus creating a secondary servlet chain as well.

Figure 4.3

JRun mime filters.

Figure 4.3

JRun mime filters.

Servlet Aliasing

Servlet aliasing allows you to create an alias for a commonly used servlet, to create a nickname for a servlet with a lengthy name, or to force the invocation of servlets when a certain file name pattern is encountered. Figure 4.4 shows the servlet aliasing tab.

Figure 4.4

JRun servlet aliasing.

For each alias you can also specify arguments, which will be supplied to the servlet when it is started, as well as whether the servlet should be loaded when the Web server starts. Preloading servlets can cut down on initial response times, especially if you have a resource-intensive init(), such as establishing database connections. Unlike mime filters and servlet aliases, you can only specify a single servlet to be invoked.

Multihoming

JRun supports multiple server hosts by allowing you to specify alternate servlet and log file directories, as shown in Figure 4.5 and described in the following list.

- Host name—This is the name of the virtual host that a browser would use to access your site. The host name is retrieved from the browser's host header and then searched for in this table. Note that "www.larryboy.com" and "larryboy" are two different virtual hosts.

- Servlet dir—This is the absolute directory path to the servlets directory for the host.

- Logging dir—This is the absolute directory path to the logging directory for the host.

Figure 4.5

JRun multihoming.

Java Settings

As shown in Figure 4.6, JRun also allows you to customize certain Java settings. Note that JRun does not recommend that you modify these settings without an understanding of how they will affect system performance. The default values given are those set by Sun.

- Native stack size—This is the size, in bytes, of the native stack.
- Java stack size—This is the size, in bytes, of the Java stack.
- Minimum heap size—This is the minimum size, in bytes, of the heap.
- Maximum heap size—This is the maximum size, in bytes, of the heap.
- Security manager—This is the full package name of a security manager to use within JRun. The default, Jrun security manager, does not impose any security restrictions, but you can create your own security manager to adhere to any specific needs.

Figure 4.6

JRun Java environment settings.

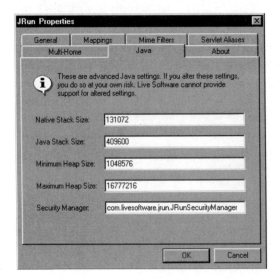

More Free Stuff

As if JRun weren't enough, Live Software also supplies a number of sample servlets to help you get started. In addition, sample projects are also included for many of the industry-leading development environments, such as JBuilder, Visual Café, and Visual Café Pro. For the latest free stuff, visit Live Software's home page (www.livesoftware.com).

Summary

In this chapter, we've taken a closer look at JRun from Live Software. JRun is a Web server add-on, which allows many leading Web servers to invoke servlets. JRun is an excellent alternative to using the Java Web server, especially when replacing an existing Web server would be impractical or impossible. JRun features servlet aliasing, servlet filtering, servlet chaining, virtual server support, dynamic reloading of modified servlets, and an intuitive administration application. Not only is JRun a super product, but Live Software provides it for free.

Next it's time to put some servlets together and perform some chaining. We'll take a look at how to chain servlets together using servlet mapping, as well as how to chain using mime types.

CHAPTER **5**

Servlet
Chaining

I n this chapter, we're going to take a look at one of the advanced features of the JavaServer architecture: servlet chaining.

What Is Servlet Chaining?

Similar to piping UNIX or DOS commands, you can chain multiple servlets together in a particular order. The output from one servlet is passed as input to the next servlet in the chain; the output from the last servlet in the chain is returned to the browser. Figure 5.1 illustrates chaining using two servlets.

Chaining Example: Table Filter

Let's jump right in and look at how to write a servlet that will be used in a chain. This servlet, table filter, will parse the output from another servlet and look for an HTML comment containing special table formatting instructions, such as the number of columns and whether the table contains a header. All lines following the table command will be formatted into an HTML table. This allows the previous servlet in the chain to simply dump out rows of comma-separated data without having to worry about formatting the data for use in an HTML table. Also,

Figure 5.1

Servlet chaining.

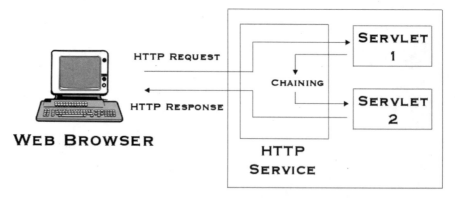

Figure 5.2

Copying header
information.

```
public class TableFilter extends HttpServlet
{
  /**
   * <p>Performs an HTTP service request
   *
   * @param req The request from the client
   * @param resp The response from the servlet
   */

  public void service(HttpServletRequest req,
                      HttpServletResponse resp)
    throws ServletException, java.io.IOException
    {
      // Get all headers set by the previous servlet and echo them

      java.util.Enumeration e = req.getHeaderNames();
      while (e.hasMoreElements()) {
        String header = (String)e.nextElement();
        String value = req.getHeader(header);
        resp.setHeader(header, value);
      }
```

if you want to change the look of the table, you only have to modify the table filter servlet.

The table filter servlet implements the HTTP service method. The first thing that needs to be done is to echo any header information set from the previous servlet. This includes information such as the content type, calling URL, remote host, and so on. Figure 5.2 shows the code necessary to set all the header information.

The next step (as shown in Figure 5.3) is to get the input stream that we can use to read the output of the previous servlet. If the content type of the input is something that we can parse (such as HTML), we'll go ahead and do so; otherwise, we'll just read all the bytes in the input stream and write them back to the browser unchanged.

Figure 5.3

Getting input and
output streams.

```
// Get the input and output streams
    ServletInputStream in = req.getInputStream();
    ServletOutputStream out = resp.getOutputStream();

    // Only process if this is a recognized MIME type
    String type = req.getContentType();

    if (type.equals("text/html") ||
        type.equals("application/x-www-form-urlencoded")) {

      // Create a buffered reader that we can use to read
      // a single line at a time
```

```
        BufferedReader br =
          new BufferedReader(new InputStreamReader(in));

        boolean inTable = false;
        int tableCols = 0;
        boolean headerRow = false;

        // Read until no more data exists

        while (true) {
          String s = br.readLine();

          // null indicates end of file

          if (s == null) {
            break;
          }

          // If we are in the middle of a table command, process
          // the line

          if (inTable) {

            // Search for the end of the table
            if (s.startsWith("<!--end table")) {
              out.println("</table></center>");
              inTable = false;
            }
            else {
              // We've got a row of a table - format it
              s = formatRow(s, tableCols, headerRow);
              headerRow = false;
            }
          }
          else {

            // Search for the start of a table
            if (s.startsWith("<!--table")) {
              int pos = s.indexOf("columns=");
              tableCols = 0;
              if (pos >= 0) {

                // Get the number of columns

                String cols = s.substring(pos + 8);
                int endPos = cols.indexOf(" ");
                if (endPos > 0) {
                  cols = cols.substring(0, endPos);
                }
                tableCols = Integer.parseInt(cols);
              }

              // Get the header flag. If 'yes' the first
              // row of data is actually a header

              pos  = s.indexOf("header=");
              if(pos >= 0) {
                String flag = s.substring(pos + 7);
```

```
                              headerRow = flag.startsWith("yes");
                          }

                          // If we have a valid number of columns, format
                          // the table

                          if (tableCols > 0) {
                            out.println(s);
                            s = "<center><table border>";
                            inTable = true;
                          }
                        }
                      }
                      out.println(s);
                  }
              } else {

                  // Unsupported MIME type; echo the contents unchanged
                  while (true) {
                    int b = in.read();
                    if (b == -1) {
                      break;
                    }
                    out.write(b);
                  }
              }

              out.close();
          }

      /**
        * <p>Formats the given line into a table row
        */

      private String formatRow(String line, int cols, boolean header)
          {
              String s = "<tr>";

              int pos = line.indexOf(",");
              int lastPos = 0;

              // Loop for each column

              for (int i = 0; i < cols; i++) {
                if (pos < 0) {
                  pos = line.length();
                }

                // Insert the proper HTML tag
                if (header) {
                  s += "<th>";
                }
                else {
                  s += "<td>";
                }

                // Find the next column data
```

```
    if (pos > 0) {
      s += line.substring(lastPos, pos);
      lastPos = pos;
      if (pos < line.length()) {
        lastPos = pos + 1;
        pos = line.indexOf(",", lastPos);
      }
      else {
        pos = 0;
      }
    }

    // Insert the proper HTML tag
    if (header) {
      s += "</th>";
    }
    else {
      s += "</td>";
    }
  }

  // Return the formatted line
  return s;
}
```

Parsing the input stream is quite simple. We'll just read each line and search for a comment line containing table-formatting information. Once found, we'll format each subsequent line as a row in the table until we find the end-of-table marker.

Triggering a Servlet Chain

Once you have assembled the servlets you will be chaining together, you can trigger the chain by aliasing, mime types, and HTML requests. Each has its own configuration issues; let's take a closer look at what it takes to configure each trigger using both the Java Web server and JRun from Live Software, although other servers can be configured in a similar manner.

Servlet Aliasing

Servlet aliasing allows you to set up a single servlet name, or alias, that represents one or more servlets. A servlet chain is given as a comma-separated list of servlets in the order in which they should be invoked.

Figure 5.4

Enabling servlet chaining in the Java Web server.

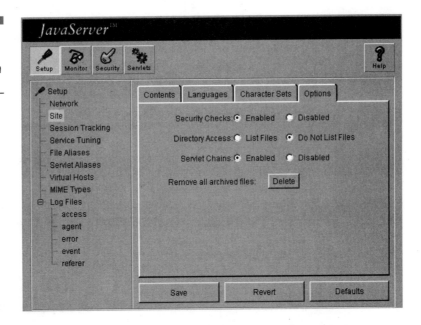

Java Web Server   Before configuring a servlet alias to trigger servlet chaining, be sure that you have enabled servlet chaining. Figure 5.4 shows the site setup administration screen, which allows you to enable chaining.

Adding a servlet alias is very straightforward. When the server receives a request for "/Elements," it will invoke the "javaservlets.samples.Elements" servlet, take the output and give it to the "javaservlets.samples.TableFilter" servlets as input, and then forward the output back to the browser. You can chain any number of servlets together simply by providing each servlet name separated by commas, as shown in Figure 5.5.

Note that at the time of this writing, Java Web server 1.1 does not properly support servlet chaining. This problem will be corrected in subsequent versions.

JRun   Configuring JRun to chain servlets is done via mapping servlets. JRun's concept of servlet aliasing is one-to-one; a single servlet can have a single alias and does not allow servlet chaining, while servlet mapping allows you to map a single name to any number of servlets, including servlet alias names. Figure 5.6 shows how to map a servlet chain in JRun.

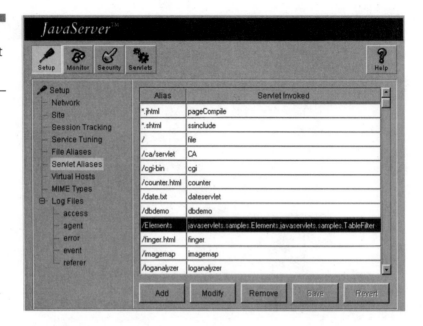

Servlet Alias Chaining Example: Elements To illustrate triggering
servlet chaining with servlet aliasing, let's write a simple servlet that will
list all the periodic elements in an HTML table. The elements servlet will

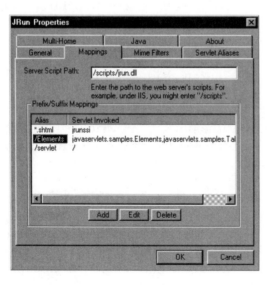

implement doGet(), which will service an HTML GET command. We'll need to set the content type and then output HTML header information. Instead of formatting the HTML table in the elements servlet, we're going to output the table-formatting information needed by the table filter servlet and then simply dump out the comma-separated data of each row (as shown in Figure 5.7).

Figure 5.7

The elements servlet.

```
public void doGet(HttpServletRequest req,
                  HttpServletResponse resp)
   throws ServletException, java.io.IOException
   {
       // Create a PrintWriter to write the response
       java.io.PrintWriter out =
         new java.io.PrintWriter(resp.getOutputStream());

       // Set the content type of the response
       resp.setContentType("text/html");

       // Print the HTML header
       out.println("<html>");
       out.println("<head>");
       out.println("<title>Java Servlets Sample - " +
                   "Periodic Elements</title>");
       out.println("</head>");
       out.println("<h2><center>");
       out.println("The Periodic Elements</center></h2>");
       out.println("<br>");

       // Output special table formatting instructions for
       // the TableFilter servlet

       out.println("<!--table columns=2 header=yes-->");

       // Output the table
       out.println("Symbol,Element");
       out.println("Ac,Actinium");
       out.println("Ag,Silver");
       out.println("Al,Aluminum");
       // Etc...
       out.println("Y,Yttrium");
       out.println("Yb,Ytterbium");
       out.println("Zn,Zinc");
       out.println("Zr,Zirconium");
       out.println("<!--end table-->");

       // Wrap up
       out.println("</html>");
       out.flush();
       out.close();
   }
```

Using the servlet mapping we configured for JRun, enter the URL for "/Elements" from your favorite browser. Figure 5.8 shows the output from the chained servlets.

To recap, the browser sent the URL request to the Web server. The Web server found a servlet mapping that matched the URL information and invoked the elements servlet. The elements servlet processed the GET request and returned the unformatted list of periodic elements back to the Web server. The Web server then discovered that a servlet chain existed and redirected the output from the elements servlet to the next servlet in the chain, table filter. Table filter then reset all the HTTP headers to match those set by the filter servlet and read all the periodic element data. These data were parsed for special table-formatting information and processed. The final product was a formatted list of periodic elements.

Figure 5.8

Output from the elements servlet chained with the table filter servlet.

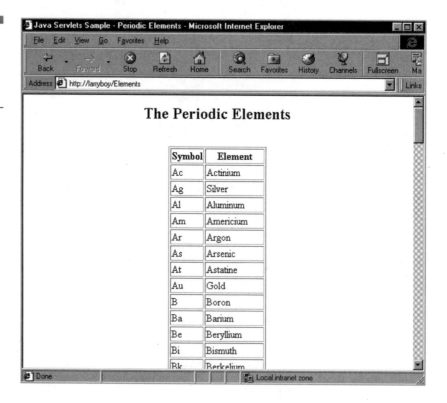

Mime Types

Another way to trigger a servlet chain is by associating a servlet with a particular mime type. When a response is generated using this mime type, the output is sent to the associated servlet. Since the mime type is specified when a servlet writes to its output stream, you can easily redirect the output to another servlet in this manner.

Java Web Server   As previously mentioned, be sure that servlet chaining is enabled for the Java Web server before continuing (see Figure 5.4). At the time of this writing, there is no Graphical User Interface (GUI) for administering mime type to servlet mappings, so you need to manually edit the "mimeservlets.properties" file. This file can be found in "<server_root>/properties/server/javawebserver/webpageservice." Figure 5.9 shows the default contents of this file. Note that the servlet name to which the mime type is mapped is actually a servlet alias name.

JRun   JRun allows mime type mappings via the administration application. As shown in Figure 5.10, you need to associate a servlet (or servlet chain) with a particular mime type.

Mime Type Chaining Example: Indy 500   To illustrate triggering a servlet chain using a mime type, let's write a servlet that will list all the

Figure 5.9

The mime "servlets.properties" configuration file.

```
# This file maps mime-types to the servlets which process them
# This is used by the filter manager to set up chains of servlets
# where the output of one servlet gets piped to the input of
# another servlet based on the mime-type that the servlet specifies
# with setContentType("mime-type")
#
# The default servlet for all mime-types is file. Do not set this
# explicitly.
#
# Entries in this file should be of the form
# mime-type/servletname
# ie.
# foo/bar=fooServlet
# where fooServlet is defined in servlets.properties
java-internal/parsed-html=ssi
java-internal/template-content=template
```

Figure 5.10

Configuring mime
type mappings with
JRun.

winners of the Indianapolis 500 since it was first run in 1911. As with the elements servlet, we'll just dump each row of the table as a comma-separated list of data and let the table filter format the HTML table for us. The only difference here is that we'll set a different mime type, which will notify the Web server to redirect the output from the Indy 500 servlet to the table filter servlet (see Figure 5.11).

Using the mime type mapping we configured in JRun, invoking the Indy 500 servlet (with its full package name) will return a formatted list of Indianapolis 500 winners (as shown in Figure 5.12). Note that we very easily could have set up an alias for the servlet instead of specifying the full package name.

To reiterate, the Web browser sends an HTTP request to the Web server containing a servlet name. The Web server invokes the servlet (Indy 500), which sets the mime type to "text/table," which we have mapped to the table filter servlet. This will cause the output from the Indy 500 to be redirected to the table filter servlet as input. The table filter servlet will format the data into an HTML table and return the output to the Web server, which, in turn, forwards the HTML page back to the browser.

Figure 5.11

The Indy 500
servlet.

```java
public class Indy500 extends HttpServlet
{
    /**
     * <p>Performs the HTTP GET operation
     *
     * @param req The request from the client
     * @param resp The response from the servlet
     */

    public void doGet(HttpServletRequest req,
                      HttpServletResponse resp)
        throws ServletException, java.io.IOException
    {
        // Create a PrintWriter to write the response
        java.io.PrintWriter out =
            new java.io.PrintWriter(resp.getOutputStream());

        // Set the content type of the response. This MIME type
        // will redirect the output to the TableFilter servlet.
        resp.setContentType("text/table");

        // Print the HTML header
        out.println("<html>");
        out.println("<head>");
        out.println("<title>Java Servlets Sample - " +
                    "Past Indianapolis 500 Winners</title>");
        out.println("</head>");
        out.println("<h2><center>");
        out.println("Past Indianapolis 500 Winners</center></h2>");
        out.println("<br>");

        // Output special table formatting instructions for
        // the TableFilter servlet

        out.println("<!--table columns=3 header=yes-->");
        out.println("Year,Driver,Average Speed");
        out.println("1997,Arie Luyendyk,145.827");
        out.println("1996,Buddy Lazier,147.956");
        out.println("1995,Jacques Villenueve,153.616");
        // Etc...
        out.println("1912,Joe Dawson,78.719");
        out.println("1911,Ray Harroun,74.602");
        out.println("<!--end table-->");

        // Wrap up
        out.println("</html>");
        out.flush();
        out.close();
    }
```

Figure 5.12
Output from the
Indy 500 servlet
chained with the
table filter servlet.

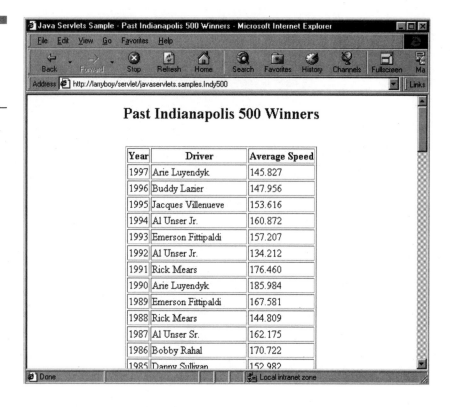

HTTP Requests

Another way to trigger servlet chaining is by specifying the servlet chain as part of the HTTP request. This may not be supported by all Web servers. To illustrate chaining with HTTP requests, let's write a simple servlet (solar system), which will return information about all the planets in our solar system. Figure 5.13 shows the code listing for the solar system servlet.

Again, the servlet will output unformatted data and let the table filter servlet format the HTML table for us. Since the Java Web server does not support triggering servlet chaining in the HTTP request, we'll use JRun. Figure 5.14 shows the output from the solar system servlet chained together with the table filter servlet.

Note that the URL specifies the servlet to be invoked. In this case it's a comma-separated list of servlets to be chained together.

Figure 5.13

The solar system
servlet.

```java
public class SolarSystem extends HttpServlet
{
  /**
   * <p>Performs the HTTP GET operation
   *
   * @param req The request from the client
   * @param resp The response from the servlet
   */

  public void doGet(HttpServletRequest req,
                    HttpServletResponse resp)
    throws ServletException, java.io.IOException
    {

      // Create a PrintWriter to write the response
      java.io.PrintWriter out =
        new java.io.PrintWriter(resp.getOutputStream());

      // Set the content type of the response
      resp.setContentType("text/html");

      // Print the HTML header
      out.println("<html>");
      out.println("<head>");
      out.println("<title>Java Servlets Sample - " +
                  "Planets In Our Solar System</title>");
      out.println("</head>");
      out.println("<h2><center>");
      out.println("Planets In Our Solar System</center></h2>");
      out.println("<br>");

      // Output special table formatting instructions for
      // the TableFilter servlet

      out.println("<!--table columns=5 header=yes-->");
      out.println("Planet,Avg. Distance from Sun," +
                  "Time to orbit,Time to spin,Moons");
      out.println("Mercury,58 million km,88 days,58.6 days,0");
      out.println("Venus,108 million km,225 days,243 days,0");
      out.println("Earth,150 million km,365.25 days,24 hours,1");
      out.println("Mars,228 million km,687 days,24.62 hours,2");
      out.println("Jupiter,778 million km,11.9 years,9.83 hours,16");
      out.println("Saturn,1427 million km,29.5 years,10.65 hours,19");
      out.println("Uranus,2870 million km,84 years,17.23 hours,15");
      out.println("Neptune,4497 million km,164.8 years,16 hours,8");
      out.println("Pluto,5913 million km,248 years,6.375 days,1");
      out.println("<!--end table-->");

      // Wrap up
      out.println("</html>");
      out.flush();
      out.close();
    }
```

Figure 5.14

Output from the
solar system servlet
chained with the
table filter servlet.

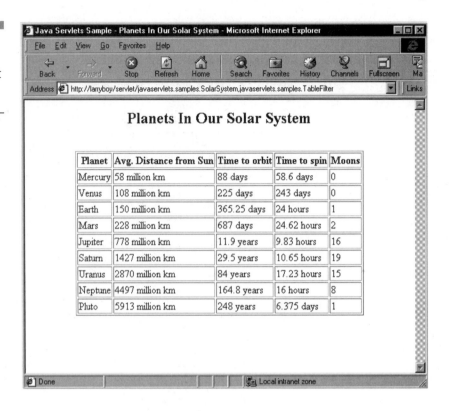

Summary

In this chapter, we've taken a look at servlet chaining, one of the advanced features of the JavaServer architecture. Servlet chaining provides the ability to pipe the output from one servlet to the input of another. Chaining allows you to divide work over a series of servlets or to combine servlets to provide new functionality.

Coming up next, we'll focus on another advanced feature of the JavaServer architecture: server-side includes. Server-side includes allow you to embed servlets within HTML documents.

Server-Side
Includes

Another advanced feature of the JavaServer architecture is server-side includes. Server-side includes enable you to embed servlets within HTML documents, allowing you to assemble a final HTML document with the aid of one or more servlets.

What Are Server-Side Includes?

As just mentioned, server-side includes allow you to embed servlets within HTML documents using a special servlet tag. This is accomplished using a special internal servlet, which processes the servlet tags, and a special suffix mapping, which invokes the server-side include servlet whenever a certain file type (.shtml being the standard) is requested. Figure 6.1 illustrates the basic flow of server-side includes. The following list describes this in more detail.

- The client browser makes a request to load an .shtml file. The Web server processes the request and invokes the file servlet to read and serve the file.

Figure 6.1

Server-side
includes.

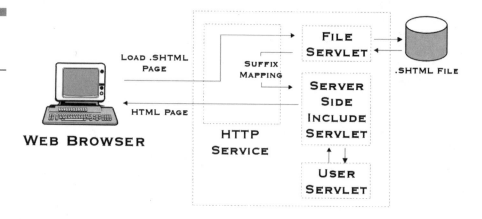

- The Web server checks its mapping table for any prefix or suffix matches. In this case, the .shtml file matches a suffix mapping, which instructs the Web server to invoke the server-side includes servlet.

- The server-side includes servlet (SSInclude) is loaded (if necessary) and invoked. The SSInclude servlet will parse the data stream that was read by the file servlet and look for servlet tags.

- For all servlet tags found, the corresponding servlet will be invoked. The output from the servlet will be merged with the data stream at the point where the servlet tag was found.

- The Web server will forward the assembled HTML page to the client.

The Servlet Tag Syntax

The following code segment is the syntax used for the servlet tag, which the server-side includes servlet will process.

```
<servlet name=SERVLET_NAME
  code=SERVLET.CLASS
  codebase=SERVLET_CODE_BASE
  INIT_PARAM1=VALUE1
  INIT_PARAM2=VALUE2
  INIT_PARAMn=VALUEn>
<param name=PARAM1 value=PARAM_VALUE1
  param name=PARAM2 value=PARAM_VALUE2
  param name=PARAMn value=PARAM_VALUEn>
</servlet>
```

Once a servlet tag is found by the server-side includes servlet, it will attempt to load the servlet as named by the "servlet name" field. If the named servlet could not be found, or no name was given, the servlet is loaded using the servlet class given in the "code" field and the servlet code base given in the "code base" field. Any remaining fields will be passed to the servlet as initialization arguments. If there are any "param" fields with the servlet tag, they will be parsed and given to the servlet as parameters that can be accessed via the servlet request object, which is provided when the servlet is invoked.

Server-Side Includes Example: Echo Servlet Tag

To illustrate the use of the servlet tag, let's take a look at a very simple server-side includes example called the echo servlet tag. This servlet will echo any initialization arguments and parameters specified in the servlet tag back to the client browser. Figure 6.2 shows the code listing for the echo servlet tag servlet.

Figure 6.2

EchoServletTag.java code listing.

```java
package javaservlets.samples;

import javax.servlet.*;

/**
 * <p>This is a simple server side include servlet that will
 * echo all of the initialization arguments and parameters specified
 * with the servlet tag of the .shtml document.
 */

public class EchoServletTag extends GenericServlet
{
  /**
   * <p>Performs the servlet service
   *
   * @param req The request from the client
   * @param resp The response from the servlet
   */

  public void service(ServletRequest req,
                      ServletResponse resp)
    throws ServletException, java.io.IOException
    {

      // Create a PrintWriter to write the response
      java.io.PrintWriter out =
        new java.io.PrintWriter(resp.getOutputStream());

      // Get an enumeration of all of the initialization
      // arguments
      java.util.Enumeration initParms= getInitParameterNames();

      // Process each argument
      while (initParms.hasMoreElements()) {

        // Get the initialization argument name
        String p = (String) initParms.nextElement();

        // Get the value
        String s = getInitParameter(p);

        // Output the name and value
        out.println("Initialization argument " + p + "=" + s);
```

```
    }
    out.println();

    // Get an enumeration of all of the parameters
    java.util.Enumeration parms = req.getParameterNames();

    // Process each parameter
    while (parms.hasMoreElements()) {

        // Get the parameter name
        String p = (String) parms.nextElement();

        // Get the value(s). Note that an array of Strings is
        // returned that may contain multiple values
        String s[] = req.getParameterValues(p);

        // Output the name and value(s)
        out.print("Parameter " + p + "=");

        if (s != null) {
          for (int i = 0; i < s.length; i++) {
            if (i > 0) {
              out.print(" AND ");
            }
            out.print(s[i]);
          }
        }
        out.println();
    }

    // Wrap up
    out.flush();
    out.close();
  }

/**
  * <p>Returns information about this servlet
  */

public String getServletInfo() {
    return "EchoServletTag - Simple Server Side Include example";
}
```

Note that I have implemented the base generic servlet class, not the HTTP servlet class we have seen in the past. This is to illustrate further that we are not performing any HTTP-specific tasks here; we are just getting arguments and parameters and dumping them to the output stream. Since we don't know the names of any of the arguments or parameters, we'll have to retrieve an enumeration and walk through them one by one.

Also notice the way that parameters are handled. Due to the fact that a single parameter can contain multiple values, the getParameterValue() method returns an array of strings. This can be a bit problematic,

Figure 6.3

EchoServlet-
Tag.shtml listing.

```
<html>
<head>
<title>Java Servlets Sample - EchoServletTag</title>
</head>
<body>
<p>The following lists the initialization arguments and
parameters specified in the servlet tag of the server side
include file that generated this HTML page.
<br><br>
<hr>
<br>
<pre>
<servlet code=javaservlets.samples.EchoServletTag
        myArg1=myValue1 myArg2=myValue2>
<param name=myParm1 value=Hello>
<param name=myParm1 value=World>
<param name=myParm2 value=myParmValue2>
</servlet>
</pre>
</body>
</html>
```

since you must always ensure that the value is nonnull before accessing an array element (such as [0]).

Figure 6.3 shows the EchoServletTag.shtml file, which we'll use to include the servlet and to specify the servlet tag values.

Unlike servlets, the .shtml file will reside in your document root directory (i.e., wwwroot). When we request the EchoServletTag.shtml file from the Web server, it will be loaded via the file servlet and the contents will be given back to the server. The server will then recognize that the name of the file ends with .shtml, which will then cause the server-side includes (SSInclude) servlet to be invoked. The SSInclude servlet will parse the data stream (which is the contents of the .shtml file) searching for all servlet tags. Once a servlet tag has been found, the corresponding servlet will be invoked and the output from the servlet will be merged into the output stream, beginning at the point where the servlet tag was found. Note that the servlet tag will not be part of the page that is returned to the client browser. Figure 6.4 shows the source of the page that is returned to the browser, and Figure 6.5 shows the browser after the page has been loaded.

Don't be surprised that the arguments and parameters aren't returned in the same order in which they were given in the servlet tag; they are stored internally in a hash table, which does not guarantee any type of ordering (other than random).

Figure 6.4

Final EchoServlet-
Tag.shtml listing.

```html
<html>
<head>
<title>Java Servlets Sample - EchoServletTag</title>
</head>
<body>
<p>The following lists the initialization arguments and
parameters specified in the servlet tag of the server side
include file that generated this HTML page.
<br><br>
<hr>
<br>
<pre>
Initialization argument code=javaservlets.samples.EchoServletTag
Initialization argument myarg2=myValue2
Initialization argument myarg1=myValue1

Parameter myParm2=myParmValue2
Parameter myParm1=Hello AND World

</pre>
</body>
</html>
```

Figure 6.5

EchoServlet-
Tag.shtml page.

Server-Side Includes Example: Standard Header and Standard Footer

Now let's take a look at a very good use for server-side includes: formatting standard headers and footers for your HTML documents. Instead of repeating the header and footer in each of your documents, you can very easily create a servlet for both the header and footer and embed them in your document with the servlet tag. Not only will this simplify writing an HTML document, but if you want to change the look and feel of your pages, you can do so in a centralized place.

Figure 6.6 shows the code listing for the standard header servlet.

Note that the title of the page will be formatted using the "title" property; this will have to be set in the servlet tag of the .shtml file.

Figure 6.7 shows the code listing for the standard footer servlet.

Now let's put our new header and footer servlets to work. Figure 6.8 shows a .shtml file that utilizes both the standard header and standard footer servlets.

Note that the "title" property is being set for the standard header servlet. I've also placed comments around the servlet tags so that you can easily see the HTML code that is generated by the included servlets. Figure 6.9 shows the page as loaded in a browser. Remember that the .shtml file and any images are loaded from your document root directory (i.e., wwwroot).

Figure 6.10 shows the source of the page that was assembled for us and returned to the browser.

▬▬ ▬▬ ▬▬ ▬▬
Figure 6.6

Standard header
listing.

```java
package javaservlets.samples;

import javax.servlet.*;

/**
 * <p>This is a simple server side include servlet that will
 * format the standard company HTML header. The title of the page
 * will be set to the value of the title property
 */

public class StandardHeader extends GenericServlet
{
  /**
    * <p>Performs the servlet service
    *
    * @param req The request from the client
    * @param resp The response from the servlet
    */

  public void service(ServletRequest req,
                        ServletResponse resp)
    throws ServletException, java.io.IOException
    {

      // Create a PrintWriter to write the response
      java.io.PrintWriter out =
        new java.io.PrintWriter(resp.getOutputStream());

      // Get the title of the page. Set to empty string if
      // no title parameter was given
      String titles[] = req.getParameterValues("title");
      String title = "";
      if (titles != null) {
        if (titles.length > 0) {
          title = titles[0];
        }
      }

      // Format the standard header
      out.println("<html>");
      out.println("<head>");
      out.println("<title>" + title + "</title>");
      out.println("</head>");
      out.println("<body>");
      out.println("<img align=\"right\"");
      out.println("     src=\"images\\CompanyLogo.jpg\"");
      out.println("     alt=\"Company Logo\">");
      out.println("<font size=\"4\" face=\"Arial\" color=\"red\">");
      out.println("<br><br>");
      out.println("<strong>" + title + "</strong></font>");
      out.println("<br><hr><br>");

      // Wrap up
      out.flush();
      out.close();
    }
```

Figure 6.7

Standard footer
listing.

```java
package javaservlets.samples;

import javax.servlet.*;

/**
 * <p>This is a simple server side include servlet that will
 * format the standard company HTML footer.
 */

public class StandardFooter extends GenericServlet
{
  /**
   * <p>Performs the servlet service
   *
   * @param req The request from the client
   * @param resp The response from the servlet
   */

  public void service(ServletRequest req, ServletResponse resp)
    throws ServletException, java.io.IOException
    {

      // Create a PrintWriter to write the response
      java.io.PrintWriter out =
        new java.io.PrintWriter(resp.getOutputStream());

      // Format the standard footer
      out.println("<br><hr>");
      out.println("<a href=\"mailto:karlmoss@mindspring.com\">");
      out.println("<img src=\"images\\mailbox.gif\"");
      out.println("     alt=\"Mailbox\">");
      out.println("</a>");
      out.println("<font size=\"-1\">");
      out.println("<i>Questions or Comments?</i></font>");
      out.println("</body>");
      out.println("</html>");

      // Wrap up
      out.flush();
      out.close();
    }
```

Figure 6.8

GollumsFifth.shtml
listing.

```
<!-- Standard Company Header -->
<servlet code=javaservlets.samples.StandardHeader>
<param name="title" value="Gollum's Fifth Riddle">
</servlet>
<!-- end -->
<dir>
This thing all things devours;<br>
Birds, beasts, trees, flowers;<br>
Gnaws iron, bites steel;<br>
Grinds hard stones to meal;<br>
Slays king, ruins town,<br>
And beats high mountain down.<br>
</dir>
<!-- Standard Company Footer -->
<servlet code=javaservlets.samples.StandardFooter>
</servlet>
<!-- end -->
```

Figure 6.9

GollumsFifth.shtml
page.

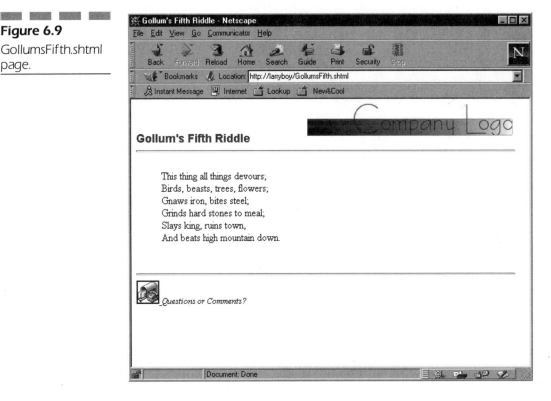

Figure 6.10

Final
GollumsFifth.shtml
listing.

```
<!-- Standard Company Header -->
<html>
<head>
<title>Gollum's Fifth Riddle</title>
</head>
<body>
<img align="right"
     src="images\CompanyLogo.jpg"
     alt="Company Logo">
<font size="4" face="Arial" color="red">
<br><br>
<strong>Gollum's Fifth Riddle</strong></font>
<br><hr><br>

<!-- end -->
<dir>
This thing all things devours;<br>
Birds, beasts, trees, flowers;<br>
Gnaws iron, bites steel;<br>
Grinds hard stones to meal;<br>
Slays king, ruins town,<br>
And beats high mountain down.<br>
</dir>
<!-- Standard Company Footer -->
<br><hr>
<a href="mailto:karlmoss@mindspring.com">
<img src="images\mailbox.gif"
     alt="Mailbox">
</a>
<font size="-1">
<i>Questions or Comments?</i></font>
</body>
</html>

<!-- end -->
```

Summary

In this chapter, we've taken a closer look at using server-side includes. Server-side includes provide us with the ability to embed servlets within documents using a special servlet tag. This servlet tag is processed by the server-side includes servlet. Whenever a servlet tag is found, the corresponding servlet is invoked and the output from the servlet is merged with the document and returned to the browser. Using server-side includes allows you to create HTML documents on the fly and can also help to centralize the source for common aspects of your documents (such as a header or footer).

Next up we'll start exploiting the power of the server by combining HTML forms with Java servlets. HTML is still a great way to gather data from a user; tie HTML with a servlet on the server and you create a dynamic data collection duo.

CHAPTER **7**

HTML Forms

I n the previous chapters, we've taken a look at the basics of servlet writing; now it's time to put these basics to use and develop a real-world example. This chapter is devoted to HTML forms, which are used to gather data from the user in many interactive Web applications.

HTML Forms or Java Applets?

We all know that HTML is a great way to deliver information on the Web, but what is the best way to gather data and deliver these data back to the server? As we'll see in later chapters, Java applets are one way to create an extremely powerful interactive Web application. However, there are some significant tradeoffs, one of which is the size of the applet, which will grow significantly as more and more functionality is added (as with any other type of program). Also, as you may well be aware, the behavior of applets can vary from browser to browser.

HTML forms, on the other hand, provide a very rich set of interactive elements and are supported by almost every browser. Most people find that HTML is very easy to write, and there are a number of HTML development environments available to make it even easier. HTML forms also have a much smaller footprint (the downloaded size of the application) than applets, which makes loading them over the Internet faster, thus reducing the amount of time that users will have to wait. Forms, coupled with a server-side program (such as a servlet), are a great way to provide robust, interactive Web applications.

Form Basics

As with every other HTML tag, forms have a start tag and an end tag. Within each form you can include any number of input elements, such as text input fields, buttons, pull-down menus, check boxes, or clickable images. You can also place regular HTML content, such as text and images, within the HTML tag. The text can be used to provide instructions for filling out the form, as well as form labels and prompts.

Once the user has filled out a form, he or she presses a Submit button, which will perform some action. This will most likely be invoking a server-side process (such as a servlet) but can also include sending an

Figure 7.1

Basic HTML form
tag structure.

```
<FORM ACTION="url" METHOD="POST or GET">

FORM contents

</FORM>
```

e-mail. Once the Submit button has been pressed, the browser will package all the input gathered from the user and send it off to a server process. The server will then route the package to the appropriate destination, which will process the data, create a response (usually another HTML page), and send the response back to the browser.

A form can be placed anywhere inside the body of an HTML page, and more than one form can be placed in a single page (although forms cannot be nested). Browsers place the form elements into the formatted HTML page as if they were small images embedded into the text. There are no special layout rules for form elements; because of this you'll need to use other HTML formatting elements (such as tables) to control where the input elements are placed on the page.

The Form Tag

Figure 7.1 shows the basic structure of the form tag.

You are required to define two form attributes: ACTION, which defines the name of the server-side process to invoke, and METHOD, which defines how parameters are to be sent to the server. Table 7.1 provides a list of all the form tag attributes.

TABLE 7.1

Form Tag
Attributes

Attribute	Required	Description
ACTION	Yes	The URL of the server-side process that will receive the data when the form is submitted
ENCTYPE		Specifies how the data are to be encoded for secure transmission
METHOD	Yes	Controls how the data are to be sent to the server

Note that there are extended form tag attributes defined by Microsoft and/or Netscape; however, we'll just be concentrating on those defined by the HTML specification.

The ACTION Attribute   The ACTION attribute, which is required, specifies the URL of the server-side process that is to receive the form data when these data are submitted. In a traditional (nonservlet) environment this would most likely point to a Common Gateway Interface (CGI) script found in the "cgi-bin" directory. In our case, since we'll be using servlets, the URL will point to a servlet on a particular server. Note that the URL may contain an actual servlet name, a servlet alias, or invoke a servlet via prefix or suffix mapping.

An example ACTION attribute would look like this.

```
<FORM ACTION="http://www.myhost.com/servlet/myServlet" …>
</FORM>
```

As an aside, you can also specify an e-mail address in place of the URL. Why would you want to do this? Some Internet providers may not allow you to place scripts on your Web site, making it impossible to use a form to invoke a CGI script or servlet. However, you can use a "mailto" URL in the ACTION attribute, which will cause all the form parameters and values to be mailed to the address given in the URL. The mail recipient can then process the form data as needed.

An example ACTION attribute with an e-mail URL would look like this.

```
<FORM ACTION="mailto:karlmoss@mindspring.com" …>
</FORM>
```

The body of the e-mail will contain the form parameter and value pairs.

```
name=Bruce Wayne
address=1 Bat Cave
```

Note that if you are using an e-mail URL in the ACTION attribute, you need to consider the following.

■ Your form will only work with browsers that support a "mailto" URL.

- After a form is submitted to an e-mail URL, the user will be left wondering if anything happened. Unlike submitting data to a script or servlet, which can respond with some type of confirmation HTML page, submitting data to an e-mail URL will simply leave the user staring at the form that was just completed. You can use JavaScript to solve this problem.

- You will want to set the ENCTYPE attribute (as described in the next section) to text/plain to ensure that the form parameters and values are in a readable format.

- You will have to process the form parameter values in the e-mail in some manner. This may include some type of batch process, which reads each e-mail, parses the values of the parameters, and then takes some action.

The ENCTYPE Attribute The Web browser will encode the form data before they are passed to the server, which, in turn, may decode the parameters or simply pass them to the application. The default encoding format is the Internet media type known as "application/x-www-form-urlencoded." You can change the default encoding type with the ENCTYPE attribute in the form tag. Table 7.2 provides a list of the valid encoding types.

TABLE 7.2

Form Tag ENCTYPE Attribute Values

Value	Description
application/x-www-form-urlencoded	The default encoding format. Converts any spaces in the form parameter values to a plus sign (+), nonalphanumeric characters to a percent sign (%) followed by the two-digit hexadecimal ASCII value of the character, and line breaks within any multiline values into %0D%0A (carriage return/line feed).
multipart/form-data	Only used with forms that contain a file-selection field. The data are sent as a single document with multiple sections.
text/plain	Only used to send the form parameters and values via e-mail. Each element in the form is placed on a single line with the name and value separated by an equal (=) sign. Line breaks within any multiline values are converted into %0D%0A (carriage return/line feed).

You will most likely not have to change the default value of "application/x-www-form-urlencoded" and can thus omit the ENCTYPE attribute.

The METHOD Attribute The METHOD attribute, which is required, specifies the method in which the Web browser sends the form values to the server. There are two methods used to send the form values: POST and GET.

The POST method will cause the Web browser to send the form values in two steps. The browser first contacts the server specified in the ACTION attribute and, once contact is made, sends the form values to the server in a separate transmission. The server is expected to read the parameters from a standard location.

The GET method will cause the Web browser to contact the server and send the form values in a single transmission. The browser will append the form values to the ACTION URL (as command-line arguments), separating the values by a question mark.

Which should you use? Here are some guidelines.

- If the form has only a small number of fields, use the GET method. Since all the data are passed in a single transmission, it is much more efficient.

- Since some servers limit the length of command-line arguments (which is how GET works), you will have to use POST for larger forms or forms that can contain long text values.

- If you are security conscious, use the POST method. Because the GET method passes the form values as command-line arguments after the URL, it is quite easy to capture the data values with network sniffers or extract the data from server log files. The POST method, on the other hand, causes the data to be encrypted and sent in a separate transmission.

Passing Additional Parameters You can very easily pass additional parameters to the ACTION URL by encoding them and adding them as command-line arguments—for example, if you have two parameters, named "a" and "b," you can encode them using the "application/x-www-form-urlencoded" style (see Table 7.2) as follows.

```
a=3&b=24
```

An example URL that uses these additional parameters would look like this.

```
<FORM ACTION="http://www.myhost.com/servlet/myServlet?a=3&b=24" ...>
</FORM>
```

But wait, there is a catch (as usual). The ampersand character is a reserved character used by HTML to specify the character-entity insertion point. To get around this, you will need to replace any ampersand characters with their character-entity values, either &#38 or &amp.

```
<FORM ACTION="http://www.myhost.com/servlet/myServlet?a=3&ampb=24"
...>
</FORM>
```

Because of this confusion, some Web servers allow you to separate parameter values with a semicolon instead.

The Input Tag

The input tag is used to define input fields for the form, such as text fields and buttons. Figure 7.2 shows the basic structure of the input tag.

The required TYPE attribute specifies the type of input field to use (as the following sections describe), as well as the required NAME attribute, which specifies the name that will be supplied to the server for the field. Note that you should take care in naming the fields; I would suggest that you shy away from using any special characters (except the underscore) and use only letters for the leading character. Specifically, don't use the +, &, or % characters, since they have special meaning when using "application/x-www-form-urlencoded."

Note that there are attribute extensions defined by Microsoft Internet Explorer and/or Netscape Navigator; however, I'll just focus on the standard attributes as defined by the HTML specification.

Figure 7.2

Basic HTML input tag structure.

```
<INPUT TYPE=input type
        NAME=parameter name
        [additional attributes] >
```

TABLE 7.3

Button
Attributes

Attribute	Required?	Description
NAME	Yes	The name of the button
VALUE	Yes	The button label

The Button Input Type By using the button input type, you can create a button that can be pressed by the user of the form but that does not submit or reset the form. Table 7.3 shows the attributes for the button input type.

You might ask what the value of a button that does not submit or reset the form might be. Well, unless you are using JavaScript to perform some action, the answer is absolutely nothing. Regardless of that, Figure 7.3 shows the HTML code for presenting the user with multiple buttons, and Figure 7.4 shows these buttons in action. Note that when the user presses a button, a parameter known as "action" will be sent to the server with the value of the button set to the label.

Figure 7.3

Example button
HTML code.

```
<html>
<head>
<title>HTML Form Input - Buttons</title>
</head>
<body>

<form>
<input type=button name=action value="Next">
<input type=button name=action value="Previous">
</form>

</body>
</html>
```

Figure 7.4

Example buttons.

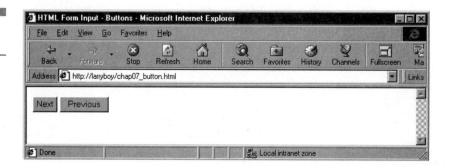

TABLE 7.4

Check Box
Attributes

Attribute	Required?	Description
CHECKED		The presence of this attribute causes the check box to be selected; no value is given.
NAME	Yes	The name of the check box
VALUE	Yes	The value that will be sent to the server if the check box is selected

The Check Box Input Type   The check box input type allows you to present the user of the form with a way to select and deselect a particular item. Table 7.4 shows the attributes for the check box input type.

An example HTML file using check boxes is shown in Figure 7.5. Note that you can (and will need to) embed HTML formatting instructions as well as other text with your input fields. Figure 7.6 shows the page loaded in a browser.

The File Input Type   The file input type allows the user to select a file stored on his or her local computer and send the contents of the file to the server when the Submit button is pressed. The Web browser will

Figure 7.5

Example check box
HTML code.

```
<html>
<head>
<title>HTML Form Input - Checkboxes</title>
</head>
<body>

<form>
Operating Systems:
<input type=checkbox name=age value="95"> Win/95
<input type=checkbox name=age value="NT"> NT
<input type=checkbox name=age value="Solaris"> Solaris
<input type=checkbox name=age value="HPUX"> HP-UX
<br><br>
Browsers:
<br><dir>
<input type=checkbox name=weight value="IE"> Internet Explorer<br>
<input type=checkbox name=weight value="NN"> Netscape Navigator<br>
</dir>
</form>

</body>
</html>
```

Figure 7.6

Example check
boxes.

create a text input field, which will accept user input, as well as a Browse
button, which will, when pressed, present the user with a platform-specific dialog, allowing a file to be selected. Table 7.5 shows the attributes
for the file input type.

Figure 7.7 shows an example HTML file that uses the file selection input type, and Figure 7.8 shows it running in a browser.

TABLE 7.5

File Selection
Attributes

Attribute	Required?	Description
ACCEPT		Sets the types of files that the user can select through a comma-separated list of mime types, such as 'image/*' to select all images.
MAXLENGTH		Maximum length (in characters) of the file name
NAME	Yes	The name of the file input field
SIZE		Size (in characters) of the input field
VALUE		Default file name

Figure 7.7

Example file selection HTML code.

```html
<html>
<head>
<title>HTML Form Input - File Selection</title>
</head>
<body>

<form>
My favorite file is:
<input type=file name=myfile size=25>
</form>

</body>
</html>
```

Figure 7.9 shows a sample platform-specific dialog presented when the user presses the Browse button.

Figure 7.8

Example file selection.

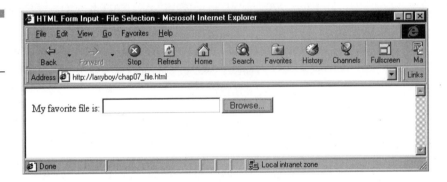

Figure 7.9

File selection dialog.

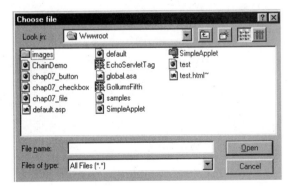

The Hidden Input Type   The hidden input type is one that is hidden from the user's view; it is a way to embed additional information into your HTML form. This information cannot be modified by the user. Why would you want to use hidden input fields?

- To embed versioning information within the form: You can use a hidden form to send a version number of the HTML form to the server.

- To embed user identification within the form: You will typically be generating HTML forms on the server to be returned to the browser so you can embed information about the current user into the HTML form.

- To embed any additional information required by the server: You may be using a single servlet to serve multiple forms and need to embed some additional information in a form for the server to be able to process it properly.

Table 7.6 shows the attributes for the hidden field input type. Whenever a form is submitted to the server, the name and value of any hidden fields are sent to the server along with any other parameters.

Figure 7.10 shows an example HTML file that uses a hidden field, and Figure 7.11 shows it running within a browser. Note that the hidden field is, and this should come as no surprise, hidden.

The Image Input Type   The image input type will create a custom button with a clickable image. This custom button will be created using the image the user specifies, and, when clicked by the user, it submits the form and sends the X and Y coordinates of the mouse click within the image to the server. The values of the X and Y coordinates will be sent as <name>.x and <name>.y. Thus, if you create an image input named "map," the X and Y coordinates will be sent to the server as map.x and map.y.

TABLE 7.6

Hidden Field
Attributes

Attribute	Required?	Description
NAME	Yes	The name of the hidden field
VALUE	Yes	The value of the hidden field

Figure 7.10

Example hidden
field HTML code.

```
<html>
<head>
<title>HTML Form Input - Hidden fields</title>
</head>
<body>

<form>
There's a hidden input field here (
<input type=hidden name=version value=1.0>
) but you can't see it!<br>
</form>

</body>
</html>
```

Figure 7.11

Example hidden
field.

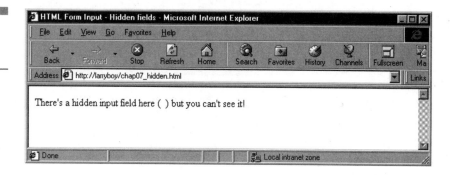

Table 7.7 shows the attributes for the clickable Image button, while Figure 7.12 shows an example HTML file using an Image button, and Figure 7.13 shows it in action.

TABLE 7.7

Image Button
Attributes

Attribute	Required?	Description
ALIGN		Image alignment with text: TOP, TEXTTOP, MIDDLE, ABSMIDDLE, CENTER, BOTTOM, BASELINE, ABSBOTTOM.
BORDER		Specifies the thickness of the image border in pixels
NAME	Yes	The name of the Image button
SRC	Yes	The URL of the image

Figure 7.12

Example clickable Image button HTML code.

```
<html>
<head>
<title>HTML Form Input - Image Button</title>
</head>
<body>

<form>
Click here to submit the form:
<input type=image name=submit src="submit.gif" align=middle>
</form>

</body>
</html>
```

Figure 7.13

Example clickable Image button.

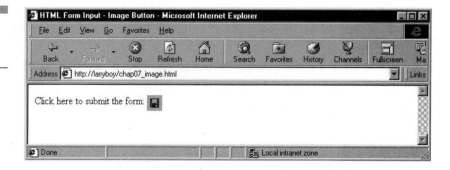

The Password Input Type   The password input type allows you to mask input from the user, as is typically done with password entry fields. Do not be misled into thinking that the password will be encrypted or that any other type of security measures will be taken with a password field; it only hides the characters from view in the browser.

Table 7.8 shows the attributes for the password input field.

TABLE 7.8

Password Attributes

Attribute	Required?	Description
MAXLENGTH		The number of total characters to accept
NAME	Yes	The name of the password field
SIZE		The width, in characters, of the input field
VALUE		Default value for the field

Figure 7.14

Example password input field HTML code.

```
<html>
<head>
<title>HTML Form Input - Password Input Fields</title>
</head>
<body>

<form>
Enter your password:
<input type=password name=password size=10>
</form>

</body>
</html>
```

Figure 7.14 shows an example HTML file using a password input field, and Figure 7.15 shows it running within a browser.

The Radio Button Input Type The Radio button input type allows you to present users with a list of choices and allow them to choose exactly one. Table 7.9 shows the attributes for the Radio button input type.

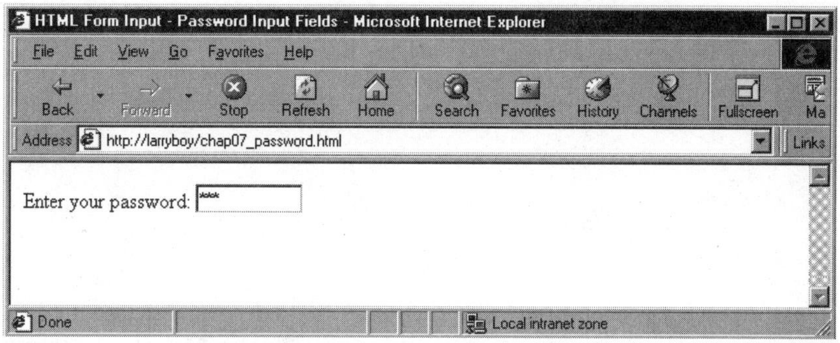

Figure 7.15

Example password input field.

TABLE 7.9

Radio Button Attributes

Attribute	Required?	Description
CHECKED		The presence of this attribute causes this item to be the default selection; no value is given.
NAME	Yes	The name of the radio button
VALUE	Yes	The value that will be sent to the server if this item is selected

Note that Radio buttons with the same name will be considered part of the same group; only one item from a given group may be selected at any time. Also, if no Radio button fields are selected, the browser will automatically select the first button in the group to be the default selection.

Figure 7.16 shows an example HTML file using a group of Radio button fields, and Figure 7.17 shows it in action.

The Reset Input Type   The Reset button input type allows you to place a Reset All Input Fields to Their Default Values button on the form. Unlike all other input types, the server is never aware of its pres-

Figure 7.16

Example Radio button HTML code.

```
<html>
<head>
<title>HTML Form Input - Radio Buttons</title>
</head>
<body>

<form>
How long have you been using Java?
<dir><dir>
<input type=radio name=time value="never" checked> Never<br>
<input type=radio name=time value="<6mo"> Less than 6 months<br>
<input type=radio name=time value="6-12"> 6 - 12 months<br>
<input type=radio name=time value=">12"> More than 12 months<br>
<input type=radio name=time value="guru"> I'm a Java guru<br>
</dir></dir>
</form>

</body>
</html>
```

Figure 7.17

Example Radio button.

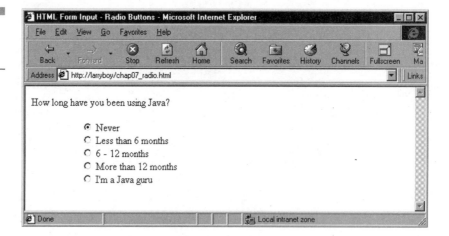

TABLE 7.10

Reset Button
Attributes

Attribute	Required?	Description
VALUE		The reset button label: The default is "Reset."

TABLE 7.11

Submit Button
Attributes

Attribute	Required?	Description
NAME		The optional name of the Submit button
VALUE		The submit button label: The default is "Submit."

ence; all the processing performed when the Reset button is pressed is done in the browser. Table 7.10 shows the one lone attribute for the Reset button.

The Submit Button Input Type   The Submit button does exactly what you would imagine; when pressed by the user it will submit the form to the server for processing. Table 7.11 shows the attributes for the Submit button.

Figure 7.18 shows an example HTML file using several Submit buttons. Note that the first Submit button will have the default label "Submit query," the second Submit button specifies its own label, and the third button specifies its own label and a button name. By supplying a button name, a parameter and value will be sent to the server when the button is pressed—in this case, `action=add`. Figure 7.19 shows all three Submit buttons in a browser.

Figure 7.18

Example Submit
button HTML code.

```
<html>
<head>
<title>HTML Form Input - Submit Buttons</title>
</head>
<body>

<form>
<input type=submit> <br><br>
<input type=submit value="Process"> <br><br>
<input type=submit value="Add" name=action>
</form>

</body>
</html>
```

Figure 7.19

Example Submit
buttons.

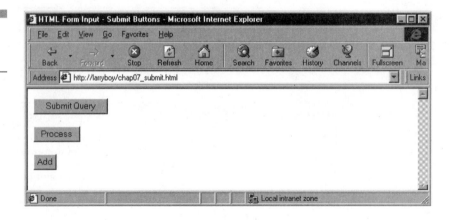

The Text Input Type   The most common input type you will use is a text input field. A text input field consists of a single input line where the user can enter up to a specified number of characters. Table 7.12 shows the attributes for the text input field.

While you don't need to specify values for the size and maximum length of the input field, I would recommend that you do, because different browsers use different defaults. If the size is less than the maximum length, then the text can be scrolled within the input field.

Figure 7.20 shows an example HTML file using input fields, and Figure 7.21 shows them in action.

OK, so it doesn't look too pretty. We'll be taking a look at how to format the layout of the input fields later using HTML tables.

TABLE 7.12

Text Field
Attributes

Attribute	Required?	Description
MAXLENGTH		The number of total characters to accept
NAME	Yes	The name of the input field
SIZE		The width, in characters, of the input field
VALUE		Default value for the field

Figure 7.20

Example text input field HTML code.

```
<html>
<head>
<title>HTML Form Input - Input Fields</title>
</head>
<body>

<form>
Name:
<input type=text name=name size=30 maxlength=30> <br><br>
Address:
<input type=text name=address size=60 maxlength=60> <br>

</form>

</body>
</html>
```

Figure 7.21

Example text input fields.

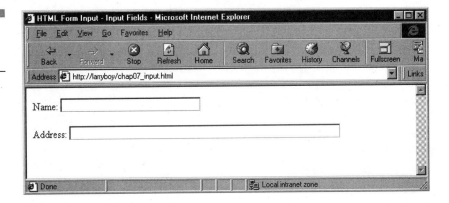

The Select Tag

Check boxes and Radio buttons are great, but what about pull-down menus and list boxes? That's where the select tag comes in. With the select tag you can very easily create pull-down menus and list boxes where the user can make selections depending upon the choices you present. Figure 7.22 shows the basic structure of the select tag.

Figure 7.22

Basic HTML select tag structure.

```
<SELECT NAME=name SIZE=n MULTIPLE>

<OPTION> tags...

</SELECT>
```

As with other input types, the NAME attribute is required; it is the name of the parameter that is sent to the server when the form is submitted. The MULTIPLE attribute directs the browser to allow multiple selections by the user; this would be used in a list box that allows the user to choose more than one item. The SIZE attribute specifies the maximum number of options visible to the user; if the SIZE attribute is less than the number of options given, then the user can scroll through the options.

Note that there are attribute extensions defined by Microsoft Internet Explorer and/or Netscape Navigator; however, I'll just focus on the standard attributes as defined by the HTML specification.

To best illustrate this, let's take a look at an HTML example, shown in Figure 7.23. The first select tag sets up a pull-down menu, and the second tag sets up a list box that allows multiple selections. Each option is specified by an option tag, which specifies the value that will be sent to the server if the option is selected. The option tag also has one optional attribute: SELECTED. If this attribute is present (it has no value), then the option will be selected by default. Note that to create a pull-down menu, the SIZE attribute should be set to one.

Figure 7.23

Example select tag HTML code.

```
<html>
<head>
<title>HTML Form Input - Pull-down menus and list boxes</title>
</head>
<body>

<form>
How long have you been using Java?
<select name=time size=1>
 <option value="never"> Never
 <option value="<6">    Less than 6 months
 <option value="6-12">  6 - 12 months
 <option value=">12">   More than 12 months
 <option value="guru">  I'm a Java guru
</select>

<br><br>
Operating Systems:
<select name=os size=4 multiple>
 <option value="95">      Win/95
 <option value="NT">      NT
 <option value="Solaris"> Solaris
 <option value="HPUX">    HP-UX
</select>

</form>

</body>
</html>
```

Figure 7.24

Example pull-down
menu and list box.

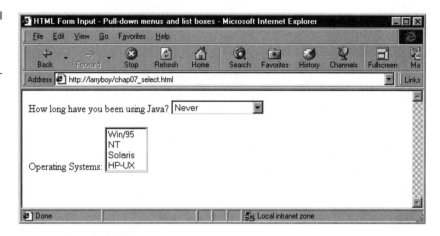

Figure 7.24 shows what the pull-down menu and list box look like in a browser. Note that if multiple selections are made in the list box, multiple parameter/value pairs will be sent to the server.

The Textarea Tag

The textarea tag will create a multiline text-entry area. This is quite useful for gathering comments or address information. Figure 7.25 shows the basic structure of the textarea tag.

Again, there are attribute extensions defined by Microsoft Internet Explorer and/or Netscape Navigator; however, I'll just focus on the standard attributes as defined by the HTML specification.

Any plain text found between the textarea tag and the end tag will be considered the initial default value of the text area; no special HTML tags are allowed—it must be plain text.

I would highly recommend that you provide values for the COLS and ROWS attributes to ensure consistent look and feel between various browsers—you may not like the defaults that are chosen for you.

Figure 7.25

Basic HTML
textarea tag
structure.

```
<TEXTAREA NAME=name COLS=n ROWS=m>

default value

</TEXTAREA>
```

Figure 7.26

Example textarea
tag HTML code.

```
<html>
<head>
<title>HTML Form Input - Textarea</title>
</head>
<body>

<form>
Comments?<br>
<textarea name=comments cols=60 rows=5>
</textarea>

</form>

</body>
</html>
```

Figure 7.27

Example text area
input field.

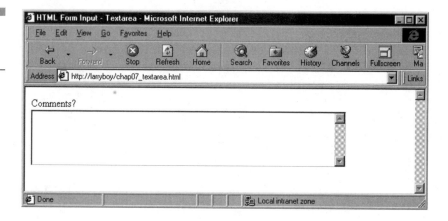

Figure 7.26 shows an example HTML file that uses a textarea tag, and Figure 7.27 shows the text area in a browser.

Putting It All Together: A Survey Form

Now that we have covered all the form input types available to you, let's put it all together by creating a user survey form. Remember that the input fields by themselves do not give us any power over controlling where the fields will be placed; we'll have to rely on other HTML capabilities to properly lay out the form. In this case I'm going to use an HTML table to ensure that everything lines up nicely (see Figure 7.28).

Figure 7.28

Survey HTML code.

```
<html>
<head>
<title>Customer Survey</title>
</head>
<body>
<h1><center>Customer Survey</center></h1>
<hr><br>

<form method=POST action="http://larryboy/servlet/EchoSurvey">
<table border=0>
 <tr>
  <td align=right>Name:</td>
  <td colspan=2 align=left><input type=text name=name size=40></td>
 </tr>
 <tr>
  <td align=right>Email Address:</td>
  <td colspan=2 align=left><input type=text name=email size=40></td>
 </tr>
 <tr valign=top>
  <td align=right>Age:</td>
  <td align=left>
   <input type=radio name=age value="<18">Less than 18<br>
   <input type=radio name=age value="18-25">18 - 25
   </td>
  <td align=left>
   <input type=radio name=age value="26-40">26-40<br>
   <input type=radio name=age value=">40">Over 40
   </td>
 </tr>
 <tr valign=top>
  <td align=right>Operating Systems:</td>
  <td align=left>
   <select name=os size=5 multiple>
    <option>Win/95
    <option>NT
    <option>Solaris
    <option>HP-UX
    <option>Other
   </select>
   </td>
 </tr>
 <tr>
  <td></td>
  <td><input type=checkbox name=more value="yes">
      Send me more information
  </td>
 </tr>
 <tr>
  <td align=right>Comments:</td>
  <td colspan=2 align=left>
   <textarea name=comments cols=40 rows=4>
   </textarea>
   </td>
 </tr>
```

```
<tr>
 <td></td>
 <td>
  <input type=reset value="Clear Form">
  <input type=submit value="Submit">
  </td>
</tr>
</table>

</form>

</body>
</html>
```

A few things to note about the HTML.

- When the form is submitted (by pressing the Submit button), the form data will be sent to the URL specified in the form tag—in this case, the EchoSurvey servlet.

- By placing the labels and input fields into a table cell, the rows are automatically aligned so that the form flows well. In some cases,

Figure 7.29

Survey page.

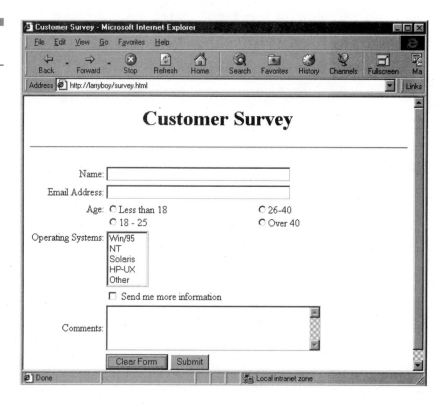

the input fields span multiple columns in order to keep the width of the overall table smaller.

■ The list box allows multiple operating systems to be selected. The servlet will have to handle multiple values for the same parameter name.

Now, let's take a look at our survey running in a browser, as shown in Figure 7.29.

Once the user fills out all the information and presses the Submit button, all the values will be sent to the server. It is important to note that HTML does not provide a mechanism for performing client-side validation of the data entered by the user (although you can use Java-Script); you'll have to validate the information on the server and return error information via an HTML page if necessary.

Let's go ahead and try out the survey page. Figure 7.30 shows a completed survey page, and Figure 7.31 shows the response from the server once the Submit button is pressed.

Figure 7.30

Completed survey page.

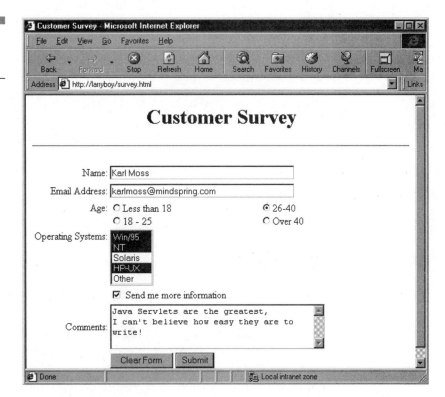

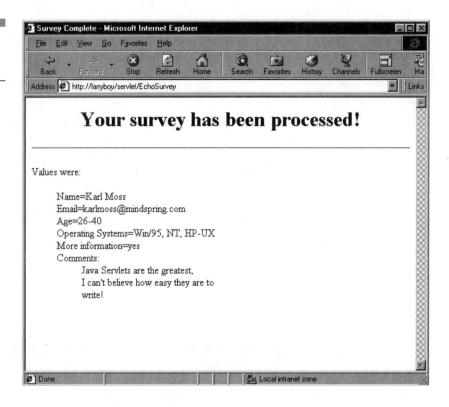

Pressing the Survey button invokes the EchoSurvey servlet, which re-
trieves all the values entered by the user on the HTML form and echoes
them back to the user. Let's take a closer look at what the servlet has to
do to get the data.

The EchoSurvey Servlet

The EchoSurvey servlet is a great example of how to retrieve parameter
values that are sent to the servlet via a form submission. The servlet API
makes it quite easy; the data are just one method call away. This method, `getParameterValues()`, takes a string argument, which is the parameter name. Remember that all the input types in the HTML form
require a name: This is the parameter name that is sent to the server. The
`getParameterValues()` method returns a string array of values for
the given parameter or null if the parameter name is not found. Re-

member that the list box input type allows multiple selections. It can send multiple values to the server for a single parameter name. Each of these values will be placed in the string array. Parameters with a single value will be returned in the first element (element 0) of the array.

Let's take a look at the servlet code, as shown in Figure 7.32. The complete source code can be found on the accompanying CD-ROM.

Figure 7.32

EchoSurvey servlet code listing.

```java
public class EchoSurvey extends HttpServlet
{
    /**
     * <p>Performs the HTTP POST operation
     *
     * @param req The request from the client
     * @param resp The response from the servlet
     */

    public void doPost(HttpServletRequest req,
                       HttpServletResponse resp)
        throws ServletException, java.io.IOException
    {
        // Set the content type of the response
        resp.setContentType("text/html");

        // Create a PrintWriter to write the response
        java.io.PrintWriter out =
          new java.io.PrintWriter(resp.getOutputStream());

        // Print a standard header
        out.println("<html>");
        out.println("<head>");
        out.println("<title>Survey Complete</title>");
        out.println("</head>");
        out.println("<body>");
        out.println("<h1><center>Your survey has been processed!");
        out.println("</center></h1><hr><br>");
        out.println("Values were:");
        out.println("<dir>");

        String values[];

        // Get the name
        String name = "";
        values = req.getParameterValues("name");
        if (values != null) {
          name = values[0];
        }
        out.println("Name=" + name + "<br>");

        // Get the email address
        String email = "";
        values = req.getParameterValues("email");
        if (values != null) {
          email = values[0];
        }
        out.println("Email=" + email + "<br>");
```

```
// Get the age
String age = "";
values = req.getParameterValues("age");
if (values != null) {
  age = values[0];
}
out.println("Age=" + age + "<br>");

// Get the operating system. There could be more than one
// value
values = req.getParameterValues("os");
out.print("Operating Systems=");
if (values != null) {
  for (int i = 0; i < values.length; i++) {
    if (i > 0) out.print(", ");
    out.print(values[i]);
  }
}
out.println("<br>");

// Get the 'more information' flag
String more = "";
values = req.getParameterValues("more");
if (values != null) {
  more = values[0];
}
out.println("More information=" + more + "<br>");

// Get the comments
String comments = "";
values = req.getParameterValues("comments");
if (values != null) {
  comments = values[0];
}
out.println("Comments:<br>");
out.println("<dir>");

// Comment lines are separated by a carriage return/line feed
// pair - convert them to an HTML line break <br>
out.println(toHTML(comments));
out.println("</dir>");

out.println("</dir>");

// Wrap up
out.println("</body>");
out.println("</html>");
out.flush();
}
```

Note that the EchoSurvey servlet extends the HttpServlet class and implements the doPost() method. This method is invoked by the Web service when an HTTP POST operation is done, which occurs when the user presses the Submit button on our survey form. Inside the doPost() method we get the output stream from the HTTP response object that is used to print the HTML page that will be sent back to the user. Once we have the output stream, it's a simple matter to retrieve all the form data and echo the values in HTML.

One thing to remember when working with a multiline text input field: The lines are separated by a carriage return/line feed pair (0x0D0A). In our example we've converted these ASCII control characters into an HTML line break command (<br>).

Don't forget that you'll have to configure the particular server you are using to use the EchoSurvey servlet.

Summary

In this chapter, we've taken an in-depth look at HTML forms and all the different types of possible input, including various types of buttons, check boxes, Radio buttons, list boxes, and text input fields. All of these types of input were explained in detail and a working example of each was provided. We then put together a customer survey form, which used many types of HTML input, and formatted the form using an HTML table so that the columns of the form would be aligned properly. A simple servlet, EchoSurvey, was used to illustrate how to process the data sent to the server when the Submit button is pressed.

Now that we have the basics of writing HTML forms, we're going to concentrate on how to use a database on the server from within a servlet. The next chapter will focus on how to use JDBC to retrieve and update database information, as well as how to manage database connections.

Using JDBC
in Servlets

One of the most common uses of servlets is to access corporate information residing in a database; some studies suggest that up to 80 percent of all applications utilize some type of data stored in a relational database. In this chapter, we'll explore JDBC, JavaSoft's API specification for connecting to databases and manipulating data, and how to use database information from within servlets.

JDBC Overview

What is JDBC? In a nutshell, JDBC, which stands for Java Database Connectivity, is an API specification that defines the following.

- How to interact with corporate data sources from Java applets, applications, and servlets
- How to use JDBC drivers
- How to write JDBC drivers

Complete books have been written on JDBC drivers (in fact, I have written one such book), but I'll attempt to cover the basics in a single chapter. With this brief overview you should have enough information to start developing data-aware Java applications.

The JDBC project was begun late in 1995 and was headed by Rick Cattel and Graham Hamilton at JavaSoft. The JDBC API is based on the X/Open CLI (Call-Level Interface), which defines how clients and servers interact with one another when using database systems. Interestingly enough, Microsoft's Open Database Connectivity (ODBC) is also based on the X/Open CLI, so you should consider it a (distant) cousin. JavaSoft wisely sought the advice and input of leading database vendors to help shape and mold the JDBC specification. In fact, JavaSoft adheres to the following process for all new API specifications, including JDBC.

1. New APIs and significant API changes are submitted to leading vendors for review and input. The fact that this step exists in the specification development process shows the maturity and wisdom of JavaSoft; they recognize that they are not experts in a given area and seek out those who are. This not only provides a very stable and functional specification, but ensures that vendors will "buy in" to the specification since they helped create it. This step may take numerous iterations and span many months.

2. After the vendor review step is complete, the specification is announced and published for public review. Anyone can download the specification from the Internet, review it, and make comments and suggestions. This step usually spans a few months and has a concrete ending date.

3. After all the public comments are reviewed and any necessary changes are made, the specification will be released and rolled into the next version of the Java Developer's Kit (JDK). Comments and suggestions from the general public are still accepted and help shape future revisions.

The JDBC specification followed all these steps and was officially released in June 1996 in the java.sql package. Because of the API review process, there were already significant vendor participation and endorsements when the API was made public.

Interoperability: The Key to JDBC

The major selling point of JDBC is database interoperability. What exactly does that mean? It means that by using the JDBC API for database access you can change the underlying database driver (or engine) without having to modify your application. Taking this one step further, you do not need to be aware of the quirks (also known as features) of a particular database system when you are developing your application; you write to the standard JDBC API specification and plug in the appropriate JDBC driver for the database that you want to use (see Figure 8.1). All the database implementation details of interfacing to a particular database system are left to the JDBC driver vendors.

Remember that the JDBC API specification is a "two-way street"; not only does it define how you, as the application developer, will interact with a database, but it also defines how a JDBC driver must be written in order to preserve interoperability. To this end, JavaSoft has developed a JDBC driver certification suite, which verifies that a JDBC adheres to the specification and behaves in a predictable manner.

The JDBC-ODBC Bridge

As previously mentioned, Microsoft's ODBC specification shares the same heritage as JDBC: the X/Open CLI. Both APIs also share the lan-

Figure 8.1
JDBC
interoperability.

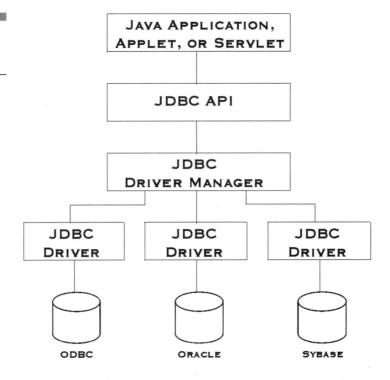

guage they use, which is SQL. SQL used to be an acronym for Structured Query Language, but it has since grown out of this acronym and is just a three-letter word with no vowels. SQL defines both how databases are defined and maintained with Data Definition Language (DDL) and how data are read and updated with Data Manipulation Language (DML).

One thing that ODBC had in 1996 that JDBC didn't was industry acceptance. ODBC, at that time, was the de facto standard for database access and had widespread popularity throughout the industry. Not only did every Microsoft database product come with an ODBC driver, but all major database vendors (such as ORACLE, Sybase, Informix, etc.) had ODBC drivers for their products as well. How could JavaSoft leverage the existing investment that companies had in ODBC and transfer some of its popularity into the realm of JDBC? The answer was the JDBC-ODBC bridge.

The JDBC-ODBC bridge is a JDBC driver that uses native (C language) libraries that make calls to an existing ODBC driver to access a database engine. As the author of the JDBC-ODBC bridge, I have frequently been asked about the "inside story" of how and why the bridge was developed.

The Inside Edition As previously mentioned, the JDBC API went through the standard JavaSoft specification review process. Early on in the vendor review stage (late 1995) the JDBC specification was sent to INTERSOLV who was (and still is) the leading ODBC driver vendor. I was part of the ODBC team at that time and had just finished developing an ODBC driver for FoxPro. Luckily I had already begun to follow Java and was writing applications in my spare time, just like everyone else (Java was still young and very few companies had resources dedicated to Java programming). I was approached by my manager and was asked (OK, I begged) to review this new database access specification known as JDBC. I think that this first draft was version 0.20 and vaguely resembled what we call JDBC today.

INTERSOLV was very interested in making a name for itself in the Java world and forged an agreement (with a signed contract) to implement a JDBC driver that would use existing ODBC drivers. In exchange for this development effort (plus one year of support) JavaSoft would issue a press release announcing this new partnership between JavaSoft and INTERSOLV; no money ever changed hands. Sounds as if JavaSoft got a good deal, doesn't it? Since I had already been reviewing the specification, I was chosen (OK, I begged again) to develop this JDBC-ODBC bridge. I started work in March 1996, and the bridge was completed in May in spite of continuous API changes and revisions.

JavaSoft's main motivation for the bridge, which it planned to distribute at no charge, was to provide JDBC developers with an immediate way to start writing JDBC applications and, in their words, to "set the hook" so that JDBC would be widely accepted. Time has proven that JavaSoft's plans have certainly paid off.

Limitations There are many limitations concerning the use of the JDBC-ODBC bridge, as well as many things that you should keep in mind.

- The bridge was never intended to be a production piece of software, and it is not officially supported by JavaSoft; it was developed as a prototyping and marketing tool. While I am aware of many corporations using the bridge for mission-critical applications, if there is another JDBC driver available for the database you are using you should evaluate it.

- The bridge uses native (C language) code, which has severe implications. The bridge cannot be used in untrusted applets, and all the native libraries must be installed and configured on each machine. This includes not only the native library that comes with the bridge (JdbcOdbc.dll or JdbcOdbc.so, depending upon the operating system) but also all the ODBC libraries, ODBC drivers, and all the libraries the ODBC driver requires to function. Once all this software is properly installed, you must also configure ODBC and create a new data source. This type of setup is a far cry from Java's "zero-install" model.

■ Since the bridge uses existing ODBC drivers, any bugs in the ODBC driver will be encountered when using the bridge.

■ If your ODBC driver can't do it, neither will the bridge when using that ODBC driver. Many people think that using the bridge and their favorite ODBC driver will "Web-enable" the ODBC driver and magically allow the database to be accessed over the Internet; this is obviously not true. Remember that the ODBC driver is running on the client machine and the way it accesses its data has not changed.

Having said all this, the bridge will continue to be the only way to access some database products (such as Microsoft Access). There are many databases that come with an ODBC driver but are not (and will not be) shipped with a corresponding JDBC driver. In this case the bridge will be the only way to get to the data, unless you are willing to write a JDBC driver of your own.

JDBC Driver Types

JavaSoft has defined four basic types of JDBC drivers. It is important to understand the qualities of each type so that you can choose the right JDBC driver to suit your needs. One of the first questions you will be asked if you go shopping for JDBC drivers is: What type do you need?

Type 1: The JDBC-ODBC Bridge   As we've already seen, the JDBC-ODBC bridge is provided by JavaSoft as part of its JDK (starting with 1.1). The bridge is part of the sun.jdbc.odbc package and is not required to be ported by vendors that provide a Java virtual machine. Remember that the bridge uses native ODBC methods and has limitations in its use. (See Figure 8.2.)

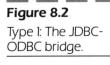

Figure 8.2

Type 1: The JDBC-
ODBC bridge.

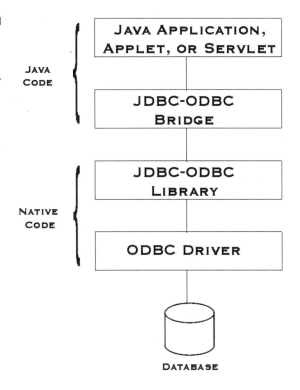

You might consider using the bridge for the following implemetations.

■ Quick system prototyping

■ Three-tier database systems (as we'll see in Chapter 13)

■ Database systems that provide an ODBC driver but no JDBC driver

■ Low-cost database solution where you already have an ODBC driver

Type 2: Java to Native API The Java to native API driver makes use of local native libraries provided by a vendor to communicate directly to the database (see Figure 8.3). This type of driver has many of the same restrictions as the JDBC-ODBC bridge, since it uses native libraries; the most severe restriction is the inability to use it in untrusted applets. Also note that since the JDBC driver uses native libraries, these libraries must

Figure 8.3

Type 2: Java to
native API.

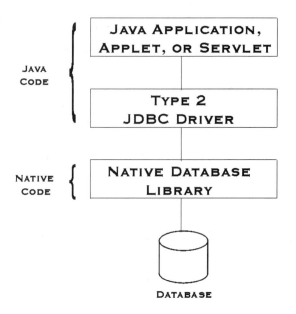

be installed and configured on each machine that will be using the driver. Most major database vendors provide a type 2 JDBC driver with their
products.

You might consider using Java to native API drivers for the following implementations.

- As an alternative to using the JDBC-ODBC bridge—type 2 drivers
  will perform better than the bridge, since they interface directly
  with the database.

- As a low-cost database solution where you are already using a major database system that provides a type 2 driver (such as ORACLE,
  Informix, Sybase, etc.)—many vendors bundle their type 2 drivers
  with the database product.

Type 3: Java to Proprietary Network Protocol   This type of JDBC
driver is by far the most flexible. It is typically used in a three-tier solution (explored in greater detail in Chapter 13) and can be deployed over
the Internet. Type 3 drivers are pure Java and communicate with some
type of middle tier via a proprietary network protocol created by the
driver vendor (see Figure 8.4). This middle tier will most likely reside on
a Web or database server and, in turn, communicates with the database
product via the JDBC-ODBC bridge, either type 2 or type 4 driver. Type
3 drivers are usually developed by companies not associated with a par-

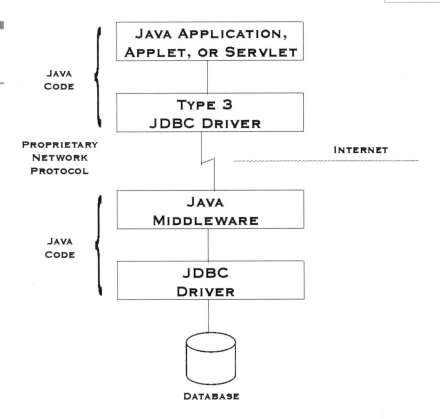

Figure 8.4

Java to proprietary network protocol.

ticular database product and may prove to be costly because of the benefits they provide.

You might consider using a Java to proprietary network protocol driver for the following implementations.

- Web-deployed applets that do not require any preinstallation or configuration of software
- Secure systems where the database product will be protected behind a middle tier
- Flexible solutions where there are many different database products in use—the middle-tier software can usually interface to any database product accessed via JDBC.
- Clients requiring a small "footprint"—the size of a type 3 driver is usually much smaller than all other types.

Type 4: Java to Native Database Protocol   Type 4 JDBC drivers are pure Java drivers that communicate directly with the database engine

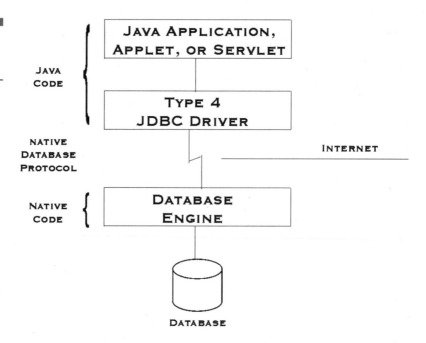

Figure 8.5

Java to native
database protocol.

via its native protocol (see Figure 8.5). These drivers may be able to be deployed over the Internet, depending on the native communication protocol. The advantage that type 4 drivers have over all the rest is performance; there are no layers of native code or middle-tier software between the client and the database engine.

You might consider using a Java to native database protocol driver for the following implementations.

- When high performance is critical
- In environments where only one database product is in use—if you do not have to worry about supporting multiple database systems, then a type 4 driver may be all you need.
- Web-deployed applets, depending upon the capabilities of the driver

And the Winner Is . . . If you've skipped ahead to find out which type of driver will solve the world's problems, then you will be greatly disappointed; the answer is "it depends." There are four types of JDBC drivers because there are many database requirements. You will just have to weigh each of your requirements with the capabilities of each driver type to find the one that best suits your needs.

There does seem to be some confusion, however, about the preference of the different driver types. Just because type 4 is the highest driver type number does not imply that it is better than types 3, 2, or 1. Only your particular requirements will be able to point you to the right JDBC driver.

The Basic JDBC Flow

All JDBC applications follow the same basic flow.

1. Establish a connection to the database.

2. Execute a SQL statement.

3. Process the results.

4. Disconnect from the database.

Let's take a closer look at each of these steps.

Establish a Connection to the Database   The first step in using a database product via JDBC is to establish a connection. JDBC connections are specified by a Uniform Resource Locator (URL), which has the general format:

```
jdbc:<subprotocol>:<subname>
```

where *subprotocol* is the kind of database connectivity being requested (such as ODBC, ORACLE, Informix, etc.) and *subname* provides additional information required to establish a connection. When a connection URL is requested from the JDBC DriverManager, each of the known JDBC drivers is asked if it can service the given URL. An example of requesting a connection to an ODBC data source named "MyData" via the JDBC-ODBC bridge is:

```
Connection con = DriverManager.getConnection("jdbc:odbc:MyData");
```

That's all fine and dandy, but how does the JDBC DriverManager know which JDBC drivers are available on the system? Good question! There are two mechanisms for notifying the DriverManager that a JDBC driver is available: the sql.drivers property and JDBC driver registration.

The sql.drivers system property is referenced by the DriverManager to get a list of JDBC drivers available on the system. It contains a colon-separated list of JDBC driver class names that the DriverManager can use in an attempt to satisfy a connection request.

Driver registration is much more common and gives you greater control over which JDBC driver you will use. All JDBC drivers are required to register themselves with the DriverManager when they are instantiated, which can be accomplished in either of two ways.

1. `Class.forName("foo.Driver").newInstance();`

2. `new foo.Driver();`

I personally prefer to use the `Class.forName()` method, but they both have the same effect; the JDBC driver will register itself with the DriverManager so that it can be used to service a connection request.

Execute a SQL Statement   Once a connection to the database has been established, you are ready to execute SQL statements that will perform some type of work. Before executing a SQL statement, you first need to create a statement object, which provides an interface to the underlying database SQL engine. There are three different types of statement objects.

1. Statement—The base statement object, which provides methods to execute SQL statements directly against the database. The statement object is great for executing one-time queries and DDL statements, such as CREATE TABLE, DROP TABLE, and so on.

2. Prepared statement—This statement object is created using a SQL statement that will be used many times, replacing only the data values to be used. Methods exist to specify the input parameters used by the statement.

3. Callable statement—This statement object is used to access stored procedures in the database. Methods exist to specify the input and output parameters used by the statement.

An example of using the statement class to execute a SQL SELECT statement is as follows.

```
Statement stmt = con.createStatement();
ResultSet rs = stmt.executeQuery("SELECT * FROM MyTable");
```

Process the Results   After executing a SQL statement, you must process the results. Some statements will only return an integer value containing the number of rows affected (such as an UPDATE or DELETE statement). SQL queries (SELECT statements) will return a result set containing the results of the query. The result set is made up of columns and rows; column values are retrieved by a series of `get` methods for each database type (such as `getString`, `getInt`, `getDate`, etc.). Once all the values are retrieved from a row, you can call the `next()` method to move to the next row in the result set. The current version of the JDBC specification (1.1) allows forward-only cursors; JDBC 2.0 will have more robust cursor control where you can move backward and position to absolute rows as well.

Disconnect from the Database   Once you are done with a result set, statement, or connection object you should close it properly. The connection object, result set object, and all the statement objects contain a `close()` method, which should be called to ensure that the underlying database system frees all the associated resources properly.

Some developers prefer to leave references hanging around and let the garbage collector take care of cleaning up the object properly. I would strongly advise that when you are finished with a JDBC object, you call the `close()` method. Doing so should minimize any memory leaks caused by dangling objects left in the underlying database system.

JDBC Example: SimpleQuery

To illustrate all the basic steps necessary when using JDBC, let's take a look at a very simple Java application, which will connect to a Microsoft Access database using the JDBC-ODBC bridge, execute a query against an employee database, display the results of the query, and perform all the necessary cleanup.

Since we will be using the JDBC-ODBC bridge (because it's part of the JDK) and Microsoft Access (if you are running Win/95 or NT you have it installed), we first need to configure an ODBC data source. For Win/95 and NT there is an ODBC administration tool that makes it easy to set up data sources; if you are using a UNIX platform, you'll have to edit the odbc.ini configuration file by hand (note that there is no Microsoft Access ODBC driver for UNIX). To start the ODBC administra-

Figure 8.6
ODBC
administration
screen.

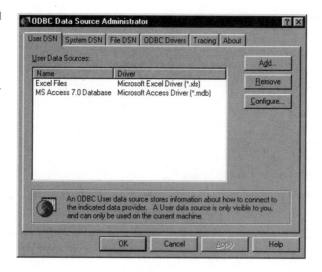

tion program, select ODBC from the control panel (Start | Settings).
Figure 8.6 shows an example ODBC administration screen.

Select the Add... button to add a new data source. You will then be presented with a list of all the installed ODBC drivers on your system (from the odbcinst.ini configuration file). An example is shown in Figure 8.7.

When you select an installed ODBC driver (such as Microsoft Access, in our case), a configuration program is invoked that is specific to that particular driver. Figure 8.8 shows the configuration screen for Microsoft Access.

Figure 8.7
Create new ODBC
data source screen.

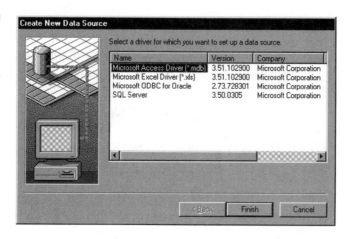

Figure 8.8

Creating a new
Microsoft Access
data source.

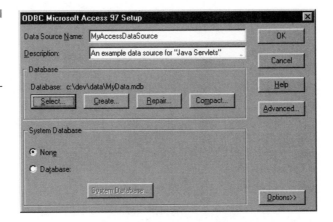

You'll need to enter the data source name and any other pertinent information required for the particular database in use. Let's use "MyAccessDataSource" as the data source name and "MyData.mdb" for the database file. MyData.mdb contains a prebuilt employee table and can be found on the accompanying CD-ROM. You can also find a Java application called javaservlets.db.BuildEmployee, which was used to build this particular database. The BuildEmployee application is a great example of generic JDBC programming; it makes no assumptions about the type of database being used and uses introspection (via DatabaseMetaData) to gain information about the database in use.

Figure 8.9 shows the code for the SimpleQuery application that will dump the contents of the Employee table from the Access database to the screen. As you can see, the four basic steps (establish a connection, execute a SQL statement, process the results, and disconnect from the database) are shown.

Figure 8.10 shows the results after executing the application.

Figure 8.9

SimpleQuery.java
code listing.

```java
public class SimpleQuery
{
    /**
     * <p>Main entry point for the application
     */
    public static void main(String args[])
    {
        try {

            // Perform the simple query and display the results
            performQuery();
        }
```

```
      catch (Exception ex) {
        ex.printStackTrace();
      }
    }

  public static void performQuery() throws Exception
    {
      // The name of the JDBC driver to use
      String driverName = "sun.jdbc.odbc.JdbcOdbcDriver";

      // The JDBC connection URL
      String connectionURL = "jdbc:odbc:MyAccessDataSource";

      // The JDBC Connection object
      Connection con = null;

      // The JDBC Statement object
      Statement stmt = null;

      // The SQL statement to execute
      String sqlStatement =
        "SELECT Empno, Name, Position FROM Employee";

      // The JDBC ResultSet object
      ResultSet rs = null;

      try {

        System.out.println("Registering " + driverName);

        // Create an instance of the JDBC driver so that it has
        // a chance to register itself
        Class.forName(driverName).newInstance();

        System.out.println("Connecting to " + connectionURL);

        // Create a new database connection. We're assuming that
        // additional properties (such as username and password)
        // are not necessary
        con = DriverManager.getConnection(connectionURL);

        // Create a statement object that we can execute queries with
        stmt = con.createStatement();

        // Execute the query
        rs = stmt.executeQuery(sqlStatement);

        // Process the results. First dump out the column
        // headers as found in the ResultSetMetaData
        ResultSetMetaData rsmd = rs.getMetaData();

        int columnCount = rsmd.getColumnCount();

        System.out.println("");
        String line = "";
        for (int i = 0; i < columnCount; i++) {
          if (i > 0) {
            line += ", ";
          }
```

```
                    // Note that the column index is 1-based
                    line += rsmd.getColumnLabel(i + 1);
                }
                System.out.println(line);

                // Count the number of rows
                int rowCount = 0;

                // Now walk through the entire ResultSet and get each row
                while (rs.next()) {
                    rowCount++;

                    // Dump out the values of each row
                    line = "";
                    for (int i = 0; i < columnCount; i++) {
                        if (i > 0) {
                            line += ", ";
                        }

                        // Note that the column index is 1-based
                        line += rs.getString(i + 1);
                    }
                    System.out.println(line);
                }

                System.out.println("" + rowCount + " rows, " +
                                        columnCount + " columns");
            }
            finally {

                // Always clean up properly!
                if (rs != null) {
                    rs.close();
                }
                if (stmt != null) {
                    stmt.close();
                }
                if (con != null) {
                    con.close();
                }
            }
        }
    }
```

Figure 8.10

SimpleQuery output.

```
java javaservlets.db.SimpleQuery

Registering sun.jdbc.odbc.JdbcOdbcDriver
Connecting to jdbc:odbc:MyAccessDataSource

Empno, Name, Position
1, Nebby K. Nezzer, President
2, Mr. Lunt, Foreman
3, Rack, Jr. Executive
4, Shack, Jr. Executive
5, Benny, Jr. Executive
6, George, Security Guard
7, Laura, Delivery Driver
7 rows, 3 columns
```

JDBC Servlet: EmployeeList

Now that you've had a whirlwind tour of JDBC, let's create a simple servlet that puts your newfound knowledge to use. Writing a servlet to use JDBC is really no different from the SimpleQuery application we just saw; we'll still use the same basic steps to connect, execute, process, and close. The real difference is in how we process the results. Instead of printing the information to the standard output device (the screen), we'll need to format the HTML that will be sent back to the client.

Figure 8.11 shows the source code for a simple servlet (EmployeeList), which will use JDBC to get all the employee information for our mythical company "Nezzer's Chocolate Factory." The results of our query will be formatted into an HTML table and returned to the client.

Figure 8.11

EmployeeList.java
code listing.

```java
public class EmployeeList extends HttpServlet
{
  /**
   * <p>Performs the HTTP GET operation
   *
   * @param req The request from the client
   * @param resp The response from the servlet
   */

  public void doGet(HttpServletRequest req,
                    HttpServletResponse resp)
    throws ServletException, java.io.IOException
    {
      // Set the content type of the response
      resp.setContentType("text/html");

      // Create a PrintWriter to write the response
      java.io.PrintWriter out =
        new java.io.PrintWriter(resp.getOutputStream());

      // Print the HTML header
      out.println("<html>");
      out.println("<head>");
      out.println("<title>Employee List</title>");
      out.println("</head>");
      out.println("<h2><center>");
      out.println("Employees for Nezzer's Chocolate Factory");
      out.println("</center></h2>");
      out.println("<br>");

      // Create any addition properties necessary for connecting
      // to the database, such as user and password
      java.util.Properties props = new java.util.Properties();
```

```
query("sun.jdbc.odbc.JdbcOdbcDriver",
        "jdbc:odbc:MyAccessDataSource",
        props,
        "SELECT Empno, Name, Position FROM Employee",
        out);

    // Wrap up
    out.println("</html>");
    out.flush();
}

/**
 * <p>Given the JDBC driver name, URL, and query string,
 * execute the query and format the results into an
 * HTML table
 *
 * @param driverName JDBC driver name
 * @param connectionURL JDBC connection URL
 * @param props Addition connection properties, such as user
 * and password
 * @param query SQL query to execute
 * @param out PrintWriter to use to output the query results
 * @return true if the query was successful
 */

private boolean query(String driverName,
                    String connectionURL,
                    java.util.Properties props,
                    String query,
                    java.io.PrintWriter out)
{
  boolean rc = true;

    // The JDBC Connection object
    Connection con = null;

    // The JDBC Statement object
    Statement stmt = null;

    // The JDBC ResultSet object
    ResultSet rs = null;

    // Keep stats for how long it takes to execute
    // the query
    long startMS = System.currentTimeMillis();

    // Keep the number of rows in the ResultSet
    int rowCount = 0;

    try {

        // Create an instance of the JDBC driver so that it has
        // a chance to register itself
        Class.forName(driverName).newInstance();
```

```java
      // Create a new database connection.
      con = DriverManager.getConnection(connectionURL, props);

      // Create a statement object that we can execute queries
      // with
      stmt = con.createStatement();

      // Execute the query
      rs = stmt.executeQuery(query);

      // Format the results into an HTML table
      rowCount = formatTable(rs, out);

    }
    catch (Exception ex) {
      // Send the error back to the client
      out.println("Exeption!");
      ex.printStackTrace(out);
      rc = false;
    }
    finally {
      try {
        // Always close properly
        if (rs != null) {
          rs.close();
        }
        if (stmt != null) {
          stmt.close();
        }
        if (con != null) {
          con.close();
        }
      }
      catch (Exception ex) {
        // Ignore any errors here
      }
    }

    // If we queried the table successfully, output some statistics
    if (rc) {
      long elapsed = System.currentTimeMillis() - startMS;
      out.println("<br><i>" + rowCount + " rows in " +
                  elapsed + "ms</i>");
    }

    return rc;
  }

  /**
   * <p>Given a JDBC ResultSet, format the results into
   * an HTML table
   *
   * @param rs JDBC ResultSet
   * @param out PrintWriter to use to output the table
   * @return The number of rows in the ResultSet
   */

  private int formatTable(java.sql.ResultSet rs,
                          java.io.PrintWriter out)
```

```java
throws Exception
{
  int rowCount = 0;

  // Create the table
  out.println("<center><table border>");

  // Process the results. First dump out the column
  // headers as found in the ResultSetMetaData
  ResultSetMetaData rsmd = rs.getMetaData();

  int columnCount = rsmd.getColumnCount();

  // Start the table row
  out.println("<tr>");

  for (int i = 0; i < columnCount; i++) {

    // Create each table header. Note that the column index
    // is 1-based
    out.println("<th>" +
                rsmd.getColumnLabel(i + 1) +
                "</th>");
  }

  // End the table row
  out.println("</tr>");

  // Now walk through the entire ResultSet and get
  // each row
  while (rs.next()) {
    rowCount++;

    // Start a table row
    out.println("<tr>");

    // Dump out the values of each row
    for (int i = 0; i < columnCount; i++) {

      // Create the table data. Note that the column index
      // is 1-based
      out.println("<td>" +
                  rs.getString(i + 1) +
                  "</td>");
    }

    // End the table row
    out.println("</tr>");
  }

  // End the table
  out.println("</table></center>");

  return rowCount;
}

}
```

Note that EmployeeList contains two very generic methods for processing JDBC information: `query()` and `formatTable()`. The parameters for the `query()` method specify everything that JDBC needs in order to instantiate the JDBC driver, establish a connection, and execute a query. The `formatTable()` method will then take the results of a query (a result set object) and create an HTML table containing all the data.

You might also notice that the total amount of time to process the HTML request is included in the HTML output. We'll be using this time as a baseline later when we start improving performance through connection pooling.

Figure 8.12 shows the results of the EmployeeList servlet. Don't forget to configure the servlet appropriately for the Web server you are using; I used JRun, so I had to add a servlet alias.

Isn't publishing data on the Web easy? I hope you are starting to see the real power of using servlets and how painless it is to convert existing applications to the servlet framework.

Figure 8.12

Results of EmployeeList servlet.

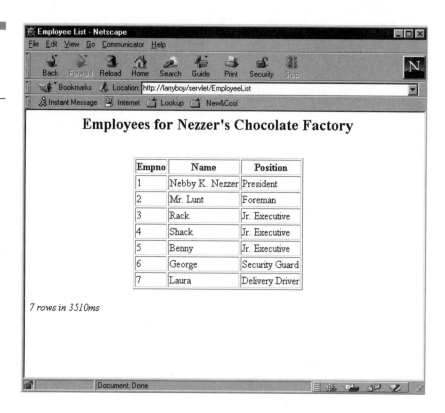

Employees for Nezzer's Chocolate Factory

Empno	Name	Position
1	Nebby K. Nezzer	President
2	Mr. Lunt	Foreman
3	Rack	Jr. Executive
4	Shack	Jr. Executive
5	Benny	Jr. Executive
6	George	Security Guard
7	Laura	Delivery Driver

7 rows in 3510ms

Limitations

Here are a few things to keep in mind about our EmployeeList servlet.

- It works well for small amounts of data. If you are working with tables that have a large amount of rows (hundreds or thousands), then it would be inefficient to dump the entire contents in a single HTML table. Not only would this take a while to complete, but from a user's perspective it would not be very useful.

- All the columns in the table are converted into a string when placed into the HTML table. This will not be appropriate for binary data such as images.

- The servlet establishes a new connection to the database with every GET request. Performing a database connection is a very expensive operation and not very efficient. In fact, creating a new connection for every new request will kill a high-traffic Web server very quickly.

Let's take a look at how we can solve these limitations.

Splitting the Output into Separate Pages If you have a large amount of data to return to the user, you certainly don't want to put it all on one page. Not only would it be difficult for the user to maneuver through the data, but it would take a long time to generate and download the HTML page. One way to solve this problem is to split data over many pages and let the user press a Next button to view the next portion of data. If you've ever used a search engine on the Web (which I know you have), you will be familiar with how this works.

Here's our plan of attack for implementing a servlet that can break up the output over multiple pages.

1. Connect to the database and submit a query.

2. Process the results of the query, only outputting up to the maximum number of rows allowed on a single page.

3. If the maximum number of rows is exceeded, place a Next button at the bottom of the page and embed information within the HTML document that can be used to reposition the result set cursor if the Next button is pressed.

4. If the Next button is pressed, a new query will be executed and the result set cursor will be repositioned to where we left off. The results are processed as before.

Let's look at the IndyList servlet, which will list all the past winners of the Indianapolis 500. The basic code is identical to that of the EmployeeList servlet (Figure 8.11), so I'll just point out the major differences.

First, we need to limit the number of rows shown when processing the result set. Figure 8.13 shows the code necessary for doing this. Note that if we had to limit the number of rows, a Submit button would be generated in the HTML. When pressed, this button will cause the servlet to be invoked again. A hidden field is added that maintains the last year shown on the page. The year is a unique key in this particular table that we can use as a starting point when called again. If we are on the last page of data for the table, the Next button is not generated.

Figure 8.13

IndyList.java result set processing code listing.

```
/**
 * <p>Given a JDBC ResultSet, format the results into
 * an HTML table
 *
 * @param rs JDBC ResultSet
 * @param out PrintWriter to use to output the table
 * @param uri Requesting URI
 * @return The number of rows in the ResultSet
 */

private int formatTable(java.sql.ResultSet rs,
                        java.io.PrintWriter out,
                        String uri)
  throws Exception
  {
    int rowsPerPage = 10;
    int rowCount = 0;

    // Keep track of the last year found
    String lastYear = "";

    // This will be true if there is still more data in the
    // table
    boolean more = false;

    // Create the table
    out.println("<center><table border>");

    // Process the results. First dump out the column
    // headers as found in the ResultSetMetaData
    ResultSetMetaData rsmd = rs.getMetaData();

    int columnCount = rsmd.getColumnCount();

    // Start the table row
    out.println("<tr>");

    for (int i = 0; i < columnCount; i++) {
```

```java
    // Create each table header. Note that the column index
    // is 1-based
    out.println("<th>" +
                rsmd.getColumnLabel(i + 1) +
                "</th>");
}

// End the table row
out.println("</tr>");

// Now walk through the entire ResultSet and get each row
while (rs.next()) {
  rowCount++;

  // Start a table row
  out.println("<tr>");

  // Dump out the values of each row
  for (int i = 0; i < columnCount; i++) {

    // Create the table data. Note that the column index
    // is 1-based
    String data = rs.getString(i + 1);
    out.println("<td>" + data + "</td>");

    // If this is the year column, cache it
    if (i == 0) {
      lastYear = data;
    }
  }

  // End the table row
  out.println("</tr>");

  // If we are keeping track of the maximum number of
  // rows per page and we have exceeded that count
  // break out of the loop
  if ((rowsPerPage > 0) &&
      (rowCount >= rowsPerPage)) {
    // Find out if there are any more rows after this one
    more = rs.next();
    break;
  }
}

// End the table
out.println("</table></center>");

if (more) {

  // Create a 'Next' button
  out.println("<form method=POST action=\"" +
              uri + "\">");
  out.println("<center>");
  out.println("<input type=submit value=\"Next " +
              rowsPerPage + " rows\">");
```

```
        out.println("</center>");
        // Page was filled. Put in the last year that we saw
        out.println("<input type=hidden name=lastYear value=" +
                    lastYear + ">");
        out.println("</form>");
    }

    return rowCount;
}
```

The Uniform Resource Indicator (URI) of the servlet was retrieved from the HTTP request object given when the servlet was invoked.

When the Next button is pressed, we need to be able to start where we left off. Using the value of the hidden field, which was generated when the result set was processed, we can create a new SQL statement with a WHERE clause that will return the proper data. Figure 8.14 shows the code necessary to retrieve the value of the hidden field.

I'm using the value of the hidden field to generate this SQL statement.

```
SELECT * from IndyWinners where year<lastYear order by Year desc
```

The default value of `lastYear` is **9999**, so if the parameter is not set (the first time the servlet is invoked) all the years will be selected. Otherwise, the search will be limited to those years that are less than the last year. Note that I'm sorting the years in descending order, so the most current winners are shown first. This type of searching is not really very efficient and has the possibility of being inaccurate. Each time the Next button is pressed, a new query is executed; this may be expensive if the database engine does not cache previous queries. Also, if another user happens to modify the table by adding, deleting, or updating a row, the new query will reflect those changes. Ideally, we should have a single result set, which we could use to move forward and backward as the user requests data. Unfortunately, JDBC 1.x does not allow for any cursor

Figure 8.14

Java code to retrieve the value of a parameter.

```
// Get the last year shown on the page that
// called us. Remember that we are sorting
// the years in descending order.
String lastYear = "9999";
String values[] = req.getParameterValues("lastYear");
if (values != null) {
    lastYear = values[0];
}
```

movement other than forward. JDBC 2.0, however, will allow drivers to expose expanded cursor support, which may make this task possible.

Also note that the only way this can work is with tables that have a unique key (the year, in our case). We have to be able to uniquely identify the last row that was displayed so that we can pick up where we left off. The absolute best way to do this is with a unique row identifier, such as ORACLE'S ROWID. This ROWID is present in all tables and you can use it to uniquely reference rows. You can query the underlying database about the presence of some type of unique identifier with `Data-baseMetaData.getBestRowIdentifier()`. If a row identifier does not exist, you will have to design your table so that a unique key is present instead. Since I'm using Microsoft Access, which does not supply a unique row identifier, I am using the unique year column instead.

Figure 8.15 shows the first page of the query, and Figure 8.16 shows the results after the Next button is pressed.

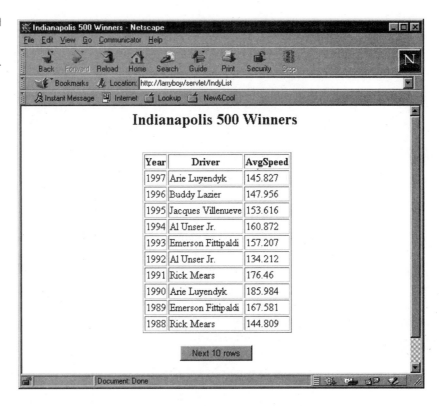

Figure 8.15

IndyList initial page.

Figure 8.16

IndyList second
page.

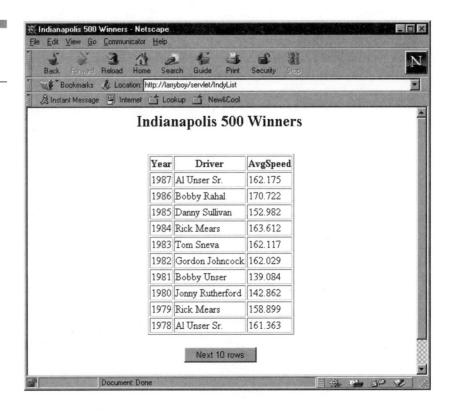

Connection Pooling

As I have previously mentioned, one of the most expensive database operations is establishing a connection. Depending upon the database engine you are using, a connection might have to perform protocol handshaking, verify user information, open disk files, create memory caches, and so on. While we can't discount the time it takes to establish a connection, we can preallocate a pool of connections ready for use. By creating this pool in a separate thread we can let another process take the performance hit and let the main application (a servlet) grab the next ready connection without having to wait.

There are many benefits to having a connection pool: You can monitor connection usage, limit the maximum number of connections allowed, establish timeout parameters for badly behaved connections, and so on.

Figure 8.17

Connection pool
configuration file.

```
#ConnectionPool.cfg
JDBCDriver=sun.jdbc.odbc.JdbcOdbcDriver
JDBCConnectionURL=jdbc:odbc:MyAccessDataSource
ConnectionPoolSize=5
ConnectionPoolMax=100
ConnectionUseCount=5
ConnectionTimeout = 2
User=karl
Password=larryboy
```

Writing the ConnectionPool Object

Let's take a look at a connection pool implementation I have named
ConnectionPool (pretty clever, huh?). The connection pool attributes are
determined by a configuration file, which, by default, is named "Con-
nectionPool.cfg" (see Figure 8.17). The attributes are as follows.

- JDBCDriver—The class name of the JDBC driver to use for the
  connection pool. The example is using the JDBC-ODBC bridge.

- JDBCConnectionURL—The URL of the connection to establish.
  The example is specifying to create an ODBC connection through
  the bridge for the data source "MyAccessDataSource."

- ConnectionPoolSize—The minimum size of the connection pool.
  The ConnectionPool object will ensure that there are always at
  least this number of connections in the pool.

- ConnectionPoolMax—The maximum size of the connection pool.
  Note that the actual size of the connection pool may be limited
  by the underlying JDBC driver as well.

- ConnectionUseCount—If nonzero, this is the maximum number
  of times the connection can be used before it is closed and a new
  connection is created in its place. Some JDBC drivers may have
  problems reusing connections for an indefinite amount of time;
  this parameter is available to work around this type of problem.

- ConnectionTimeout—If nonzero, this is the number of minutes a
  connection may be idle (with no users) before it is terminated and
  a new connection is created in its place. This can prevent "stale"
  connections.

- Other properties—Any other properties found in the configuration file (user and password, in our case) are considered properties
  that must be passed on to the JDBC driver when establishing a
  connection.

Figure 8.18 shows the source code used to create the initial pool (the complete source code can be found on the accompanying CD-ROM).

Figure 8.18

Creating an initial connection pool.

```java
/**
 * <p>Creates the initial connection pool. A timer thread
 * is also created so that connection timeouts can be
 * handled.
 *
 * @return true if the pool was created
 */
private void createPool() throws Exception
{
    // Sanity check our properties
    if (m_JDBCDriver == null) {
        throw new Exception("JDBCDriver property not found");
    }
    if (m_JDBCConnectionURL == null) {
        throw new Exception("JDBCConnectionURL property not found");
    }
    if (m_ConnectionPoolSize < 0) {
        throw new Exception("ConnectionPoolSize property not found");
    }
    if (m_ConnectionPoolSize == 0) {
        throw new Exception("ConnectionPoolSize invalid");
    }
    if (m_ConnectionPoolMax < m_ConnectionPoolSize) {
        trace("WARNING - ConnectionPoolMax is invalid and will " +
                "be ignored");
        m_ConnectionPoolMax = -1;
    }
    if (m_ConnectionTimeout < 0) {
        // Set the default to 30 minutes
        m_ConnectionTimeout = 30;
    }

    // Dump the parameters we are going to use for the pool.
    // We don't know what type of servlet environment we will
    // be running in - this may go to the console or it
    // may be redirected to a log file
    trace("JDBCDriver = " + m_JDBCDriver);
    trace("JDBCConnectionURL = " + m_JDBCConnectionURL);
    trace("ConnectionPoolSize = " + m_ConnectionPoolSize);
    trace("ConnectionPoolMax = " + m_ConnectionPoolMax);
    trace("ConnectionUseCount = " + m_ConnectionUseCount);
    trace("ConnectionTimeout = " + m_ConnectionTimeout +
            " seconds");

    // Also dump any additional JDBC properties
    java.util.Enumeration enum = m_JDBCProperties.keys();
    while (enum.hasMoreElements()) {
        String key = (String) enum.nextElement();
        String value = m_JDBCProperties.getProperty(key);
        trace("(JDBC Property) " + key + " = " + value);
    }
```

```java
        // Attempt to create a new instance of the specified
        // JDBC driver. Well behaved drivers will register
        // themselves with the JDBC DriverManager when they
        // are instantiated
        trace("Registering " + m_JDBCDriver);
        java.sql.Driver d = (java.sql.Driver)
          Class.forName(m_JDBCDriver).newInstance();

        // Create the vector for the pool
        m_pool = new java.util.Vector();

        // Bring the pool to the minimum size
        fillPool(m_ConnectionPoolSize);
    }

/**
  * <p>Adds a new connection to the pool
  *
  * @return Index of the new pool entry, or -1 if an
  * error has occurred
  */
private int addConnection()
    {
        int index = -1;

        try {
          // Calculate the new size of the pool
          int size = m_pool.size() + 1;

          // Create a new entry
          fillPool(size);

          // Set the index pointer to the new connection if one
          // was created
          if (size == m_pool.size()) {
            index = size - 1;
          }
        }
        catch (Exception ex) {
          ex.printStackTrace();
        }
        return index;
    }

/**
  * <p>Brings the pool to the given size
  */
private synchronized void fillPool(int size) throws Exception
    {
        trace("Filling pool to " + size);

        // Loop while we need to create more connections
        while (m_pool.size() < size) {

          trace("Creating connection " + (m_pool.size() + 1));

          ConnectionObject co = new ConnectionObject();
```

```
    // Create the connection
    co.con =
        java.sql.DriverManager.getConnection(m_JDBCConnectionURL,
                                             m_JDBCProperties);

    // Do some sanity checking on the first connection in
    // the pool
    if (m_pool.size() == 0) {

        // Get the maximum number of simultaneous connections
        // as reported by the JDBC driver
        java.sql.DatabaseMetaData md = co.con.getMetaData();
        m_MaxConnections = md.getMaxConnections();
    }

    // Give a warning if the size of the pool will exceed
    // the maximum number of connections allowed by the
    // JDBC driver
    if ((m_MaxConnections > 0) &&
        (size > m_MaxConnections)) {
        trace("WARNING: Size of pool will exceed safe maximum of " +
            m_MaxConnections);
    }

    // Clear the in use flag
    co.inUse = false;

    // Set the last access time
    touch(co);

    m_pool.addElement(co);
    }
}
```

As you can see, the connections are kept in a small wrapper object (called ConnectionObject), which contains the JDBC connection as well as the use count and last access time. The ConnectionObjects are kept in a global vector. Note how the DatabaseMetaData is used to query the JDBC driver for the maximum number of concurrent connections allowed. Note also that a timer thread was created that will call back into the ConnectionPool object so that connection timeouts and general housekeeping can be performed. One of the most vital is to check for connections that were closed outside of the connection pool; an application could have inadvertently closed a connection. With each timer tick (every 20 seconds) all the connections are checked to make sure they are still open; if a connection is no longer open, it is removed from the pool and a new one is created in its place.

Figure 8.19 shows the all-important getConnection method, which will find an available connection in the pool (or create one if necessary) and return it to the caller.

Figure 8.19

getConnection
source code.

```java
/**
 * <p>Gets an available JDBC Connection. Connections will be
 * created if necessary, up to the maximum number of connections
 * as specified in the configuration file.
 *
 * @return JDBC Connection, or null if the maximum
 * number of connections has been exceeded
 */
public synchronized java.sql.Connection getConnection()
{
    // If there is no pool it must have been destroyed
    if (m_pool == null) {
        return null;
    }

    java.sql.Connection con = null;
    ConnectionObject connectionObject = null;
    int poolSize = m_pool.size();

    // Get the next available connection
    for (int i = 0; i < poolSize; i++) {

        // Get the ConnectionObject from the pool
        ConnectionObject co = (ConnectionObject)
            m_pool.elementAt(i);

        // If this is a valid connection and it is not in use,
        // grab it
        if (co.isAvailable()) {
            connectionObject = co;
            break;
        }
    }

    // No more available connections. If we aren't at the
    // maximum number of connections, create a new entry
    // in the pool
    if (connectionObject == null) {
        if ((m_ConnectionPoolMax < 0) ||
            ((m_ConnectionPoolMax > 0) &&
             (poolSize < m_ConnectionPoolMax))) {

            // Add a new connection.
            int i = addConnection();

            // If a new connection was created, use it
            if (i >= 0) {
                connectionObject = (ConnectionObject)
                    m_pool.elementAt(i);
            }
        }
        else {
            trace("Maximum number of connections exceeded");
        }
    }

    // If we have a connection, set the last time accessed,
    // the use count, and the in use flag
```

```
    if (connectionObject != null) {
      connectionObject.inUse = true;
      connectionObject.useCount++;
      touch(connectionObject);
      con = connectionObject.con;
    }

    return con;
  }
```

Figure 8.20 shows the `close` method. Closing a connection with the ConnectionPool `close` method does not necessarily close the connection; it just may be placed back into the connection pool ready for another use.

Figure 8.20

close source code.

```
/**
 * <p>Places the connection back into the connection pool,
 * or closes the connection if the maximum use count has
 * been reached
 *
 * @param Connection object to close
 */
public synchronized void close(java.sql.Connection con)
  {
    // Find the connection in the pool
    int index = find(con);

    if (index != -1) {
      ConnectionObject co = (ConnectionObject)
        m_pool.elementAt(index);

      // If the use count exceeds the max, remove it from
      // the pool.
      if ((m_ConnectionUseCount > 0) &&
          (co.useCount >= m_ConnectionUseCount)) {
        trace("Connection use count exceeded");
        removeFromPool(index);
      }
      else {
        // Clear the use count and reset the time last used
        touch(co);
        co.inUse = false;
      }
    }
  }
```

ConnectionPool Example: A Local Pool One use for our new ConnectionPool object is to embed it within a servlet. Let's rewrite the EmployeeList servlet we saw earlier in this chapter to use the ConnectionPool—we'll call it "FastEmployeeList1." First, we need to define a ConnectionPool instance variable to hold our local copy of the connection pool (as shown in Figure 8.21).

Even though it is spelled out in the comment block above the instance variable, it's worth repeating: You should consider instance variables as global in nature to all invocations of the servlet. The reason is that there are multiple threads executing using only one instance of the servlet.

Now we can override the init and destroy methods of the servlet to create and destroy the connection pool (Figure 8.22).

Next, we can simply modify the original code to use the ConnectionPool object to get a connection, instead of requesting one from the JDBC DriverManager. When we are finished with the query, we also need to call the close method on the ConnectionPool object to release it back into the pool. This is shown in Figure 8.23.

After the servlet has been compiled and configured for your particular Web server, you should see a dramatic improvement in performance over the original EmployeeList servlet (as seen in Figure 8.24). Take a look back at Figure 8.12; note the time it took to execute the query and compare it to the time in Figure 8.24. All I can say is "wow!"

Figure 8.21

Defining an
instance variable.

```
/**
 * <p>This is a simple servlet that will use JDBC to gather all
 * of the employee information from a database and format it
 * into an HTML table. This servlet uses a local connection
 * pool.
 */

public class FastEmployeeList1 extends HttpServlet
{
    // Our connection pool. Note that instance variables are
    // actually global to all clients since there is only
    // one instance of the servlet that has multiple threads
    // of execution
    javaservlets.jdbc.ConnectionPool m_connectionPool;
```

Figure 8.22

Overriding the
init and destroy
methods.

```
/**
 * <p>Initialize the servlet. This is called once when the
 * servlet is loaded. It is guaranteed to complete before any
 * requests are made to the servlet
 *
 * @param cfg Servlet configuration information
 */

public void init(ServletConfig cfg)
  throws ServletException
  {
    super.init(cfg);

    // Create our connection pool
    m_connectionPool = new javaservlets.jdbc.ConnectionPool();

    // Initialize the connection pool. This will start all
    // of the connections as specified in the connection
    // pool configuration file
    try {
      m_connectionPool.initialize();
        //("javaservlets.db.FastEmployeeList.cfg");
    }
    catch (Exception ex) {
      // Convert the exception
      ex.printStackTrace();
      throw new ServletException
        ("Unable to initialize connection pool");
    }
  }

/**
 * <p>Destroy the servlet. This is called once when the servlet
 * is unloaded.
 */

public void destroy()
  {
    // Tear down our connection pool if it was created
    if (m_connectionPool != null) {
      m_connectionPool.destroy();
    }
    super.destroy();
  }
```

All the time necessary to create the connection pool is taken in the init method of the servlet. Remember that the init method is called once when the servlet is first loaded; you may want to configure your Web server to preload the servlet when the system is started, so that the first user doesn't have to wait for the pool to be created.

Figure 8.23

Using the
ConnectionPool
object.

```
try {
  // Get an available connection from our connection pool
  con = m_connectionPool.getConnection();

  // Create a statement object that we can execute queries
  // with
  stmt = con.createStatement();

  // Execute the query
  rs = stmt.executeQuery(query);

  // Format the results into an HTML table
  rowCount = formatTable(rs, out);

}
catch (Exception ex) {
  // Send the error back to the client
  out.println("Exeption!");
  ex.printStackTrace(out);
  rc = false;
}
finally {
  try {
    // Always close properly
    if (rs != null) {
      rs.close();
    }
    if (stmt != null) {
      stmt.close();
    }
    if (con != null) {
      // Put the connection back into the pool
      m_connectionPool.close(con);
    }
  }
  catch (Exception ex) {
    // Ignore any errors here
  }
}
```

ConnectionPool Example: A Global Pool How could things possibly get any better? The previous example used a connection pool that was local to the servlet; let's look at a way we can make the connection pool global to any servlet. We can do this by writing a simple servlet that owns the connection pool and is loaded when the system is started. Servlets can reference other running servlets in the same virtual machine by using standard API calls.

Figure 8.24

Results of
FastEmployeeList1
servlet.

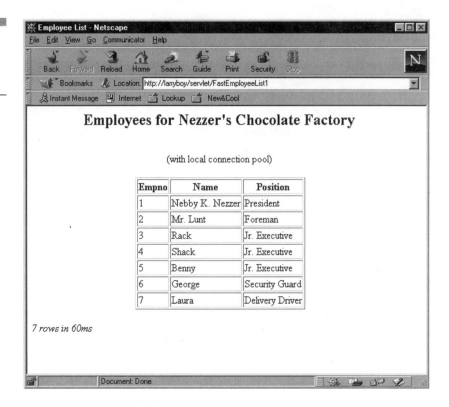

Figure 8.25 shows the servlet (ConnectionServlet) that houses the connection pool.

Figure 8.25

ConnectionServlet
source code.

```
/**
 * <p>This is a simple servlet that hold a global connection
 * pool.
 */
public class ConnectionServlet extends HttpServlet
{
    // Our connection pool.
    javaservlets.jdbc.ConnectionPool m_connectionPool;

    /**
     * <p>Get a JDBC connection from the pool
     *
     * @return JDBC connection
     */
    public java.sql.Connection getConnection() throws Exception
    {
        java.sql.Connection con = null;
```

```
        if (m_connectionPool != null) {
          con = m_connectionPool.getConnection();
        }
        return con;
    }

/**
  * <p>Closes the given JDBC connection
  *
  * @param con JDBC Connection
  */
public void close(java.sql.Connection con)
    {
      if (m_connectionPool != null) {
        m_connectionPool.close(con);
      }
    }
/**
  * <p>Initialize the servlet. This is called once when the
  * servlet is loaded. It is guaranteed to complete before any
  * requests are made to the servlet
  *
  * @param cfg Servlet configuration information
  */

public void init(ServletConfig cfg)
    throws ServletException
    {
      super.init(cfg);

      // Create our connection pool
      m_connectionPool = new javaservlets.jdbc.ConnectionPool();

      // Initialize the connection pool.This will start all
      // the connections as specified in the connection
      // pool configuration file
      try {
        m_connectionPool.initialize();
          //("javaservlets.db.FastEmployeeList.cfg");
      }
      catch (Exception ex) {
        // Convert the exception
        ex.printStackTrace();
        throw new ServletException
          ("Unable to initialize connection pool");
      }
    }

/**
  * <p>Destroy the servlet. This is called once when the servlet
  * is unloaded.
  */

public void destroy()
    {
      // Tear down our connection pool if it was created
```

```
    if (m_connectionPool != null) {
      m_connectionPool.destroy();
    }
    super.destroy();
  }

}
```

Again, we have created the connection pool in the `init` method and destroyed it in the `destroy` method. Note that two methods have been added to permit public access to the `getConnection` and `close` methods.

Figure 8.26

Referencing other servlets.

```
// Get the ConnectionServlet that holds the
// connection pool
ServletConfig config = getServletConfig();
ServletContext context = config.getServletContext();
Servlet servlet = context.getServlet("ConnectionServlet");
if (servlet == null) {
    throw new ServletException("ConnectionServlet not started");
}
ConnectionServlet conServlet = (ConnectionServlet) servlet;
```

Figure 8.27

Results of FastEmployeeList2 servlet.

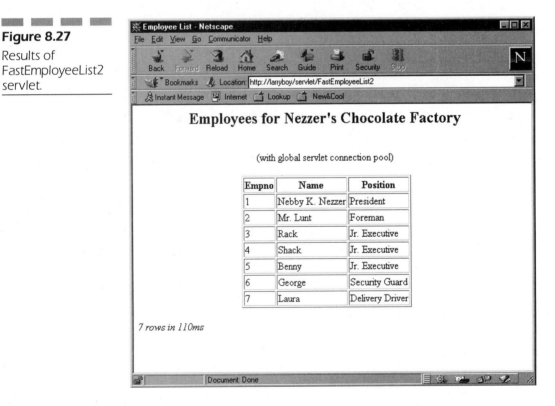

Using this new ConnectionServlet servlet is quite easy. All we need to do is look up the servlet by name to get a reference to the object (as shown in Figure 8.26).

The rest of the servlet (called FastEmployeeList2) is basically the same as FastEmployee1. When configuring your Web server with the ConnectionServlet servlet, you will definitely want to have it loaded when the system is started; otherwise, the call to "getServlet" will fail.

Figure 8.27 shows output from the FastEmployeeList2 servlet.

Working with Images

A very important aspect of any Web page is the visual content, including images. The employee table we have been working with contains a column that stores the image of each employee. Moving the image over the Web is as easy as reading the picture with JDBC, setting the HTTP response header, and dumping the raw data back to the client. The client will be responsible for rendering the image properly within the browser.

Image Example: ImageServer

In order to process image data from a database, let's take a look at a generic servlet, named "ImageServer," which will accept the parameters that specify the location of the image and return the image back to the client. We've already seen how to use connection pooling, which will be used to ensure adequate performance. The main logic in the servlet consists of executing the query, reading the binary data, and writing to the output stream, which eventually winds up back at the client (see Figure 8.28).

Figure 8.28

Processing database images.

```
/**
 * <p>Reads the database for an image and outputs that image
 * to the client
 *
 * @param resp The response from the servlet
 * @param table The name of the table containing the data
 * @param column The column name of the stored image
 * @param where The SQL where clause to uniquely identify the row
 */
```

```
        private void getImage(HttpServletResponse resp,
                              String table, String column,
                              String where)
    throws java.io.IOException
    {

      // Format the SQL string
      String sql = "select " + column + " from " + table +
        " where " + where;

      // The JDBC Connection object
      Connection con = null;

      // The JDBC Statement object
      Statement stmt = null;

      // The JDBC ResultSet object
      ResultSet rs = null;

      try {

        // Get an available connection from our connection pool
        con = m_connectionPool.getConnection();

        // Create a statement object that we can execute queries
        // with
        stmt = con.createStatement();

        // Execute the query
        rs = stmt.executeQuery(sql);

        // If this is an empty result set, send back a nice
        // error message
        if (!rs.next()) {
          resp.setContentType("text/html");
          // Create a PrintWriter to write the response
          java.io.PrintWriter pout =
            new java.io.PrintWriter(resp.getOutputStream());

          pout.println("No matching record found");
          pout.flush();
          pout.close();
        }

        // We have results! Read the image and write it to
        // our output stream
        resp.setContentType("image/gif");

        // Get the output stream
        javax.servlet.ServletOutputStream out =
          resp.getOutputStream();

        // Get an input stream to the stored image
        java.io.InputStream in = rs.getBinaryStream(1);

        // Some database systems may not be able to tell us
        // how big the data actuall is. Let's read all of it
        // into a buffer.
```

```java
java.io.ByteArrayOutputStream baos =
  new java.io.ByteArrayOutputStream();

byte b[] = new byte[1024];
while (true) {
  int bytes = in.read(b);

  // If there was nothing read, get out of loop
  if (bytes == -1) {
    break;
  }

  // Write the buffer to our byte array
  baos.write(b, 0, bytes);
}

// Now we have the entire image in the buffer. Get
// the length and write it to the output stream
b = baos.toByteArray();

resp.setContentLength(b.length);
out.write(b, 0, b.length);
out.flush();
out.close();
}
catch (Exception ex) {
  // Set the content type of the response
  resp.setContentType("text/html");

  // Create a PrintWriter to write the response
  java.io.PrintWriter pout =
    new java.io.PrintWriter(resp.getOutputStream());

  pout.println("Exception!");
  ex.printStackTrace(pout);
  pout.flush();
  pout.close();
}
finally {
  try {
    // Always close properly
    if (rs != null) {
      rs.close();
    }
    if (stmt != null) {
      stmt.close();
    }
    if (con != null) {
      // Put the connection back into the pool
      m_connectionPool.close(con);
    }
  }
  catch (Exception ex) {
    // Ignore any errors here
  }
}
}
```

Notice how the content header is set for the response. If an exception or error occurs, the content type is set to "text/html" so that we can send back a readable message. If the image is read properly, the content type is set to "image/gif," which notifies the client that image data will follow. We also have to set the length of the raw image data. The most reliable way to determine this from JDBC is to read the entire contents of the binary column into a ByteArrayOutputStream, which will cache all the data in a byte array. Once all the data have been read, we can set the content length and then dump the cache to the output stream.

The ImageServer servlet takes three parameters.

1. `table`—the name of the database table to query.
2. `column`—the name of the column that holds the image.
3. `where`—the SQL WHERE clause that will cause the required row to be selected.

Here is an example.

```
servlet/ImageServer?table=Employee&column=Picture&where=Empno=1
```

Note that the parameters list is separated from the servlet name with a question mark, and parameters are separated by an ampersand.

Adding Images to EmployeeList

Now that we have a servlet that will return image data, let's update the EmployeeList servlet to include a link to an image of the employee. This new servlet will be called EmployeeList2 and can be found with the rest of the source code on the accompanying CD-ROM. Figure 8.29 shows

Figure 8.29

Using the ImageServer servlet.

```
// Add a special column in the table for the picture
out.println("<td>Click ");
out.println("<a href=/servlet/ImageServer?" +
            "table=Employee&amp" +
            "column=Picture&amp" +
            "where=Empno=" + empno + ">here</a>");
out.println("</td>");
```

Figure 8.30

Results of the
EmployeeList2
servlet.

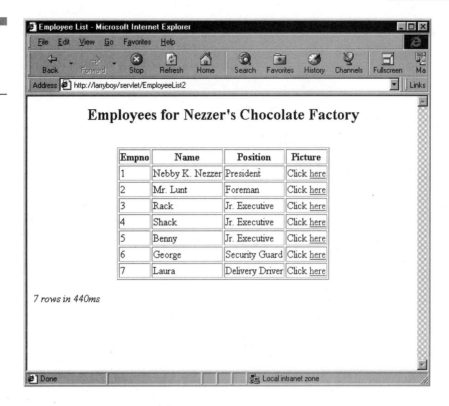

the Java code that will insert a new column into the HTML table. When clicked, this will invoke the ImageServer servlet, which will return the image.

Note that the "&" character separating each parameter has been expanded to "&amp." This is because the "&" character is reserved in HTML to specify the character-entity insertion point. To get around this you will need to replace any ampersand character with its character-entity value, either &#38 or &amp.

After configuring your Web server for the ImageServer and EmployeeList2 servlets, invoking the EmployeeList2 servlet will produce the results shown in Figure 8.30.

Notice the new column in the table that contains a link to the image of the employee. Figure 8.31 shows the results when one of the columns is clicked. Note the complete URL in the browser's address field.

Figure 8.31

Image data from
ImageServer.

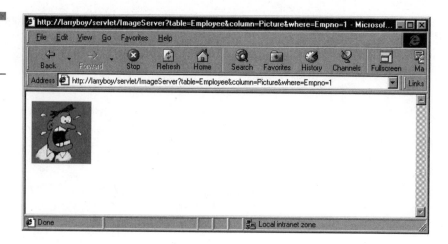

Summary

We've really covered a lot of ground in this chapter. JDBC is no small topic, but I hope that you now have a firm grasp of what it is, what types of JDBC drivers are available, and what the basic steps are in writing a JDBC application. I hope that you also realize how easy it is to publish database information on the Web by using servlets. This is exciting stuff!

We also covered ways to improve usability and performance by splitting output between multiple pages and using connection pooling. Both of these techniques are important building blocks when creating an industrial-strength JDBC solution for the Web.

The next chapter will combine the knowledge you now possess about HTML forms and JDBC to create an on-line content provider. I'm sure you have seen examples of these types of systems in your wanderings on the Web; now it's your turn to write one.

# CHAPTER 9

Putting It All Together: The Servlet Connection

N̲ow that you have HTML forms and JDBC under control, it's time to put them together and create an integrated Web application.

The Challenge

You are tasked to create a new Web site that will provide content for servlet developers. This new Web site, the Servlet Connection, will provide Frequently Asked Question (FAQ) lists, software downloads, and other information pertinent to developers working with servlets. The Web site will be provided free of charge, but all users are required to set up a user account so that their activity can be tracked.

The Servlet Connection

It might help to take a look at the finished product first, before exploring the details of how to create the servlet that handles all the requests.

When a user first visits the "Servlet Connection," he or she will be presented with a login screen (see Figure 9.1). The user can either enter a user ID and password to log in to the system or set up a new account.

Pressing the Login button will submit the form, and the database will be read to ensure that a valid user ID and password were entered. Once the account information has been validated, the user will be taken to the main content page.

Pressing the New Account button will take the user to a new page where account information can be entered (see Figure 9.2). All the fields are required, and the user must enter a valid user ID that is not already in use.

The form is submitted to the server when the user presses the Add Account button. At this time all the data entered by the user are validated, and the user database is searched to ensure that the account number is unique. Once all the validation steps have been successfully completed, a new user record will be inserted into the database and the user will be taken to the main content page, shown in Figure 9.3.

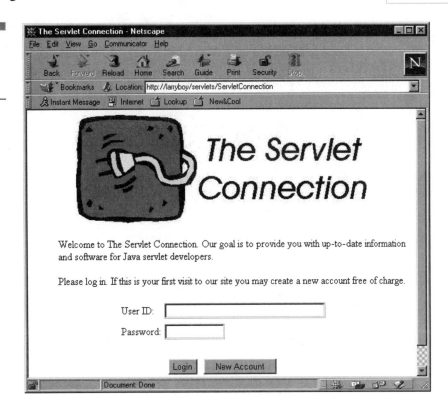

There really isn't much content on the main page, but you get the idea. Let's break the Servlet Connection servlet apart and see what makes it tick.

Creating the Database

At the heart of just about every business application beats a database. The Servlet Connection servlet is a rather simple application and only uses one database table. Creating this table for a specific database is quite simple; format the CREATE TABLE statement in SQL and submit it to the database engine for processing. But what if you don't know which database will be used? The answer is metadata.

Metadata Are Your Friend   What are metadata? Quite simply, they are data describing data or, in the case of JDBC, metadata describe the

Figure 9.2

The Servlet
Connection add
user account page.

database. If you have taken a good look through the JDBC specification, you have noticed that many pages are devoted to describing metadata. All this discussion is not because the developers wanted a thick specification (although that has been suggested) but because all these metadata are vitally important in enabling developers to create robust, generic applications. These applications can ask the database engine questions at run time about its contents and gather information about how it functions; this is quite different from making assumptions about the database engine at design time when you are compiling the application.

JDBC has divided the metadata into two areas.

1. DatabaseMetaData—There are well over 100 methods in the DatabaseMetaData class that provide important information about the behavior and settings of the database. These methods describe minimum and maximum settings, types of supported data, descriptors used for keywords, and the contents of the database (catalogs, tables, views, etc.).

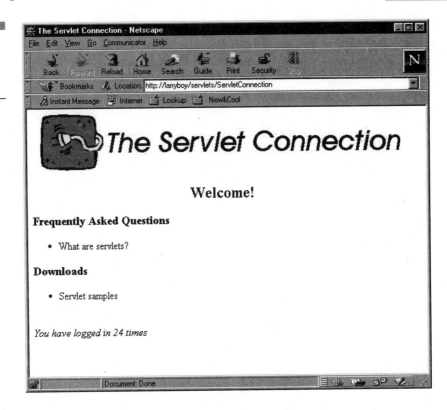

2. ResultSetMetaData—The ResultSetMetaData class contains methods that describe the results of a SQL query, such as the number of columns, column labels, and column attributes (data type, length, decimal places, etc.). Chapter 8 contains examples using ResultSetMetaData to discover information about a result set generated from a SQL query.

Generic Table Creation

Let's take a look at one way to generically create a database table. It might not sound as if this is very important—until you have to work with multiple database engines. For the most part, SQL is SQL regardless of the database engine. This is very true for Data Manipulation Language (DML), which defines how to retrieve and modify data in the database (SELECT, UPDATE, and DELETE) and is dictated by the ANSI SQL specification. Unfortunately, this is not true for Data Definition

Language (DDL), which defines how to create and modify database structures (CREATE, DROP, and ALTER catalogs, tables, and indices).

If the DDL necessary to create a new table differs among database engines, how do you create a new table through a generic application? The answer, of course, is by using database metadata. Each column in the table will have certain attributes: data type, length, decimal places, and name. The data type defines the type of data that will be stored in the column, such as character, integer, numeric, and so on. Here's where the problem begins: Different database engines describe the same basic data type in different ways with different types of parameters. In general columns are described by:

```
<Column Name> <Data Type Name>[Optional creation parameters]
```

For instance, one database may define a character column of width 30 as "CHAR(30)," while another database may define this as "VAR-CHAR(30)," and yet another may define this as "TEXT." How do you know which one is correct? The answer to this dilemma is to ask the database how it describes a given type of data; this is done by using database metadata. Table 9.1 describes the valid JDBC data types.

TABLE 9.1

JDBC Data Types

Data Type	Description
BIGINT	Large (eight-byte) signed integer value
BINARY	Binary (noncharacter) data, such as images
BIT	A single bit of data; also known as Boolean
CHAR	A single character of data
DATE	Date (month, day, year) value
DECIMAL	Signed, exact numeric value with a fixed number of decimal places
DOUBLE	Signed, approximate value (15 digits of mantissa precision)
FLOAT	Signed, approximate value (15 digits of mantissa precision)
INTEGER	Signed integer value
LONGVARBINARY	Large (some databases support gigabytes) variable-length binary data

TABLE 9.1

(cont.)

Data Type	Description
LONGVARCHAR	Large (some databases support gigabytes) variable-length character data
NULL	No value
NUMERIC	Signed, exact numeric value with a fixed number of decimal places
OTHER	Database-specific data type
REAL	Signed, approximate values (seven digits of mantissa precision)
SMALLINT	Small (two-byte) signed integer value
TIME	Time (hours, minutes, seconds, and sometimes milliseconds) value
TIMESTAMP	Date and time (month, day, year, hours, minutes, seconds, and sometimes milliseconds) value
TINYINT	Small (one-byte) signed integer value
VARBINARY	Variable-length binary data
VARCHAR	Variable-length character data

For each column you want to create in a table, you can define the JDBC data type of that column and ask the database for the data type name. Figure 9.4 shows the Java code that will perform this function.

The routine begins by getting a list of all the data types supported by the database (a database connection was previously established). We can then go through the data type list and find a matching entry. Once a match has been found, the name and optional parameters can be retrieved. This routine is the basic building block for generating a database-specific CREATE TABLE SQL statement without writing any database-specific code.

The BuildUser Application Let's now take a look at an application that uses these database metadata to create the user table required for the Servlet Connection servlet. I've created a helper class (cleverly named SQLHelper), which contains methods to get the data type names and to build SQL statements on the fly. The BuildUser application uses

Figure 9.4

Code for looking up
a data type name.

```java
/**
 * <p>Given a JDBC SQL type, return the type name as known by
 * the database and any creation parameters that it requires
 *
 * @param type JDBC SQL type
 * @return SQL type name
 */
public String getTypeName(int type) throws Exception
{
    if (m_con == null) {
        return null;
    }

    String name = null;

    // Get the database meta data
    java.sql.DatabaseMetaData md = m_con.getMetaData();

    // Get a list of all of the SQL types supported by
    // the data source
    java.sql.ResultSet rs = md.getTypeInfo();

    // Now loop through and find the first type name for the
    // given JDBC type
    while (rs.next()) {

        // Get the name of the column. We may not need it but
        // to ensure that we work against all types of data sources
        // we have to get the columns in order
        String typeName = rs.getString(1);

        // Get the type of the column
        int sqlType = rs.getInt(2);

        // Get the creation parameters
        String params = rs.getString(6);

        // Compare
        if (sqlType == type) {
            name = typeName.trim();

            if (params != null) {
                name += "(" + params.trim() + ")";
            }

            break;
        }
    }

    return name;
}
```

SQLHelper to build and execute a CREATE TABLE SQL statement to
create the user table (see Figure 9.5).

Figure 9.5

Building a database
table.

```java
/**
 * <p>Build the database table
 *
 * @param driver JDBC driver class name
 * @param url JDBC connection URL
 * @param user User name
 * @param password User password
 */
private void build(String driver, String url,
                   String user, String password)
{
    java.sql.Connection con = null;
    java.sql.PreparedStatement ps = null;

    try {

        // Attempt to create a new instance of the specified
        // JDBC driver. Well behaved drivers will register
        // themselves with the JDBC DriverManager when they
        // are instantiated
        trace("Registering " + driver);
        java.sql.Driver d = (java.sql.Driver)
          Class.forName(driver).newInstance();

        // Create a connection to the given URL
        con = java.sql.DriverManager.getConnection(url, user,
                                                   password);

        // Create a new helper class
        SQLHelper helper = new SQLHelper(con);

        // Drop the table
        trace("Dropping existing " + m_tableName + " table");
        helper.drop(m_tableName);

        // Setup the columns
        ColumnDesc cols[] = new ColumnDesc[5];
        cols[0] = new ColumnDesc("User", Types.VARCHAR);
        cols[1] = new ColumnDesc("Password", Types.VARCHAR);
        cols[2] = new ColumnDesc("Email", Types.VARCHAR);
        cols[3] = new ColumnDesc("GetEmail", Types.VARCHAR);
        cols[4] = new ColumnDesc("Logins", Types.INTEGER);

        // Create the table
        trace("Creating table " + m_tableName);
        helper.create(m_tableName, cols);

    }
    catch (Exception ex) {
        ex.printStackTrace();
    }
    finally {

        try {
            // Make sure we always clean up after ourselves
            if (ps != null) {
                ps.close();
```

```
      }
      if (con != null) {
        con.close();
      }
    }
    catch (Exception ex) {
    }
  }

}
```

The basic steps in the build routine are as follows.

1. Establish a database connection.

2. Drop the user table if it exists.

3. Create a list of columns for the table. The JDBC data type is defined—not the data type name. The data type name will be retrieved from the database metadata.

4. Invoke the `helper` method to create the user table according to the column definitions.

5. Gracefully close the connection.

Of additional interest is the create routine (shown in Figure 9.6), which will actually piece together the SQL statement necessary to create the table for the current database system.

Figure 9.6

Assembling a
CREATE TABLE SQL
statement.

```
/**
 * <p>Creates the given table with the given column descriptions
 *
 * @param name Table name to create
 * @param colDesc Array of ColumnDesc objects describing each
 * column in the table
 */
public void create(String name, ColumnDesc cols[])
  throws Exception
  {
    if (cols == null) {
      return;
    }

    boolean didCreate = false;

    String sql = "create table " + name + " (";

    // Loop for each column description

    for (int i = 0; i < cols.length; i++) {
      ColumnDesc c = cols[i];

      if (c == null) {
        continue;
      }
```

```
    // Get the type name
    String typeName = getTypeName(c.getType());

    // Format the SQL string

    // If this isn't the first column, separate with a comma
    if (i > 0) {
      sql += ",";
    }

    // Add the column name
    sql += c.getName() + " ";

    // Add the length and decimal places if necessary
    sql += formatType(typeName, c);
  }
  sql += ")";

  java.sql.Statement stmt = null;

  try {
    // Create a statement object
    stmt = m_con.createStatement();

    System.out.println("Executing " + sql);

    // Submit the drop table statement to the database
    stmt.executeUpdate(sql);
    didCreate = true;
  }
  finally {
    if (!didCreate) {

      // The table did not get created. Display the sql
      // statement for debugging purposes
      System.out.println(sql);
    }

    // Ensure that we always close the statement properly
    if (stmt != null) {
      try {
        stmt.close();
      }
      catch (Exception ex) {
      }
    }
  }
}
```

Notice how the SQL statement is assembled using each column that was defined. To better illustrate what is going on in this routine, let's take a look at the output generated when the BuildUser application is invoked (note that the lines have been split to improve readability).

```
java javaservlets.servletCon.BuildUser sun.jdbc.odbc.JdbcOdbcDriver
        jdbc:odbc:ServletConnection
```

```
BuildUser: Registering sun.jdbc.odbc.JdbcOdbcDriver
BuildUser: Dropping existing User table
BuildUser: Creating table User
Executing create table User (User TEXT,Password TEXT,Email TEXT,
           GetEmail TEXT,Logins LONG)
```

Note that the BuildUser application takes four parameters: the JDBC driver class name, the JDBC connection URL, the user, and the password. We're using the JDBC-ODBC bridge with an ODBC data source named "Servlet Connection"; the ODBC data source does not require a user ID or password, so the parameters were omitted. The JDBC driver is then registered, the old table is dropped if it existed, and a new user table is created. The SQL statement generated is shown in the last line. This method of creating the user table should work for just about any JDBC-compliant database system.

Connection Pooling

Now that the database has been properly created, we can focus on the Servlet Connection servlet. We took a close look at connection pooling in the previous chapter, and we will be using it again in the Servlet Connection servlet. The pool will be created in the `init` method of the servlet and closed down in the `destroy` method (see Figure 9.7).

To refresh your memory, the connection pool will preallocate a set number of JDBC connections to a specified URL and hold them in a pool. The servlet will then request a connection from the pool, use it, and then place it back into the pool. This is a tremendous performance booster, since establishing a database connection can be one of the most costly of all JDBC operations. Parameters for the connection pool are specified in a configuration file, which, in our case, is named "javaservlets/servletCon/ServletConnection.cfg." The configuration will be found by searching the current CLASSPATH, just as if it were a Java class file.

Session Tracking

Yet another advantage Java servlets have over conventional CGI scripts is the ability to preserve state via session tracking. By this I mean that information can be maintained between server requests without having to embed additional information into the client. By using HTTP session

Figure 9.7

Servlet Connection
init and destroy
methods.

```java
/**
 * <p>Initialize the servlet. This is called once when the
 * servlet is loaded. It is guaranteed to complete before any
 * requests are made to the servlet
 *
 * @param cfg Servlet configuration information
 */
public void init(ServletConfig cfg)
  throws ServletException
  {
    super.init(cfg);

    // Create our connection pool
    m_connectionPool = new javaservlets.jdbc.ConnectionPool();

    // Initialize the connection pool. This will start all
    // of the connections as specified in the connection
    // pool configuration file
    try {
      m_connectionPool.initialize
        ("javaservlets/servletCon/ServletConnection.cfg");
    }
    catch (Exception ex) {
      // Convert the exception
      ex.printStackTrace();
      throw new ServletException
        ("Unable to initialize connection pool");
    }
  }

/**
 * <p>Destroy the servlet. This is called once when the servlet
 * is unloaded.
 */
public void destroy()
  {
    // Tear down our connection pool if it was created
    if (m_connectionPool != null) {
      m_connectionPool.destroy();
    }
    super.destroy();
  }
```

tracking you can add your own objects to a master session object; this master session object is guaranteed to be maintained for the life of a client's session. In other words, as long as a user maintains a connection to your Web server with his or her Web browser a unique session will also be maintained.

In the case of the Servlet Connection servlet we will be maintaining user information in the HTTP session object. Once a user has logged in to our site, he or she will remain logged in for the lifetime of the session.

Figure 9.8

Retrieving an HTTP
session object.

```
// Get the session object or create one if it does not
// exist. A session will persist as long as the client
// browser maintains a connection to the server.
HttpSession session = req.getSession(true);

// We should always get a session back
if (session == null) {
  out.println("ERROR: Internal servlet problem - no session");
  out.flush();
  out.close();
  return;
}

// Get the current user info. If we get back a null, the
// user is not currently logged in
UserInfo info = (UserInfo) session.getValue(USER);
```

Figure 9.8 shows a code segment that gets the current session object (or creates a new session object if this is the user's first hit to the Web server) and then attempts to retrieve user information from the session by a string key.

The first time a user invokes the servlet a new HTTP session object will be created. When we attempt to get the UserInfo object from the session object, it will be null, since we have not placed any information into the session. After the user successfully logs in, we can add the User-Info to the session, as shown in Figure 9.9.

As we'll see in later chapters, HTTP session tracking is an invaluable tool for maintaining server-side information for each client.

The Login Page

The first thing the user will see when accessing the Servlet Connection site is the login page (refer to Figure 9.1). The page is generated from within the Servlet Connection servlet, as shown in Figure 9.10.

Figure 9.9

Adding values to
the HTTP session
object.

```
// Create a new user info object
info = new UserInfo();
info.setUser(user);
info.setLoginCount(loginCount(user));

// Set the current user info for the session
session.putValue(USER, info);
```

Figure 9.10

Creating the login page.

```java
/**
 * <p>Formats the Servlet Connection login screen
 *
 * @param out Output stream
 * @param uri Requesting URI
 */
public void login(java.io.PrintWriter out, String uri)
  {
    out.println("<html>");
    out.println("<head>");
    out.println("<title>The Servlet Connection</title>");
    out.println("</head>");
    out.println("<center>");
    out.println("<img src=\"/images/ServletConnection.jpg\">");
    out.println("</center>");
    out.println("<br><dir>");
    out.println("<p>Welcome to The Servlet Connection. Our goal");
    out.println("is to provide you with up-to-date information");
    out.println("and software for Java servlet developers.</p>");
    out.println("<p>Please log in. If this is your first visit");
    out.println("to our site you may create a new account free");
    out.println("of charge.</p>");
    out.println("</dir>");
    out.println("<form method=POST action=\"" + uri + "\">");
    out.println("<center>");
    out.println("<table>");
    out.println("<tr><td>User ID:</td>");
    out.println("<td><input type=text name=" +
                FIELD_USER + " size=30></td>");
    out.println("</tr>");
    out.println("<tr><td>Password:</td>");
    out.println("<td><input type=password name=" +
                FIELD_PASSWORD + " size=10></td>");
    out.println("</tr>");
    out.println("</table>");
    out.println("<br>");
    out.println("<table>");
    out.println("<tr><td>");
    out.println("<input type=submit name=" + ACTION + " value=\"" +
                ACTION_LOGIN + "\">");
    out.println("</td><td>");
    out.println("<input type=submit name=" + ACTION + " value=\"" +
                ACTION_NEW_ACCOUNT + "\">");
    out.println("</td></tr>");
    out.println("</table>");
    out.println("</center>");
    out.println("</form>");

    out.println("</html>");
  }
```

The output stream has already been retrieved from the HTTP response object, as well as the URI used to invoke the servlet. We need to know the URI, since the Servlet Connection servlet is used to service all the requests for the site; any HTML form actions will invoke the Servlet Connection servlet again with form-specific data. We can determine the state of the client through a combination of the values stored in the HTTP session object and values supplied by the HTML form.

Using the Database

The Servlet Connection servlet needs to use the database to query and modify the user table using JDBC. Let's review the basic steps in writing a JDBC application.

1. Establish a connection to the database.
2. Execute a SQL statement.
3. Process the results.
4. Disconnect from the database.

Since we are using a connection pool, connecting to and disconnecting from the database is already handled for us. That leaves executing a SQL statement and processing the results; how could it get any easier?

Figure 9.11 shows the code segment used to add a new user to the database. This shows JDBC programming at its finest; getting a connection from the connection pool, creating a prepared statement, setting parameters on the statement, executing the statement, and cleaning up.

Forcing HTML Refresh

Most Web browsers today have intelligent HTML page caching; this can be very beneficial for performance reasons but it can also pose problems when you want to ensure that the Web browser reads an HTML page from the Web instead of from a cache. There are several different ways to force the browser to bypass the cache and load exclusively from the Web, but Figure 9.12 shows the most reliable method.

Figure 9.11

Adding a user to
the database.

```
// The JDBC Connection object
Connection con = null;

// The JDBC PreparedStatement object
PreparedStatement ps = null;

boolean rc = false;

try {

  // Get an available connection from our connection pool
  con = m_connectionPool.getConnection();

  // Create a statement object that we can execute queries
  // with
  ps = con.prepareStatement
    ("INSERT into User" +
     "(User, Password, Email, GetEmail, Logins) " +
     "values (?,?,?,?,?)");

  // Set the statement values
  ps.setString(1, user);
  ps.setString(2, password);
  ps.setString(3, email);
  ps.setString(4, getmail);
  ps.setInt(5, 1);

  // Execute the statement
  ps.execute();
  rc = true;
}
catch (Exception ex) {
  // Send the error back
  formatError(out, ex.getMessage());
}
finally {
  try {
    // Always close properly
    if (ps != null) {
      ps.close();
    }
    if (con != null) {
      // Put the connection back into the pool
      m_connectionPool.close(con);
    }
  }
  catch (Exception ex) {
    // Ignore any errors here
  }
}
```

■■ ■■ ■■ ■■

Figure 9.12

Forcing an HTML
page to be read
from the Web
instead of a cache.

```
// Set the response header to force the browser to
// load the html from the Web instead of it's cache
resp.setHeader("Expires", "Tues, 01 Jan 1980 00:00:00 GMT");
```

If the date and time of the client are past the date given, the Web browser will consider any cached data for the Web site to be expired and will reload the page exclusively from the Web.

Servicing the Request

We've taken a look at all the pieces of the puzzle; now it's time to tie them all together. Figure 9.13 shows the doGet() method, which is invoked by the Web server to service a request. The doPost() method simply calls doGet(), so they are identical. Most of the doGet() method is devoted to figuring out what action the user has taken. This is done by examining the actions taken by submitting various HTML forms and using the HTTP session tracking mechanism to preserve state. Once the state of the client is determined, the appropriate routine is invoked to perform some type of form data validation and present the user with the next Web page.

■■ ■■ ■■ ■■

Figure 9.13

Servlet Connection
doGet() method.

```
/**
 * <p>Performs the HTTP GET operation
 *
 * @param req The request from the client
 * @param resp The response from the servlet
 */
public void doGet(HttpServletRequest req,
                  HttpServletResponse resp)
   throws ServletException, java.io.IOException
   {
      // Set the content type of the response
      resp.setContentType("text/html");

      // Create a PrintWriter to write the response
      java.io.PrintWriter out =
        new java.io.PrintWriter(resp.getOutputStream());

      // Get the session object or create one if it does not
      // exist. A session will persist as long as the client
      // browser maintains a connection to the server.
      HttpSession session = req.getSession(true);
```

```
// We should always get a session back
if (session == null) {
  out.println("ERROR: Internal servlet problem - no session");
  out.flush();
  out.close();
  return;
}

// Get the current user info. If we get back a null, the
// user is not currently logged in
UserInfo info = (UserInfo) session.getValue(USER);

// Get the requesting URI - that should be us
// Get our URI
String uri = req.getRequestURI();

// Get the action command (if one exists)
String action = getParameter(req, ACTION);

try {

  // Figure out what was requested

  if ((action != null) &&
      action.equals(ACTION_NEW_ACCOUNT)) {

    // Creating a new account.
    createAccount(out, uri);
  }
  else if ((action != null) &&
           action.equals(ACTION_ADD_ACCOUNT)) {

    // Adding a new account - validate the data
    boolean rc = validateAccount(out, req);

    // The data is valid and the account was added
    if (rc) {

      // Get the user from the request
      String user = getParameter(req, FIELD_USER);

      // Create a new user info object
      info = new UserInfo();
      info.setUser(user);
      info.setLoginCount(1);

      // Set the current user info for the session
      session.putValue(USER, info);

      // Take the user to the main page
      createMain(out, uri, info);
    }
  }
  else if ((action != null) &&
           action.equals(ACTION_LOGIN)) {

    // Login the user
    boolean rc = login(out, req);
```

```
        // The user was valid
        if (rc) {

            // Get the user from the request
            String user = getParameter(req, FIELD_USER);

            // Create a new user info object
            info = new UserInfo();
            info.setUser(user);
            info.setLoginCount(loginCount(user));

            // Set the current user info for the session
            session.putValue(USER, info);

            // Take the user to the main page
            createMain(out, uri, info);
        }
    }
    else {

        if (info == null) {
            // No action was given from a page. Present the
            // initial login page.
            login(out, uri);
        }
        else {

            // We have a user for the session. Display the
            // main page
            createMain(out, uri, info);
        }
    }

}
catch (Exception ex) {
    // Catch any exceptions and send the stack trace back
    // to the client
    ex.printStackTrace(out);
}

// Set the response header to force the browser to
// load the html from the Web instead of it's cache
resp.setHeader("Expires", "Tues, 01 Jan 1980 00:00:00 GMT");

// Wrap up
out.flush();
out.close();
}
```

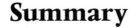 **Summary**

In this chapter, we have focused on the details involved in creating a Web site to provide content to servlet developers. One of the most important new concepts introduced was HTTP session tracking, which allows you to preserve state information for the duration of a browser's connection to the Web server. We also covered metadata and how using metadata is critical in developing generic database applications.

In the next chapter, we will move away from the static world of HTML pages and into the dynamic world of Java applets. We'll take a look at how to invoke servlet methods from an applet by using HTTP tunneling.

HTTP
Tunneling

I n this chapter, we're going to take a look at how to use server-side objects from Java applets. Java's Remote Method Invocation (RMI) specification defines how this is done using TCP/IP over a secure network; however, we'll be using a process known as HTTP tunneling, which will allow us to make remote method calls over an unsecure network such as the Internet.

HTTP

HTTP (HyperText Transfer Prototcol) is an Internet client/server protocol designed for the delivery of hypertext materials such as HTML, images, and sounds. All HTTP communication uses 8-bit characters, which ensures the safe transmission of all forms of data; this will become an important point later when we start sending and receiving binary data. Let's take a look at the basic steps in servicing an HTTP service request.

1. Open the connection. It is very important to remember that HTTP is a stateless protocol, which means that each request is treated as an independent entity. Because of this a new connection must be made for each request. This is quite unlike TCP/IP, for example, where a connection can be maintained for the life of a given client session. We'll see later that using servlet session tracking will solve the stateless server problem.

2. Send a request. The client will send a message to the Web server requesting some type of service. The request contains HTTP request headers, which define the type and length of the request packet and are followed by the request data.

3. Service the request. The Web server will service the request. In our case we'll be writing a new servlet to process the request.

4. Send the response. The server will send (or forward) a response to the client. The response contains the response headers, which define the type and length of the response packet and are followed by the response data.

5. Close the connection. Remember that HTTP is stateless; connections cannot be preserved between requests.

You might think that HTTP is used just for requesting and downloading documents from a secure server over the Internet. This is certainly the most common use of HTTP; however, we can use it to serve other purposes as well, such as method call tunneling.

What Is Tunneling?

I like to think of tunneling as a way to use an existing road of communication (HTTP) and create a subprotocol within it to perform specific tasks. The subprotocol we'll be creating will contain all the information necessary to create an object on the Web server, invoke methods on that object, and return results back to the client. The great thing about using HTTP tunneling is that you can concentrate on the specifics of the subprotocol without having to be concerned about transporting the data packets between the client and server—HTTP was designed for this very purpose and does it quite well.

The Basic Flow

To further illustrate this concept of tunneling, let's expand upon the basic HTTP flow.

1. Open the HTTP connection. Always remember that HTTP is a stateless protocol; because of this you will have to open a new connection for each request.

2. Format the method request. This will include some type of method indicator that describes which method to invoke and any parameters required by the method.

3. Set the HTTP request headers. This includes the type of data being sent (binary) and the total length of the data.

4. Send the request. Write the binary stream to the server.

5. Read the request. The target servlet will be invoked and given the HTTP request data. The servlet can then extract the method to invoke any necessary parameters. Note that if this is the first request for a given client a new instance of the server object will be created.

6. Invoke the method. The method will be called on the server object.

7. Format the method response. If the invoked method throws an exception, the error message will be sent to the client; otherwise, the return type (if any) will be sent.

8. Set the HTTP response headers. As with the request headers, the type and length of the data being sent must be set.

9. Send the request. The binary data stream will be sent to the Web server and, in turn, will be returned to the client.

10. Close the connection.

That's a lot of work just to send a single request. For performance reasons you should always try to pass as much information as possible with each request/response; the weak link in the HTTP tunneling chain is creating a new connection for each request.

Tunneling for Java 1.0.2

A great deal of focus has been placed on the current versions of the Java Developer's Kit (JDK), whether it is JDK 1.1 or JDK 1.2 (or later). Don't forget about the first official release of the JDK: version 1.0.2. You might not think it is important to use this version, but I have found that later versions of the JDK are not totally supported in some browsers and the behavior is (at best) unpredictable. Applets created with JDK 1.0.2, on the other hand, seem quite well behaved in all the Java-enabled browsers I have tried. Sure, there's a lot of new functionality in the later versions of the JDK, but if you have basic applet requirements that can be satisfied using version 1.0.2, you may want to consider using it—especially if you will be distributing your applet over the Internet (as opposed to an intranet) where you do not have control over the type or version of browser in use.

Marshaling Parameters and Return Values

Just exactly what is marshaling? Quite simply, it is the process of packaging a piece of data for transmission and unpackaging it after it has been received. Later in this chapter, you will discover that starting with JDK 1.1 this is made very easy with serialization; this is not so with JDK 1.0.2. Java 1.0.2 provides us with a mechanism to read and write all the basic scalar data types (boolean, char, byte, short, int, long, float, double, and string); all other types of data must be marshaled as a combination of these types. Also, when you write a particular type of data the reader must know what type of data to expect. You can get around this by preceding each piece of data with some type of indicator, but there is no generic way to determine what type of data is present.

Using DataOutputStream and DataInputStream   To illustrate how to marshal data with any version of the JDK, let's take a look at a simple client application that uses java.io.DataOutputStream for writing the request data and java.io.DataInputStream for reading the response data. The flow of our client application is as follows.

1. Open an HTTP connection.
2. Format the request data.
3. Send the request to the server.
4. Read the response data.
5. Close the HTTP connection.

The server (which we'll look at later) will simply read the request data and echo these data back to the client.

Figure 10.1 shows the complete application. To invoke the application you must supply the URL of the server process that will echo the data (a servlet, of course!):

```
java javaservlets.tunnel.TestDataStream
    http://larryboy/servlet/javaservlets.tunnel.DataStreamEcho
```

Note that the command has been split over two lines to improve readability; it should be entered as a single line. We will be using the "larryboy" server to invoke the DataStreamEcho servlet found in the javaservlets.tunnel package. You may have to configure your Web server and specify a servlet alias for the DataStreamEcho servlet; I'm using JRun from Live Software, which allows me to specify the full package name of the servlet without preregistering.

Figure 10.1

The
TestDataStream
application.

```
package javaservlets.tunnel;

import java.io.*;

/**
 * <p>This application shows how to read data from and write data
 * to a servlet using data input/output streams.
 */

public class TestDataStream
{
  /**
   * <p>Application entry point. This application requires
   * one parameter, which is the servlet URL
   */
  public static void main(String args[])
    {
      // Make sure we have an argument for the servlet URL
      if (args.length == 0) {
        System.out.println("\nServlet URL must be specified");
        return;
      }

      try {

        System.out.println("Attempting to connect to " + args[0]);

        // Get the server URL
        java.net.URL url = new java.net.URL(args[0]);

        // Attempt to connect to the host
        java.net.URLConnection con = url.openConnection();

        // Initialize the connection
        con.setUseCaches(false);
        con.setDoOutput(true);
        con.setDoInput(true);

        // Data will always be written to a byte array buffer so
        // that we can tell the server the length of the data
        ByteArrayOutputStream byteOut = new ByteArrayOutputStream();

        // Create the output stream to be used to write the
        // data to our buffer
        DataOutputStream out = new DataOutputStream(byteOut);

        System.out.println("Writing test data");

        // Write the test data
        out.writeBoolean(true);
        out.writeByte(1);
        out.writeChar(2);
        out.writeShort(3);
        out.writeInt(4);
        out.writeFloat(5);
        out.writeDouble(6);
        out.writeUTF("Hello, Karl");

        // Flush the data to the buffer
```

```
        out.flush();

        // Get our buffer to be sent
        byte buf[] = byteOut.toByteArray();

        // Set the content that we are sending
        con.setRequestProperty("Content-type",
                               "application/octet-stream");

        // Set the length of the data buffer we are sending
        con.setRequestProperty("Content-length",
                               "" + buf.length);

        // Get the output stream to the server and send our
        // data buffer
        DataOutputStream dataOut =
          new DataOutputStream(con.getOutputStream());
        //out.write(buf, 0, buf.length);
        dataOut.write(buf);

        // Flush the output stream and close it
        dataOut.flush();
        dataOut.close();

        System.out.println("Reading response");

        // Get the input stream we can use to read the response
        DataInputStream in =
          new DataInputStream(con.getInputStream());

        // Read the data from the server
        boolean booleanValue = in.readBoolean();
        byte byteValue = in.readByte();
        char charValue = in.readChar();
        short shortValue = in.readShort();
        int intValue = in.readInt();
        float floatValue = in.readFloat();
        double doubleValue = in.readDouble();
        String stringValue = in.readUTF();

        // Close the input stream
        in.close();

        System.out.println("Data read: " +
                           booleanValue + " " +
                           byteValue + " " +
                           ((int) charValue) + " " +
                           shortValue + " " +
                           intValue + " " +
                           floatValue + " " +
                           doubleValue + " " +
                           stringValue);
      }
      catch (Exception ex) {
        ex.printStackTrace();
      }

    }
  }
```

Figure 10.2

TestDataStream
output.

```
Attempting to connect to http://larryboy/servlet/
javaservlets.tunnel.DataStreamEcho
Writing test data
Reading response
Data read: true 1 2 3 4 5.0 6.0 Hello, Karl
```

Notice how the request data are actually being written to an in-memory buffer (java.io.ByteArrayOutputStream). We could have written the data directly to the HTTP output stream, but then you could not set the request length in the request header properly. To be able to do this we write all the data to a buffer and then retrieve the raw byte array from which we can get the length. After the request headers are set, we can get the HTTP output stream from the URLConnection object and write the entire contents of the internal buffer. Once these data have been sent, we can request an input stream from the URLConnection object that will be used to read the response. Note that requesting the input stream will block execution on the thread until the response is received. Once we have the input stream, we can simply read the data and display what was echoed by the servlet. Figure 10.2 shows the output from our application.

What about the servlet? By looking at the client you should be able to write the servlet quite easily, since the process is very similar.

1. Wait for a service request from a client.

2. Read the request data.

3. Write the response using the data read from the request.

Figure 10.3 shows the source code for the DataStreamEcho servlet. It is very important to remember to read the data in the same order they were written by the client.

Figure 10.3

DataStreamEcho
servlet.

```
package javaservlets.tunnel;

import javax.servlet.*;
import javax.servlet.http.*;
import java.io.*;

/**
 * <p>This servlet shows how to read data from and write data
 * to a client using data input/output streams.
 */

public class DataStreamEcho extends HttpServlet
{
```

```
/**
 * <p>Services the HTTP request
 *
 * @param req The request from the client
 * @param resp The response from the servlet
 */
public void service(HttpServletRequest req,
                    HttpServletResponse resp)
  throws ServletException, java.io.IOException
  {
    // Get the input stream for reading data from the client
    DataInputStream in =
      new DataInputStream(req.getInputStream());

    // We'll be sending binary data back to the client so
    // set the content type appropriately
    resp.setContentType("application/octet-stream");

    // Data will always be written to a byte array buffer so
    // that we can tell the client the length of the data
    ByteArrayOutputStream byteOut = new ByteArrayOutputStream();

    // Create the output stream to be used to write the
    // data to our buffer
    DataOutputStream out = new DataOutputStream(byteOut);

    // Read the data from the client.
    boolean booleanValue = in.readBoolean();
    byte byteValue = in.readByte();
    char charValue = in.readChar();
    short shortValue = in.readShort();
    int intValue = in.readInt();
    float floatValue = in.readFloat();
    double doubleValue = in.readDouble();
    String stringValue = in.readUTF();

    // Write the data to our internal buffer.
    out.writeBoolean(booleanValue);
    out.writeByte(byteValue);
    out.writeChar(charValue);
    out.writeShort(shortValue);
    out.writeInt(intValue);
    out.writeFloat(floatValue);
    out.writeDouble(doubleValue);
    out.writeUTF(stringValue);

    // Flush the contents of the output stream to the
    // byte array
    out.flush();

    // Get the buffer that is holding our response
    byte[] buf = byteOut.toByteArray();

    // Notify the client how much data is being sent
    resp.setContentLength(buf.length);

    // Send the buffer to the client
    ServletOutputStream servletOut = resp.getOutputStream();
```

```
    // Wrap up
    servletOut.write(buf);
    servletOut.close();
  }
}
```

The Base Tunnel Client Class

Now that you know how to get data back and forth between the client and server, let's get started on some supporting classes to make method tunneling much easier. Since I had the distinct advantage of looking ahead in this chapter, I know that we are going to write two types of clients: a "lite" version (for marshaling scalar types only) and a full version (using Java serialization). Because of this, I think it would be an excellent idea to implement an abstract base class, which these two types of clients can extend.

What types of methods will the client need? All clients will definitely need to initialize themselves. Since we are invoking methods on the server, part of this initialization step should be to instantiate the server-side object. Figure 10.4 shows the initialization method from the base client class.

All this method does is send a message packet to the server instructing it to instantiate a new server-side object (we'll get to that later). It's important to note the basic steps involved in sending our data packet to the server.

1. Create a new in-memory buffer to hold the contents of the data stream.

2. Invoke a `helper` method to create the packet header. We're going to invoke remote methods by assigning each method an ordinal (a number), which will uniquely identify a particular method. The ordinal –1 is reserved to indicate that the request is not to invoke a method but rather to initialize the server.

3. Invoke a `helper` method to send the request packet to the server. This method will return an input stream, which we can then use to read any return values from the server.

If you think back to the TestDataOutput sample application presented earlier, this should all sound quite familiar.

Figure 10.5 shows the code necessary to create the packet header, which will be used on every tunneled method request.

Figure 10.4

Base client
initialization.

```java
/**
 * <p>Initializes the client. Also makes a server request
 * to initialize the server as well.
 */
public void _initialize() throws TunnelException
{
    try {
        // Create a new buffer that will hold our data
        ByteArrayOutputStream buffer = new ByteArrayOutputStream();

        // Create a method header. An ordinal value of -1 is
        // reserved for initializing the server
        _createHeader(buffer, -1);

        // Invoke the method. This will send the initialization
        // header to the server
        DataInput in = _invokeMethod(buffer.toByteArray());

        // We're not expecting any type of response. If the
        // server was not initialized an exception would
        // have been thrown.
        _close(in);
    }
    catch (IOException ex) {
        // Re-throw as a tunnel exception
        ex.printStackTrace();
        throw new TunnelException(ex.getMessage());
    }
}
```

Figure 10.5

Creating the
request packet
header.

```java
/**
 * <p>Starts a method by creating the method header.
 * The header consists of the method ordinal to invoke.
 *
 * @param buffer Buffer to hold the header data
 * @param ordinal Method ordinal to invoke on the server
 * @return Output stream to be used to send parameters
 */
public DataOutput _createHeader(ByteArrayOutputStream buffer,
                                int ordinal)
    throws TunnelException
{
    try {
        // Get an output stream use to write data to the buffer
        DataOutput out = _getOutputStream(buffer);

        // Write the method ordinal
        out.writeInt(ordinal);
        _flush(out);
        return out;
    }
    catch (IOException ex) {
        // Re-throw as a tunnel exception
        ex.printStackTrace();
        throw new TunnelException(ex.getMessage());
    }
}
```

Not a lot of magic going on here—just opening an output stream, writing the method ordinal, and flushing the data to the output stream. But wait! What are these _getOutputStream and _flush methods? Each client that extends the base client will have to implement these abstract methods to create the proper type of output stream and to flush the data if necessary. By defining these methods as abstract, we can write a very generic base class, which can be reused for different types of tunnel clients.

The last method we need to look at from the base class is the one that actually sends the packet to the server (see Figure 10.6).

Figure 10.6

Sending the request packet.

```
/**
 * <p>Sends the given buffer that will cause a remote
 * method to be invoked.
 *
 * @param buffer Buffer containing data to send to the server
 * @return Input stream to be used to read the response from
 * the server
 */
public DataInput _invokeMethod(byte buf[])
   throws TunnelException
   {
     DataInput in = null;

     try {
       // Get the server URL
       java.net.URL url = _getURL();
       if (url == null) {
         throw new IOException("Server URL has not been set");
       }

       // Attempt to connect to the host
       java.net.URLConnection con = url.openConnection();

       // Initialize the connection
       con.setUseCaches(false);
       con.setDoOutput(true);
       con.setDoInput(true);

       // Set the content that we are sending
       con.setRequestProperty("Content-type",
                                 "application/octet-stream");

       // Set the length of the data buffer we are sending
       con.setRequestProperty("Content-length",
                                 "" + buf.length);

       // Get the output stream to the server and send our
       // data buffer
       DataOutputStream out =
         new DataOutputStream(con.getOutputStream());
       out.write(buf);

       // Flush the output stream and close it
```

```
          out.flush();
          out.close();

          // Get the input stream we can use to read the response
          in = _getInputStream(con.getInputStream());

          // The server will always respond with an int value
          // that will either be the method ordinal that was
          // invoked, or a -2 indicating an exception was thrown
          // from the server
          int ordinal = in.readInt();

          // Check for an exception on the server.
          if (ordinal == -2) {
            // Read the exception message and throw it
            String msg = in.readUTF();
            throw new TunnelException(msg);
          }

        }
        catch (IOException ex) {
          // Re-throw as a tunnel exception
          ex.printStackTrace();
          throw new TunnelException(ex.getMessage());
        }

        // Return the input stream to be used to read the rest
        // of the response from the server
        return in;
      }
```

The first thing we must do is connect to a given URL. The URL is set when the tunnel client is instantiated (which we'll discuss later). Part of connecting to a particular URL is initializing the connection settings. Of note here is the setUseCaches method, which tells the browser whether to use internal caching for information or to always read directly from the connection itself. In our case we will turn off all browser caching capabilities. Next, we'll set the request headers (the data type and data length) and write the data buffer to the server. After the request is sent, we will block until a response is available. Notice that the _getInputStream method will return the type of input stream being used by the client; it is an abstract method and must be implemented by each tunnel client. Once the response has arrived, we can read the response header, which will always be prefixed with the same method ordinal that was sent in the request header. A returning ordinal value of –2 indicates that an exception was encountered during the execution of the remote method. If this is the case, we can read the exception message from the input stream and throw a new exception to the client. If all goes well, we can return the input stream back to the caller so that it can read any additional data sent by the server.

The Tunnel "Lite" Client

Writing the client implementation for our "lite" tunnel client is very straightforward (see Figure 10.7). Remember that our definition of a "lite" client is one that uses DataInputStream and DataOutputStream to marshal data. This type of client can be used with any version of the JDK.

Figure 10.7

Tunnel "lite" client implementation.

```java
package javaservlets.tunnel.client;

import java.io.*;

/**
 * <p>This class implements the necessary TunnelClientInterface
 * methods for 'tunnel lite' which is intended for use by
 * JDK 1.0.2 clients. The marshalling of data is done with
 * simple output streams and writing basic scalar data types.
 */

public class TunnelLiteClient extends BaseTunnelClient
{

  /**
   * <p>Gets an input stream to be used for reading data
   * from the connection. The lite version uses a standard
   * data input stream for reading data.
   *
   * @param in Input stream from the connection URL
   * @return Input stream to read data from the connection
   */
  public DataInput _getInputStream(InputStream in)
    throws IOException
    {
      // Create a new DataInputStream for reading data from
      // the connection.
      return new DataInputStream(in);
    }

  /**
   * <p>Gets an output stream to be used for writing data to
   * an internal buffer. The buffer will be written to the
   * connection. The lite version uses a standard data
   * output stream for writing data.
   *
   * @param buffer Buffer to hold the output data
   * @return Output stream to write data to the buffer
   */
  public DataOutput _getOutputStream(ByteArrayOutputStream buffer)
    throws IOException
    {
      // Create a new DataOutputStream for writing data to
      // the buffer.
      return new DataOutputStream(buffer);
    }

  /**
```

```
 * <p>Flushes the any buffered data to the output stream
 *
 * @param out Output stream to flush
 */
public void _flush(DataOutput out) throws IOException
  {
    // Flush the data to the buffer
    ((DataOutputStream) out).flush();
  }
}
```

The Base Tunnel Servlet Class

In the same manner that we created an abstract base client class, let's create a base servlet class as well. Similar to the client, it will contain abstract methods to create input and output streams specific to the type of marshaling being used. Figure 10.8 shows the service method of the base servlet class.

Figure 10.8

Base servlet service method.

```
/**
 * <p>Services the HTTP request
 *
 * @param req The request from the client
 * @param resp The response from the servlet
 */
public void service(HttpServletRequest req,
                    HttpServletResponse resp)
  throws ServletException, java.io.IOException
  {
    // Get the input stream for reading data from the client
    DataInput in = _getInputStream(req.getInputStream());

    // Get the session object or create one if it does not
    // exist. A session will persist as long as the client
    // browser maintains a connection to the server.
    HttpSession session = req.getSession(true);

    // Get the server object bound to the session. This may be
    // null if this is the first request. If so the request
    // should be to initialize the server.
    Object serverObject = session.getValue(SERVER_OBJECT);

    // We'll be sending binary data back to the client so
    // set the content type appropriately
    resp.setContentType("application/octet-stream");

    // Data will always be written to a byte array buffer so
    // that we can tell the client the length of the data
    ByteArrayOutputStream byteOut = new ByteArrayOutputStream();

    // Create the output stream to be used to write the
    // data to our buffer
```

```
DataOutput out = _getOutputStream(byteOut);

// Read the method ordinal from the input stream. All
// request headers contain a method ordinal
int ordinal = in.readInt();

// Evaluate the ordinal. -1 is reserved for initializing
// the server
switch (ordinal) {
case -1:

  // Create a new instance of the server object
  serverObject = _getNewInstance();

  // Add the server object to the HTTP session
  session.putValue(SERVER_OBJECT, serverObject);

  // Send the response back to the client indicating
  // that the server object is ready for method
  // calls.
  out.writeInt(ordinal);
  break;

default:

  // We have to have a server object in order to invoke
  if (serverObject == null) {
    throwException(out, "Invalid server object");
  }
  else {

    try {

      // The response needs to always include the ordinal
      // that was invoked.
      out.writeInt(ordinal);
      _flush(out);

      // Invoke the method for the given ordinal
      _invokeMethod(serverObject, ordinal, in, out);
    }
    catch (Exception ex) {

      // Any exceptions thrown by invoking the server
      // method should be sent back to the client. Make
      // sure we are working with a 'pure' output stream
      // that does not contain any other data
      byteOut = new ByteArrayOutputStream();
      out = _getOutputStream(byteOut);
      throwException(out, ex.getMessage());
    }

  }
}

// Flush the contents of the output stream to the
// byte array
_flush(out);
```

```
        // Get the buffer that is holding our response
        byte[] buf = byteOut.toByteArray();

        // Notify the client how much data is being sent
        resp.setContentLength(buf.length);

        // Send the buffer to the client
        ServletOutputStream servletOut = resp.getOutputStream();

        // Wrap up
        servletOut.write(buf);
        servletOut.close();
    }
```

The basic flow of the service method is as follows.

1. Create an input stream to read the request from the client. The server implementation that extends the base servlet will create the proper type of input stream.

2. Get the instance of the server-side object from the session.

3. Set up the response header.

4. Create an in-memory buffer to hold the raw data of the response. We need to set the length of the response in the response header, so we'll cache the response data in an internal buffer and then get the length.

5. Read the method ordinal indicating which method to invoke on the server object. An ordinal of –1 directs us to initialize the server by instantiating a new server object and placing it in the session object.

6. Invoke the method. The server implementation will evaluate the method ordinal, read any parameters, and invoke the proper method. Once the method has been invoked, the server implementation will write any return value to the output stream so that it can be forwarded to the client.

7. Send the response buffer to the client.

The Tunnel "Lite" Server

Writing the server implementation for our "lite" tunnel server (shown in Figure 10.9) is very similar to writing the implementation for the "lite" client.

Note that we are using DataInputStream and DataOutputStream just as we did for the client.

Figure 10.9

Tunnel "lite" server
implementation.

```java
/**
 * <p>This is the base object to be extended by server objects
 * that are using HTTP lite tunneling.
 */
public abstract class TunnelLiteServer extends BaseTunnelServlet
{
    /**
     * <p>Creates an input stream to be used to read data
     * sent from the client.
     *
     * @param servletInput Servlet input stream from the servlet
     * request header
     * @return Input stream to read data from the client
     */
    public DataInput _getInputStream(ServletInputStream servletInput)
        throws IOException
        {
            // Create a new DataInputStream for reading data from
            // the client.
            return new DataInputStream(servletInput);
        }

    /**
     * <p>Gets an output stream to be used for writing data to
     * an internal buffer. The buffer will be written to the
     * client
     *
     * @param buffer Buffer to hold the output data
     * @return Output stream to write data to the buffer
     */
    public DataOutput _getOutputStream(ByteArrayOutputStream buffer)
        throws IOException
        {
            // Create a new DataOutputStream for writing data to
            // the buffer.
            return new DataOutputStream(buffer);
        }

    /**
     * <p>Flushes the any buffered data to the output stream
     *
     * @param out Output stream to flush
     */
    public void _flush(DataOutput out) throws IOException
        {
            // Flush the data to the buffer
            ((DataOutputStream) out).flush();
        }
}
```

Tunneling Example: RemoteMathLite

To bring all these pieces together, let's write a very simple applet that will perform some simple math operations (add, subtract, multiply). Big deal, right? The exciting aspect of this applet is that all the calculations will be performed on the server via HTTP tunneling.

Writing the Server Interface   I always like to begin by defining an interface that describes the methods available on a particular server object. While this is not necessary for what we are doing now, it will be critically important in Chapter 11 when we start automating the creation remote objects. If you have worked with CORBA, you are already used to writing the Interface Definition Language (IDL) necessary to generate CORBA proxies and stubs; in essence, we will be doing the same thing.

Figure 10.10 shows the interface definition for our math object.

As you can see, we have three methods: add, subtract, and multiply.

Figure 10.10

The Math interface.

```
package javaservlets.tunnel;

/**
 * <p>This interface defines the methods available for
 * performing math
 */

public interface MathInterface
{
    /**
     * <p>Adds two numbers
     */
    int add(int a, int b);

    /**
     * <p>Subtracts two numbers
     */
    int subtract(int a, int b);

    /**
     * <p>Multiplies two numbers
     */
    int multiply(int a, int b);

}
```

Writing the Server Object   Implementing the three math methods is, as you would expect, no difficult task (see Figure 10.11). Note that there is nothing special about implementing the server object even though we will be using it via HTTP tunneling.

Writing the Client Proxy   We now have to implement the client proxy. A proxy is defined by Webster as "the agency, function, or power of a person authorized to act as the deputy or substitute for another." What we are interested in is creating a proxy to take the place of the real math object and instead tunnel any method calls to the server where they will be processed. Our client math proxy (RemoteMathLiteClient) will extend our "lite" client class and implement the math interface we defined earlier. We then have to implement each method in the interface, and, using methods in the base class, write any parameters to the output stream that will be sent to the server. After invoking the remote

Figure 10.11

The math
implementation.

```
package javaservlets.tunnel;

/**
 * <p>This class performs simple math functions in order to
 * illustrate remote method tunneling.
 */

public class Math implements MathInterface
{
  /**
   * <p>Adds two numbers
   */
  public int add(int a, int b)
    {
      return (a + b);
    }

  /**
   * <p>Subtracts two numbers
   */
  public int subtract(int a, int b)
    {
      return (a - b);
    }

  /**
   * <p>Multiplies two numbers
   */
  public int multiply(int a, int b)
    {
      return (a * b);
    }

}
```

method, an input stream, which we can use to read any return values
from the method call, will be returned. This is shown in Figure 10.12.

Figure 10.12

The math client
proxy.

```
package javaservlets.tunnel;

import java.io.*;
import javaservlets.tunnel.client.*;

/**
 * <p>This class implements the 'lite' client for tunneling
 * calls to the Math object.
 */

public class RemoteMathLiteClient
  extends TunnelLiteClient
  implements MathInterface
{

  /**
   * <p>Constructs a new RemoteMathLiteClient for the
   * given URL. The URL should contain the location of
   * servlet scripts (i.e. http://larryboy/servlet/).
   */
  public RemoteMathLiteClient(String url)
    throws TunnelException, IOException
    {
      // Append the remote 'lite' server name
      url += "RemoteMathLiteServer";

      // Set the URL
      _setURL(new java.net.URL(url));

      // Initialize the client and server
      _initialize();
    }

  /**
   * <p>Adds two numbers
   */
  public int add(int a, int b)
    {
      int n = 0;
      try {
        // Create an internal buffer
        ByteArrayOutputStream baos = new ByteArrayOutputStream();

        // Create an output stream to write the request
        DataOutputStream out =
          (DataOutputStream) _createHeader(baos, 0);

        // Output the parameters
        out.writeInt(a);
        out.writeInt(b);

        // Invoke the method and read the response
        DataInputStream in =
          (DataInputStream) _invokeMethod(baos.toByteArray());
```

```
      // Read the return value
      n = in.readInt();

      // Wrap up
      out.close();
      in.close();
    }
    catch (Exception ex) {
      ex.printStackTrace();
    }
    return n;
  }
```

Note that the initialize routine specifies the name of the servlet to invoke; we'll be creating this next. Also, I've only shown the code for the add method; subtract and multiply are identical except for the method ordinal.

Writing the Server Stub   The server stub will extend the base "lite" server and implement the _getNewInstance and _invokeMethod routines. Though it may not look like it the stub is actually the servlet that will be invoked; all the servlet details have already been implemented in the base class that the stub extends. The _getNewInstance method will return an instance of the server object that will be persisted with the HTTP session object in the Web server. In our case, this is the math object with the implementation for all the math routines (add, subtract, multiply).

The _invokeMethod method will be given an instance of the server object (retrieved from the HTTP session), the method ordinal of the method to invoke on the server object, an input stream to read parameters from, and an output stream to write return values. The complete code is shown in Figure 10.13.

Figure 10.13

The math server stub.

```
package javaservlets.tunnel;

import javax.servlet.*;
import javax.servlet.http.*;
import java.io.*;
import javaservlets.tunnel.server.*;

/**
 * <p>This class implements the 'lite' server for tunneling
 * remote Math method calls
 */

public class RemoteMathLiteServer
  extends TunnelLiteServer
{
  /**
```

```
   * <p>Creates a new instance of the server object.
   *
   * @return Instance of the server object
   */
public Object _getNewInstance()
  throws ServletException
  {
    return new Math();
  }


/**
   * <p>Invokes the method for the ordinal given. If the method
   * throws an exception it will be sent to the client.
   *
   * @param Object Server object
   * @param ordinal Method ordinal
   * @param in Input stream to read additional parameters
   * @param out Output stream to write return values
   */
public void _invokeMethod(Object serverObject, int ordinal,
                          DataInput in, DataOutput out)
  throws Exception
  {
    // Cast the server object
    Math math = (Math) serverObject;

    // Cast the input/output streams
    DataInputStream dataIn = (DataInputStream) in;
    DataOutputStream dataOut = (DataOutputStream) out;

    // Evaluate the ordinal
    switch (ordinal) {
    case 0: // add
      int a0 = dataIn.readInt();
      int b0 = dataIn.readInt();
      int n0 = math.add(a0, b0);
      out.writeInt(n0);
      break;

    case 1: // subtract
      int a1 = dataIn.readInt();
      int b1 = dataIn.readInt();
      int n1 = math.subtract(a1, b1);
      out.writeInt(n1);
      break;

    case 2: // multiply
      int a2 = dataIn.readInt();
      int b2 = dataIn.readInt();
      int n2 = math.multiply(a2, b2);
      out.writeInt(n2);
      break;

    default:
      throw new Exception("Invalid ordinal: " + ordinal);
    }
  }
}
```

Writing the Applet   To test this "lite" remote object I'll be using JDK
1.0.2 to prove that it works as described. Because of this our MathLite-
Applet will use the "handleEvent" applet method instead of the JDK 1.1
event model. Don't worry, we'll be writing an applet using the event
model later in this chapter. Since this is not a book about applet programming (there are plenty of those around), I won't spend too much
time diving into the particulars of applet development. The critical
piece of this applet is how to create our remote object. In essence, all we
need to do is create an instance of our client proxy and cast it to the
math interface we have defined. This is another great benefit of using
interfaces; you can invoke the remote object by making calls on the interface without having to know (or care) that it is, indeed, a remote object. This makes remote object programming much easier, because there
is no special syntax to learn; just make method calls on an object—the
client proxy is hiding all the work.

Figure 10.14 shows the complete code for the applet. Again, note how
the client proxy is instantiated and how making remote method calls is
done with a simple call on the interface.

Figure 10.14

The MathLiteApplet
applet.

```java
package javaservlets.tunnel;

import java.applet.*;
import java.awt.*;

/**
 * <p>This applet demonstrates how to use the tunnel clients
 * to perform remote method calls using JDK 1.0.2
 * style events.
 */

public class MathLiteApplet extends Applet
{
  // Define our global components
  TextField op1 = new TextField(10);
  TextField op2 = new TextField(10);
  Choice operator = new Choice();
  TextField result = new TextField(10);
  Button calc = new Button("Calculate");
  MathInterface math;

  /**
   * <p>Initialize the applet
   */
  public void init()
    {
      // Don't allow the result to be edited
      result.setEditable(false);

      // Use a grid bag layout
      GridBagLayout gridbag = new GridBagLayout();
```

```
    GridBagConstraints gbcon = new GridBagConstraints();
    setLayout(gridbag);

    // Setup the reusable constraint
    gbcon.weightx = 1.0;
    gbcon.weighty = 0.0;
    gbcon.anchor = gbcon.CENTER;
    gbcon.fill = gbcon.NONE;
    gbcon.gridwidth = gbcon.REMAINDER;

    // Add the components
    add(new Label("Enter first value:"));
    gridbag.setConstraints(op1, gbcon);
    add(op1);

    operator.addItem("Plus");
    operator.addItem("Minus");
    operator.addItem("Times");
    operator.select(0);
    add(new Label("Select operation:"));
    gridbag.setConstraints(operator, gbcon);
    add(operator);

    add(new Label("Enter second value:"));
    gridbag.setConstraints(op2, gbcon);
    add(op2);

    add(new Label("Press to calculate"));
    gridbag.setConstraints(calc, gbcon);
    add(calc);

    add(new Label("Result from server:"));
    gridbag.setConstraints(result, gbcon);
    add(result);

    // Create an instance of our remote object
    try {
      math = new RemoteMathLiteClient(getCodeBase() + "servlet/");
    }
    catch (Exception ex) {
      ex.printStackTrace();
    }
  }

/**
  * <p>Handle events
  */
public boolean handleEvent(Event event)
  {
    // Handle the 'Calculate' button press
    if (event.target == calc) {

      // If the math object was not created, get out
      if (math == null) {
        return false;
      }

      // Get the values
      int a = 0;
```

```
        int b = 0;
        try {
          a = Integer.parseInt(op1.getText());
          b = Integer.parseInt(op2.getText());
        }
        catch (Exception ex) {
        }

        // Figure out what to do
        int n = 0;
        int index = operator.getSelectedIndex();
        switch(index) {
        case 0:
          n = math.add(a, b);
          break;
        case 1:
          n = math.subtract(a, b);
          break;
        case 2:
          n = math.multiply(a, b);
          break;
        }
        result.setText("" + n);
        return true;
      }
      return false;
    }
}
```

See It in Action   After adding the RemoteMathLiteServer servlet to the Web server (via an alias) and writing a simple HTML page to load our applet (shown in Figure 10.15), it's time to give it a test drive. Don't forget to place the applet and all supporting classes on your Web server's CLASSPATH so that the client browser can locate them (or jump ahead

Figure 10.15

HTML for
MathLiteApplet.

```
<HTML>
<HEAD>
<TITLE>Math Lite Applet</TITLE>
</HEAD>
<BODY>
<dir>
<h2>Simple calculator applet that makes remote method calls
using HTTP tunneling.</h2>
</dir>
<center>
<HR>
<APPLET WIDTH=300
        HEIGHT=200
        NAME="MathLiteApplt"
        CODE="javaservlets.tunnel.MathLiteApplet"></APPLET>
</center>
</BODY>
</HTML>
```

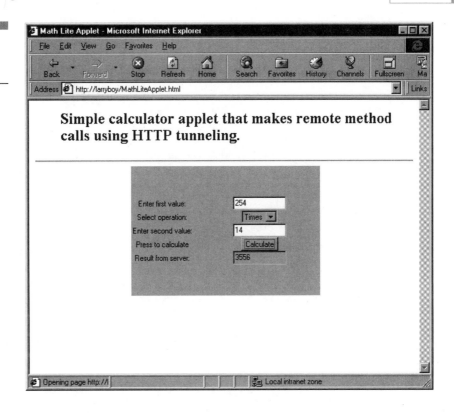

Figure 10.16

MathLiteApplet in action.

to Chapter 12 to find out how to automatically create an archive file for distributing the applet). After entering values and selecting an operator type, pressing the Calculate button will tunnel a method call to the servlet, which will then invoke the proper method on the server-side object. The return value is then read from the server and placed in the result field (see Figure 10.16).

New for Java 1.1: Serialization

Starting with JDK 1.1, we have a new option for marshaling data between a client and a server: serialization. Serialization is the process of storing (serializing) and retrieving (deserializing) the internal state of an object without having to be aware of the internal structure of that object. In other words, the Java virtual machine handles the writing of all the properties of an object and can, given this stored information, recreate the object at a later time and place. JavaSoft added serialization to the JDK to enable Remote Method Invocation (RMI) to pass objects between a client and a server; we'll take this built-in functionality and put it to use in a new version of our tunneling client and server.

Before going too far, be aware that there are a few pitfalls when using serialization.

- Not all objects are serializable. An object must implement the java.io.Serializable interface in order to be serializable. Remember that the whole purpose of serialization is to save the state of an object so that it can be recreated later; for some types of objects this does not make sense (such as database connections, open file handles, etc.).

- Serialization will add a significant amount of overhead to the size of a request/response packet. Serializing an object not only writes the properties, but it also generates versioning and class file information. This may not be a big concern for you, but these additional data may have a small impact on performance.

- Serialization errors can occur if the version of the object that was serialized differs from the one present when the object is deserialized. An example of this is a new copy of an object on the client and an older (or missing) version of the object on the server.

- Some browsers (especially older versions) may not fully support serialization. Remember that serialization is a JDK 1.1 feature; but even if a browser claims to support 1.1, it may not properly support serialization.

Using ObjectOutputStream and ObjectInputStream

To illustrate how to marshal data with version 1.1 (or later) of the JDK, let's take a look at a simple client application that uses java.io.ObjectOutputStream for writing the request data and java.io.ObjectInputStream for reading the response data. This application is basically the same as the TestDataStream application we saw earlier. To recap, the flow of our client application is as follows.

1. Open an HTTP connection.
2. Format the request data.

3. Send the request to the server.

4. Read the response data.

5. Close the HTTP connection.

The server will simply read the request data and echo these data back to the client.

Figure 10.17 shows the complete client application. To invoke the application you must supply the URL of the servlet that will echo the data:

```
java javaservlets.tunnel.TestObjectStream
     http://larryboy/servlet/javaservlets.tunnel.ObjectStreamEcho
```

Note that the command has been split over two lines to improve readability; it should be entered as a single line. We will be using the "larryboy" server to invoke the ObjectStreamEcho servlet found in the javaservlets.tunnel package. The output from the application is shown in Figure 10.18.

Figure 10.17

The TestObject-
Stream application.

```java
package javaservlets.tunnel;

import java.io.*;

/**
 * <p>This application shows how to read data from and write data
 * to a servlet using object input/output streams.
 */

public class TestObjectStream
{
  /**
   * <p>Application entry point. This application requires
   * one parameter, which is the servlet URL
   */
  public static void main(String args[])
    {
      // Make sure we have an argument for the servlet URL
      if (args.length == 0) {
        System.out.println("\nServlet URL must be specified");
        return;
      }

      try {

        System.out.println("Attempting to connect to " + args[0]);

        // Get the server URL
        java.net.URL url = new java.net.URL(args[0]);

        // Attempt to connect to the host
        java.net.URLConnection con = url.openConnection();

        // Initialize the connection
```

```
con.setUseCaches(false);
con.setDoOutput(true);
con.setDoInput(true);

// Data will always be written to a byte array buffer so
// that we can tell the server the length of the data
ByteArrayOutputStream byteOut = new ByteArrayOutputStream();

// Create the output stream to be used to write the
// data to our buffer
ObjectOutputStream out = new ObjectOutputStream(byteOut);

System.out.println("Writing test objects");

// Write the test data
out.writeObject(new Boolean(true));
out.writeObject(new Byte((byte) 1));
out.writeObject(new Character((char) 2));
out.writeObject(new Short((short) 3));
out.writeObject(new Integer(4));
out.writeObject(new Float(5));
out.writeObject(new Double(6));
out.writeObject("Hello, Karl");

// Flush the data to the buffer
out.flush();

// Get our buffer to be sent
byte buf[] = byteOut.toByteArray();

// Set the content that we are sending
con.setRequestProperty("Content-type",
                       "application/octet-stream");

// Set the length of the data buffer we are sending
con.setRequestProperty("Content-length",
                       "" + buf.length);

// Get the output stream to the server and send our
// data buffer
DataOutputStream dataOut =
  new DataOutputStream(con.getOutputStream());
//out.write(buf, 0, buf.length);
dataOut.write(buf);

// Flush the output stream and close it
dataOut.flush();
dataOut.close();

System.out.println("Reading response");

// Get the input stream we can use to read the response
ObjectInputStream in =
  new ObjectInputStream(con.getInputStream());

// Read the data from the server
Boolean booleanValue = (Boolean) in.readObject();
Byte byteValue = (Byte) in.readObject();
Character charValue = (Character) in.readObject();
```

```
        Short shortValue = (Short) in.readObject();
        Integer intValue = (Integer) in.readObject();
        Float floatValue = (Float) in.readObject();
        Double doubleValue = (Double) in.readObject();
        String stringValue = (String) in.readObject();

        // Close the input stream
        in.close();

        System.out.println("Data read: " +
                            booleanValue + " " +
                            byteValue + " " +
                            ((int) charValue.charValue()) + " " +
                            shortValue + " " +
                            intValue + " " +
                            floatValue + " " +
                            doubleValue + " " +
                            stringValue);
      }
    catch (Exception ex) {
      ex.printStackTrace();
    }


  }
}
```

Figure 10.18

TestObjectStream
output.

```
Attempting to connect to http://larryboy/servlet/
javaservlets.tunnel.ObjectStreamEcho
Writing test objects
Reading response
Data read: true 1 2 3 4 5.0 6.0 Hello, Karl
```

As with the TestDataStream application the data are being written to an in-memory buffer. Notice how we are using the generic write-Object method found in the ObjectInputStream class. The following description is given in the JDK documentation for "writeObject:" Write the specified object to the ObjectOutputStream. The class of the object, the signature of the class, and the values of the nontransient and non-static fields of the class and all of its supertypes are written. Default serialization for a class can be overridden using the writeObject and the readObject methods. Objects referenced by this object are written transitively so that a complete equivalent graph of objects can be reconstructed by an ObjectInputStream.

What this means is that "writeObject" causes the object to be serialized to the underlying output stream, which then must be deserialized using the readObject method of the ObjectInputStream class. The object should be read in the same order that it was written. However, serialization has one distinct advantage over the simple marshaling we have seen earlier: You can read a generic object and reflect upon the object to determine what type it is (such as using the instance of comparison operator).

The servlet used to read the response and echo the data is very similar to what we have seen before. Instead of using data input and output streams we'll be using object input and output streams. Figure 10.19 shows the source code for the ObjectStreamEcho servlet.

Figure 10.19

ObjectStreamEcho
servlet.

```
package javaservlets.tunnel;

import java.io.*;

/**
 * <p>This servlet shows how to read data from and write data
 * to a client using object input/output streams.
 */

public class ObjectStreamEcho extends HttpServlet
{
  /**
   * <p>Services the HTTP request
   *
   * @param req The request from the client
   * @param resp The response from the servlet
   */
  public void service(HttpServletRequest req,
                      HttpServletResponse resp)
    throws ServletException, java.io.IOException
    {
      // Get the input stream for reading data from the client
      ObjectInputStream in =
        new ObjectInputStream(req.getInputStream());

      // We'll be sending binary data back to the client so
      // set the content type appropriately
      resp.setContentType("application/octet-stream");

      // Data will always be written to a byte array buffer so
      // that we can tell the client the length of the data
      ByteArrayOutputStream byteOut = new ByteArrayOutputStream();

      // Create the output stream to be used to write the
      // data to our buffer
      ObjectOutputStream out = new ObjectOutputStream(byteOut);

      // Read the objects from the client.
      try {
        Boolean booleanValue = (Boolean) in.readObject();
        Byte byteValue = (Byte) in.readObject();
        Character charValue = (Character) in.readObject();
        Short shortValue = (Short) in.readObject();
        Integer intValue = (Integer) in.readObject();
        Float floatValue = (Float) in.readObject();
        Double doubleValue = (Double) in.readObject();
        String stringValue = (String) in.readObject();
```

```
                      // Write the data to our internal buffer.
                      out.writeObject(booleanValue);
                      out.writeObject(byteValue);
                      out.writeObject(charValue);
                      out.writeObject(shortValue);
                      out.writeObject(intValue);
                      out.writeObject(floatValue);
                      out.writeObject(doubleValue);
                      out.writeObject(stringValue);
                  }
                  catch (ClassNotFoundException ex) {
                      // Serialization can throw a ClassNotFoundException.
                      ex.printStackTrace();
                  }

                  // Flush the contents of the output stream to the
                  // byte array
                  out.flush();

                  // Get the buffer that is holding our response
                  byte[] buf = byteOut.toByteArray();

                  // Notify the client how much data is being sent
                  resp.setContentLength(buf.length);

                  // Send the buffer to the client
                  ServletOutputStream servletOut = resp.getOutputStream();

                  // Wrap up
                  servletOut.write(buf);
                  servletOut.close();
              }
          }
```

A Tunnel Client Class for Serialization

Writing the client implementation for our tunnel client that uses serialization is also very straightforward (see Figure 10.20). The only real difference between this tunnel client and our "lite" client is the type of
input and output streams that will be used. The base tunnel client does
not need to change, since you had the foresight to separate the creation
of the input and output streams from the base code (great job!).

Figure 10.20

Tunnel client
implementation.

```
package javaservlets.tunnel.client;

import java.io.*;

/**
 * <p>This class implements the necessary TunnelClientInterface
 * methods for a JDK 1.1 tunneled client. The marshaling of
 * data is done with serialization.
 */
```

```
public abstract class TunnelClient extends BaseTunnelClient
{

  /**
   * <p>Gets an input stream to be used for reading data
   * from the connection. The lite version uses a standard
   * data input stream for reading data.
   *
   * @param in Input stream from the connection URL
   * @return Input stream to read data from the connection
   */
  public DataInput _getInputStream(InputStream in)
    throws IOException
    {
      // Create a new DataInputStream for reading data from
      // the connection.
      return new ObjectInputStream(in);
    }

  /**
   * <p>Gets an output stream to be used for writing data to
   * an internal buffer. The buffer will be written to the
   * connection. The lite version uses a standard data
   * output stream for writing data.
   *
   * @param buffer Buffer to hold the output data
   * @return Output stream to write data to the buffer
   */
  public DataOutput _getOutputStream(ByteArrayOutputStream buffer)
    throws IOException
    {
      // Create a new DataOutputStream for writing data to
      // the buffer.
      return new ObjectOutputStream(buffer);
    }

  /**
   * <p>Flushes the any buffered data to the output stream
   *
   * @param out Output stream to flush
   */
  public void _flush(DataOutput out) throws IOException
    {
      // Flush the data to the buffer
      ((ObjectOutputStream) out).flush();
    }

  /**
   * <p>Closes the input stream
   *
   * @param in Input stream to close
   */
  public void _close(DataInput in) throws IOException
    {
      ((ObjectInputStream) in).close();
    }
}
```

A Tunnel Server Class for Serialization

As you might expect, the implementation for the tunnel server that uses serialization is the same as the "lite" version, except that object input and output streams are used (see Figure 10.21).

Figure 10.21

Tunnel server
implementation.

```java
package javaservlets.tunnel.server;

import javax.servlet.*;
import javax.servlet.http.*;
import java.io.*;

/**
 * <p>This is the base object to be extended by server objects
 * that are using HTTP tunneling.
 */

public abstract class TunnelServer extends BaseTunnelServlet
{
  /**
    * <p>Creates an input stream to be used to read data
    * sent from the client.
    *
    * @param servletInput Servlet input stream from the servlet
    * request header
    * @return Input stream to read data from the client
    */
  public DataInput _getInputStream(ServletInputStream servletInput)
    throws IOException
    {
      // Create a new DataInputStream for reading data from
      // the client.
      return new ObjectInputStream(servletInput);
    }

  /**
    * <p>Closes the input stream
    *
    * @param in Input stream to close
    */
  public void _close(DataInput in) throws IOException
    {
      ((ObjectInputStream) in).close();
    }

  /**
    * <p>Gets an output stream to be used for writing data to
    * an internal buffer. The buffer will be written to the
    * client
    *
    * @param buffer Buffer to hold the output data
    * @return Output stream to write data to the buffer
    */
  public DataOutput _getOutputStream(ByteArrayOutputStream buffer)
    throws IOException
    {
```

```
        // Create a new DataOutputStream for writing data to
        // the buffer.
        return new ObjectOutputStream(buffer);
    }

    /**
     * <p>Flushes the any buffered data to the output stream
     *
     * @param out Output stream to flush
     */
    public void _flush(DataOutput out) throws IOException
    {
        // Flush the data to the buffer
        ((ObjectOutputStream) out).flush();
    }
}
```

Tunneling Example: RemoteIndy

To further illustrate the use of Java serialization, let's develop a simple applet that will use HTTP tunneling to make method calls to a server-side object that will retrieve data from a database. The database contains a row for each year that the Indianapolis 500 was run; each row contains the year, the name of the winning driver, and the average speed of the winning car.

Writing the Server Interface   Let's start by writing an interface that describes the services available for our server-side object. By services I mean the methods, parameter types, and return types of the server object. Our server object will provide the following services.

- Initialize—Calling the `initialize` method will cause a database connection to be established and ready the object for use.

- Query—The `query` method will accept a single parameter that will be used to form a SQL WHERE clause to select data from the database. An object containing the selected data will be returned to the caller.

- Close—Calling the `close` method will close the database connection and perform any necessary cleanup in the server object.

Figure 10.22 shows the code listing for the Indy interface. Notice that the `query` method returns an IndyRecord object. This object (shown in Figure 10.23) contains a public attribute for each column in the database. Notice that it implements java.io.Serializable; by doing so Java can properly serialize and deserialize the object.

■■ ■■ ■■ ■■

Figure 10.22

The Indy interface.

```
package javaservlets.tunnel;

/**
 * <p>This interface defines the methods available for
 * performing queries on the Indianapolis 500 database
 */

public interface IndyInterface
{
  /**
   * <p>Connects to the database.
   *
   * @return True if the database connection was established
   */
  boolean connect();

  /**
   * <p>Closes the database connection
   */
  void close();

  /**
   * <p>Given the year return the corresponding Indianapolis
   * 500 record
   *
   * @param year Year of the race
   * @return Indy 500 record or null if not found
   */
  IndyRecord query(int year);

}
```

Note that to be JavaBeans compliant the IndyRecord class should really contain a `get` and `set` method for each of the properties; I have chosen to just make the properties public so you can get the values directly.

Writing the Server Object   The beauty of writing the server object is that you do not need to know (or care) that the object will be used by

■■ ■■ ■■ ■■

Figure 10.23

The IndyRecord
class.

```
package javaservlets.tunnel;

/**
 * <p>This object encapsulates a single Indianapolis 500 record
 */

public class IndyRecord implements java.io.Serializable
{
  public int year;
  public String driver;
  public double speed;
}
```

HTTP tunneling; all we need to be concerned about is implementing the interface. Figure 10.24 shows the implementation for the Indy object.

Figure 10.24

The Indy class.

```
package javaservlets.tunnel;

import java.sql.*;

/**
 * <p>Implements the IndyInterface to provide query capabilities
 * into the Indianapolis 500 database.
 */

public class Indy implements IndyInterface
{
  // The JDBC Connection
  Connection m_connection = null;

  // A prepared statement to use to query the database
  PreparedStatement m_ps = null;

  /**
   * <p>Connects to the database.
   *
   * @return True if the database connection was established
   */
  public boolean connect()
    {
      boolean rc = false;

      try {

        // Load the Bridge
        Class.forName("sun.jdbc.odbc.JdbcOdbcDriver").newInstance();

        // Connect to the Access database
        m_connection =
          DriverManager.getConnection("jdbc:odbc:MyAccessDataSource");

        // Go ahead and create a prepared statement
        m_ps = m_connection.prepareStatement
          ("SELECT Year, Driver, AvgSpeed from IndyWinners " +
          "WHERE Year = ?");

        rc = true;
      }
      catch (Exception ex) {
        ex.printStackTrace();
      }

      return rc;
    }

  /**
   * <p>Closes the database connection
   */
  public void close()
    {
```

```
      // Close the connection if it was opened
      if (m_connection != null) {
        try {
          m_connection.close();
        }
        catch (SQLException ex) {
          ex.printStackTrace();
        }
        m_connection = null;
      }
    }

/**
  * <p>Given the year return the corresponding Indianapolis
  * 500 record
  *
  * @param year Year of the race
  * @return Indy 500 record or null if not found
  */
public IndyRecord query(int year)
  {
    IndyRecord record = null;

    try {

      // Set the year parameter
      m_ps.setInt(1, year);

      // Execute the query
      ResultSet rs = m_ps.executeQuery();

      // Make sure a record exists
      if (rs.next()) {

        // Create a new IndyRecord object
        record = new IndyRecord();

        // Set the values
        record.year = rs.getInt(1);
        record.driver = rs.getString(2);
        record.speed = rs.getDouble(3);
      }
      rs.close();
    }
    catch (SQLException ex) {
      ex.printStackTrace();
      record = null;
    }

    return record;
  }
}
```

Notice that the `initialize` method is creating a database connection using the JDBC-ODBC bridge and an Access database. Also, a JDBC PreparedStatement object is being created as well. Preparing a SQL statement is a great way to boost performance for queries you will be using multiple times. In our case, we'll be reexecuting the same query over and over with a different year value (this is done in the `query` method).

Note also how the data are being gathered from the result of the SELECT statement in the `query` method. You should always retrieve column data in order, and each column should only be retrieved once; some JDBC drivers are rather strict in enforcing this requirement, especially the bridge (due to the way ODBC functions).

The `close` method simple ensures that the database connection is properly terminated. Make sure that you always close the database so that you don't have any unwanted memory leaks or wasted resources on the server.

Writing the Client Proxy   The client proxy is responsible for marshaling method and parameter data to the server and reading the return value from the response stream. Remember that we've already done a lot of work in the base client object, so the client proxy is quite simple (see Figure 10.25). The constructor takes the base servlet URL (such as http://larryboy/servlet/) and causes a new server-side object to be instantiated. The rest of the client proxy implementation is very repetitive; because of this, I've only included the `query` method.

Figure 10.25

The Indy client proxy.

```
package javaservlets.tunnel;

import java.io.*;
import javaservlets.tunnel.client.*;

/**
 * <p>This class implements the client for tunneling
 * calls to the Indy object.
 */

public class RemoteIndyClient
  extends TunnelClient
  implements IndyInterface
{

  /**
   * <p>Constructs a new RemoteMathLiteClient for the
   * given URL. The URL should contain the location of
   * servlet scripts (i.e. http://larryboy/servlet/).
   */
  public RemoteIndyClient(String url)
    throws TunnelException, IOException
    {
      // Append the remote server name
      url += "RemoteIndyServer";

      // Set the URL
      _setURL(new java.net.URL(url));
```

```
      // Initialize the client and server
      _initialize();
  }

/**
  * <p>Given the year return the corresponding Indianapolis
  * 500 record
  *
  * @param year Year of the race
  * @return Indy 500 record or null if not found
  */
public IndyRecord query(int year)
  {
    IndyRecord record = null;
    try {
      // Create an internal buffer
      ByteArrayOutputStream baos = new ByteArrayOutputStream();

      // Create an object stream to write the request
      ObjectOutputStream out =
        (ObjectOutputStream) _createHeader(baos, 2);

      // Write the parameters
      out.writeObject(new Integer(year));

      // Invoke the method and read the response
      ObjectInputStream in =
        (ObjectInputStream) _invokeMethod(baos.toByteArray());

      // Read the return value
      record = (IndyRecord) in.readObject();

      // Wrap up
      out.close();
      in.close();
    }
    catch (Exception ex) {
      ex.printStackTrace();
    }

    return record;
  }
```

Note that the method ordinal is unique within the method and is used to create the method header. Note also how the object input and output streams are used to marshal data back and forth to the server.

Writing the Server Stub The server stub (which is also the servlet that will be invoked) implements the _getNewInstance and _invokeMethod routines. The _getNewInstance method will return an instance of the Indy object that will be persisted with the HTTP session object in the Web server.

The _invokeMethod method will be given an instance of the server object (retrieved from the HTTP session), the method ordinal of the method to invoke on the server object, an input stream to read parameters from, and an output stream to write return values. The RemoteIndyServer code is shown in Figure 10.26.

Figure 10.26

The Indy server stub.

```
package javaservlets.tunnel;

import javax.servlet.*;
import javax.servlet.http.*;
import java.io.*;
import javaservlets.tunnel.server.*;

/**
 * <p>This class implements the server for tunneling
 * remote Indy method calls
 */

public class RemoteIndyServer
  extends TunnelServer
{
  /**
   * <p>Creates a new instance of the server object.
   *
   * @return Instance of the server object
   */
  public Object _getNewInstance()
    throws ServletException
    {
      return new Indy();
    }

  /**
   * <p>Invokes the method for the ordinal given. If the method
   * throws an exception it will be sent to the client.
   *
   * @param Object Server object
   * @param ordinal Method ordinal
   * @param in Input stream to read additional parameters
   * @param out Output stream to write return values
   */
  public void _invokeMethod(Object serverObject, int ordinal,
                            DataInput in, DataOutput out)
    throws Exception
    {
      // Cast the server object
      Indy indy = (Indy) serverObject;

      // Cast the input/output streams
      ObjectInputStream objectIn = (ObjectInputStream) in;
      ObjectOutputStream objectOut = (ObjectOutputStream) out;

      // Evaluate the ordinal
      switch (ordinal) {
      case 0: // connect
```

```
        boolean b0 = indy.connect();
        objectOut.writeObject(new Boolean(b0));
        break;

    case 1: // close
      indy.close();
      break;

    case 2: // query
      Integer i2 = (Integer) objectIn.readObject();
      IndyRecord record = indy.query(i2.intValue());
      objectOut.writeObject(record);
      break;

    default:
      throw new Exception("Invalid ordinal: " + ordinal);
    }
  }
}
```

Writing the Applet   Now it's time to put our remote object to use by writing a simple applet that uses the client proxy. Most of the work involved is in formatting the display; calling methods on the remote object is nothing more than instantiating a new client proxy and making Java method calls on the Indy interface. Figure 10.27 shows the code for the Indy applet.

Figure 10.27

The IndyApplet applet.

```
package javaservlets.tunnel;

import java.applet.*;
import java.awt.*;
import java.awt.event.*;

/**
 * <p>This applet demonstrates how to use the tunnel clients
 * to perform remote method calls using serialization
 */

public class IndyApplet
  extends Applet
  implements ActionListener
{
  // Define our global components
  TextField year = new TextField(10);
  TextField driver = new TextField(20);
  TextField speed = new TextField(10);
  Button query = new Button("Query");
  IndyInterface indy;

  /**
   * <p>Initialize the applet
   */
  public void init()
    {
      // Don't allow the results to be edited
```

```
        driver.setEditable(false);
        speed.setEditable(false);

        // Use a grid bag layout
        GridBagLayout gridbag = new GridBagLayout();
        GridBagConstraints gbcon = new GridBagConstraints();
        setLayout(gridbag);

        // Setup the reusable constraint
        gbcon.weightx = 1.0;
        gbcon.weighty = 0.0;
        gbcon.anchor = gbcon.CENTER;
        gbcon.fill = gbcon.NONE;
        gbcon.gridwidth = gbcon.REMAINDER;

        // Add listeners
        query.addActionListener(this);

        // Add the components
        add(new Label("Enter the year:"));
        gridbag.setConstraints(year, gbcon);
        add(year);

        add(new Label("Press to query:"));
        gridbag.setConstraints(query, gbcon);
        add(query);

        add(new Label("Driver(s):"));
        gridbag.setConstraints(driver, gbcon);
        add(driver);

        add(new Label("Average Speed:"));
        gridbag.setConstraints(speed, gbcon);
        add(speed);

        // Create an instance of our remote object
        try {
          indy = new RemoteIndyClient(getCodeBase() + "servlet/");

          // Open the database connection
          boolean rc = indy.connect();
          if (!rc) {
            System.out.println("Connection not initialized");
            indy = null;
          }

        }
        catch (Exception ex) {
          ex.printStackTrace();
        }
    }

/**
  * <p>Called when the applet is being destroyed
  */
public void destroy()
    {
        // If the remote object was created close the connection
```

```
      if (indy != null) {
        indy.close();
        indy = null;
      }
    }

  /**
   * <p>Process an action
   */
  public void actionPerformed(ActionEvent event)
    {
      Object o = event.getSource();

      // Figure out which component caused the event
      if (o == query) {

        // If the indy object was not created, get out
        if (indy == null) {
          return;
        }

        // Clear the display fields
        driver.setText("");
        speed.setText("");

        // Get the year entered by the user
        int n = 0;
        try {
          n = Integer.parseInt(year.getText());
        }
        catch (Exception ex) {
        }

        // Get the indy record
        IndyRecord r = indy.query(n);

        // Populate
        if (r != null) {
          driver.setText(r.driver);
          speed.setText("" + r.speed);
        }

      }
    }
}
```

Note that the applet implements the ActionListener interface; doing so will force us to implement the actionPerformed method. After registering the applet as an action listener for the button (addActionListener), the actionPerformed method will be called whenever the button is pressed. We can then perform our query, which will return the results from the database.

```
<HTML>
<HEAD>
<TITLE>Indy Applet</TITLE>
</HEAD>
<BODY>
<dir>
<h2>Simple applet that makes remote method calls
using HTTP tunneling to query an Indianapolis 500 database.</h2>
</dir>
<center>
<HR>
<APPLET WIDTH=300
        HEIGHT=200
        NAME="IndyApplet"
        CODE="javaservlets.tunnel.IndyApplet"></APPLET>
</center>
</BODY>
</HTML>
```

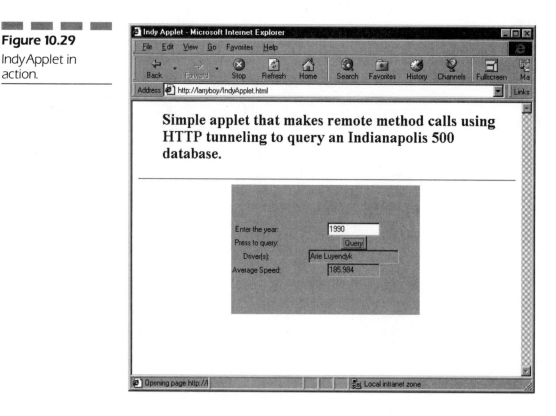

See It in Action   After adding the RemoteIndyServer servlet to the Web server (via an alias) and writing a simple HTML page to load our applet (shown in Figure 10.28), it's time to give it a test drive. Don't forget to place the applet and all supporting classes on your Web server's CLASSPATH so that the client browser can locate them (or check out Chapter 12 to find out how to automatically create an archive file for distributing the applet). After entering the year, pressing the Query button will tunnel a method call to the servlet and display the results (see Figure 10.29).

Summary

In this chapter, we've discussed how to make remote method calls using HTTP tunneling. We've seen how to marshal data generically for all versions of the JDK (which we called the "lite" version), as well as how to marshal data specifically for JDK 1.1 and higher. Along the way a base class was developed for both the client and server, which made writing client proxies and server stubs much easier. We also wrote applets to exercise the remote objects that were developed; these applets can be deployed over the Internet very easily.

In the next chapter, we'll make developing remote objects painless by automating the process. You may have noticed that writing client proxies and server stubs was somewhat repetitive; we'll be developing an application that will automatically generate the source code for these classes by using Java reflection to discover the methods, parameters, and return types of the server object.

Automating
Servlet
Programming

I n the previous chapter, we took a look at how to tunnel method calls using HTTP and Java servlets. In this chapter, we'll take this one step further and use the computer to automatically generate the client and server source code necessary to make remote method calls. This is what I call real "power programming"; program your computer to generate programs for you.

Figure 11.1

A single "lite" HTTP tunneling method call on the client.

```
/**
 * <p>Adds two numbers
 */
public int add(int a, int b)
  {
    int n = 0;
    try {
      // Create an internal buffer
      ByteArrayOutputStream baos = new ByteArrayOutputStream();

      // Create an output stream to write the request
      DataOutputStream out =
        (DataOutputStream) _createHeader(baos, 0);

      // Output the parameters
      out.writeInt(a);
      out.writeInt(b);

      // Invoke the method and read the response
      DataInputStream in =
        (DataInputStream) _invokeMethod(baos.toByteArray());

      // Read the return value
      n = in.readInt();

      // Wrap up
      out.close();
      in.close();
    }
    catch (Exception ex) {
      ex.printStackTrace();
    }
    return n;
  }
```

Writing the Client Is Always the Same

You may have noticed in the previous chapter that writing the client proxy was very repetitive. To recap, the basic steps for each method call are as follows.

1. Create a new in-memory buffer to hold the contents of the data stream.

2. Invoke a helper method to create the packet header.

3. Invoke a helper method to send the request packet to the server. This method will return an input stream, which we can then use to read any return values from the server.

These steps are consistent for both the "lite" and regular versions of HTTP tunneling. Remember that the "lite" version uses basic data input and output streams and can be used with all JDK versions (including 1.0.2). Figure 11.1 shows a single method call using "lite" tunneling, and Figure 11.2 shows a single method call using regular tunneling.

Figure 11.2

A single HTTP tunneling method call on the client.

```
/**
 * <p>Given the year return the corresponding Indianapolis
 * 500 record
 *
 * @param year Year of the race
 * @return Indy 500 record or null if not found
 */
public IndyRecord query(int year)
{
    IndyRecord record = null;
    try {
        // Create an internal buffer
        ByteArrayOutputStream baos = new ByteArrayOutputStream();

        // Create an object stream to write the request
        ObjectOutputStream out =
            (ObjectOutputStream) _createHeader(baos, 2);

        // Write the parameters
        out.writeObject(new Integer(year));

        // Invoke the method and read the response
        ObjectInputStream in =
            (ObjectInputStream) _invokeMethod(baos.toByteArray());

        // Read the return value
        record = (IndyRecord) in.readObject();

        // Wrap up
        out.close();
        in.close();
    }
    catch (Exception ex) {
        ex.printStackTrace();
    }

    return record;
}
```

The actual method calls being made are not important; what is important is the process flow for each type of client. The helper methods were developed in Chapter 10; we'll be reusing them here.

Writing the Server Is Always the Same

As with the client proxy, writing the server-side stub is tedious and repetitive. To refresh your memory the basic server-side steps are as follows.

1. Create an input stream to read the request from the client.
2. Get the instance of the server-side object from the session.
3. Set up the response header.
4. Create an in-memory buffer to hold the raw data of the response.
5. Read the method ordinal indicating which method to invoke on the server object.
6. Invoke the method. The server implementation will evaluate the method ordinal, read any parameters, and invoke the proper method. Once the method has been invoked, the server implementation will write any return value to the output stream so that it can be forwarded to the client.
7. Send the response buffer to the client.

Most of this work is being done by the base classes we developed in Chapter 10, so all we need to be concerned with is the server implementation. Figure 11.3 shows the server implementation for "lite" tunneling, and Figure 11.4 shows the implementation for regular tunneling.

Again, the actual method calls being made are not important. Note that the main difference between the two types of server implementation is the different types of input and output streams being used, which dictates how data are marshaled between the client and the server. As with the client, we will be reusing the base classes we developed in Chapter 10.

Figure 11.3

Server
implementation for
"lite" HTTP
tunneling.

```java
/**
 * <p>Invokes the method for the ordinal given. If the method
 * throws an exception it will be sent to the client.
 *
 * @param Object Server object
 * @param ordinal Method ordinal
 * @param in Input stream to read additional parameters
 * @param out Output stream to write return values
 */
public void _invokeMethod(Object serverObject, int ordinal,
                          DataInput in, DataOutput out)
    throws Exception
{
    // Cast the server object
    Math math = (Math) serverObject;

    // Cast the input/output streams
    DataInputStream dataIn = (DataInputStream) in;
    DataOutputStream dataOut = (DataOutputStream) out;

    // Evaluate the ordinal
    switch (ordinal) {
    case 0: // add
      int a0 = dataIn.readInt();
      int b0 = dataIn.readInt();
      int n0 = math.add(a0, b0);
      out.writeInt(n0);
      break;

    case 1: // subtract
      int a1 = dataIn.readInt();
      int b1 = dataIn.readInt();
      int n1 = math.subtract(a1, b1);
      out.writeInt(n1);
      break;

    case 2: // multiply
      int a2 = dataIn.readInt();
      int b2 = dataIn.readInt();
      int n2 = math.multiply(a2, b2);
      out.writeInt(n2);
      break;

    default:
      throw new Exception("Invalid ordinal: " + ordinal);
    }
}
```

Figure 11.4

Server
implementation for
HTTP tunneling.

```java
/**
 * <p>Invokes the method for the ordinal given. If the method
 * throws an exception it will be sent to the client.
 *
 * @param Object Server object
 * @param ordinal Method ordinal
 * @param in Input stream to read additional parameters
 * @param out Output stream to write return values
 */
public void _invokeMethod(Object serverObject, int ordinal,
                          DataInput in, DataOutput out)
   throws Exception
{
   // Cast the server object
   Indy indy = (Indy) serverObject;

   // Cast the input/output streams
   ObjectInputStream objectIn = (ObjectInputStream) in;
   ObjectOutputStream objectOut = (ObjectOutputStream) out;

   // Evaluate the ordinal
   switch (ordinal) {
   case 0: // connect
     boolean b0 = indy.connect();
     objectOut.writeObject(new Boolean(b0));
     break;

   case 1: // close
     indy.close();
     break;

   case 2: // query
     Integer i2 = (Integer) objectIn.readObject();
     IndyRecord record = indy.query(i2.intValue());
     objectOut.writeObject(record);
     break;

   default:
     throw new Exception("Invalid ordinal: " + ordinal);
   }
}
```

Let Java Write the Client and Server for You

Since there is a lot of repetitive programming going on with writing the client and server tunneling code, wouldn't it be nice to put someone else to work writing this code for you? Instead of *someone* else, how about *something* else: your computer? Let's outline the steps that need to take place and see if we can come up with a solution for each problem.

1. The server-side object that method calls are being tunneled to must be defined.

2. A new process must be defined that will interpret the server-side object and enumerate all the methods to be called.

3. For each method to be called, the appropriate tunneling code must be generated.

The first step is easy. In the previous chapter, we discussed how to use Java interfaces to describe the services available for a particular object. The interface describes the signatures (name, parameter[s], and return type) for each method available to outside consumers (such as an applet). By using an interface on the client side we do not need to know (or care) about the actual implementation, whether it is the actual object or some type of client proxy.

The second step may seem like an impossible task, but by the end of this chapter you will consider it quite easy. Starting with 1.1, JavaSoft has included something called the Reflection API in the JDK. The Reflection API, which is in the java.lang.reflect package, allows applications to inspect the internal makeup of other classes. Using reflection you can get a list of all the constructors, methods, and fields of any class, as well as invoke methods on the fly. The Reflection API is dynamic, as opposed to static, in that you discover things about classes at run time instead of compile time. I consider the Reflection API to be one of the most powerful aspects of the Java language, giving you abilities not found in other high-level languages (such as C). Stay tuned, we'll start using the Reflection API in the next section.

The third step involves generating Java source code and saving it to a disk file. While this is not a difficult task, we'll take a look at making things easier by creating a template file to serve as the starting point for the generated source code. As you will see later, we'll actually be creating several different source code generators to handle both the "lite" and regular versions of HTTP tunneling for the client and the server.

Using the Reflection API: ShowClass

As mentioned previously, the Reflection API included with the JDK (starting with version 1.1) enables Java applications to gather information about any other Java classes. You may not realize it, but the Reflection API is built into every class; its starting point is java.lang.Class, which is the base for all Java classes. Table 11.1 shows a partial listing of the methods found in java.lang.Class that are part of the Reflection API.

TABLE 11.1

Reflection
Methods in
java.lang.Class.

Method	Description
getConstructors	Returns an array of Constructor objects representing the public constructors found in the current class. This includes all declared and inherited constructors.
getDeclaredConstructors	Returns an array of Constructor objects representing the declared public constructors found in the current class.
getDeclaredFields	Returns an array of Field objects representing the declared fields found in the current class.
getDeclaredMethods	Returns an array of Method objects representing the declared methods found in the current class.
getFields	Returns an array of Field objects representing the fields found in the current class. This includes all declared and inherited fields.
getInterfaces	Returns an array of Class objects representing all of the interfaces directly implemented or extended by the current class.
getMethods	Returns an array of Method objects representing the methods found in the current class. This includes all declared and inherited methods.
getModifiers	Returns an encoded integer describing the Java language modifiers (such as abstract, public, class, interface, etc).
getName	Returns the fully qualified name of the current class.
getPackage	Returns the package of the current class.
getSuperclass	Returns a Class object representing the superclass of the current class, or null for java.lang.Object.

As you can see, once you have a reference to a class object you can discover just about everything you would ever want to know. Note that using the Reflection API is considered a security violation by most browsers, so you will be restricted in its use from applets.

To further illustrate the use of the Reflection API let's develop a simple application, ShowClass, which will take the place of the Java utility javap. The javap utility shows the superclass, interface, and method information for a given class. Gathering this information using the Reflection API is a breeze.

Let's take a look at the basic flow of the ShowClass application.

1. Get the class name supplied as a command-line argument.

2. Using the class name get a class object.

3. Get the list of all the superclasses for the class.

4. Get the list of all the interfaces implemented or extended by the class.

5. Get the list of all the declared fields in the class.

6. Get the list of all the declared methods in the class.

7. Display all the information.

Figure 11.5 shows the main routine that will gather and display all the class information. Remember that the complete source code for the ShowClass application can be found on the accompanying CD-ROM.

Figure 11.5

Main routine for the ShowClass application.

```
/**
 * <p>Given a class name display the classes extended,
 * interfaces implemented, and declared methods
 *
 * @param className Name of the class to process
 */
public void go(String className)
    {
      try {

        // Attempt to load the given class
        Class c = Class.forName(className);

        // Get the list of classes that it extends
        java.util.Vector extendList = getSuperClasses(c);

        // Get the list of interfaces that this class implements
        java.util.Vector interfaceList = getInterfaces(c);

        // Get the list of declared fields for this class
        java.util.Vector fields = getFields(c);
```

```java
        // Get the list of declared constructors for this class
        java.util.Vector ctors = getConstructors(c);

        // Get the list of declared methods for this class
        java.util.Vector methods = getMethods(c);

        // Display the class information
        System.out.println("\n" +
                            getModifierString(c.getModifiers()) +
                            " " + c.getName());

        // Display the extend list
        String indent = "   ";
        for (int i = 0; i < extendList.size(); i++) {
          if (i == 0) {
            System.out.println(" extends:");
          }
          System.out.println(indent +
                                ((String) extendList.elementAt(i)));
          indent += " ";
        }

        // Display the implements list
        for (int i = 0; i < interfaceList.size(); i++) {
          if (i == 0) {
            System.out.println(" implements:");
          }
          System.out.println("   " +
                                ((String) interfaceList.elementAt(i)));
        }

        // Display the fields
        for (int i = 0; i < fields.size(); i++) {
          if (i == 0) {
            System.out.println(" Fields:");
          }
          System.out.println("   " + ((String) fields.elementAt(i)));
        }

        // Display the constructors
        for (int i = 0; i < ctors.size(); i++) {
          if (i == 0) {
            System.out.println(" Constructors:");
          }
          System.out.println("   " + ((String) ctors.elementAt(i)));
        }

        // Display the methods
        for (int i = 0; i < methods.size(); i++) {
          if (i == 0) {
            System.out.println(" Methods:");
          }
          System.out.println("   " + ((String) methods.elementAt(i)));
        }

      }
      catch (ClassNotFoundException ex) {
        System.out.println("Class '" + className + "' not found.");
      }
```

```
      catch (Exception ex) {
        ex.printStackTrace();
      }
    }
```

Note how a class object is created using the `Class.forName()` method, which will attempt to locate the given class name on the current CLASSPATH. A ClassNotFoundException will be thrown if the given class name cannot be located. Once the class object has been created, the Reflection API can be used to gather the class information. Figure 11.6 shows the routine that gets all the superclasses for the class.

Note how we continue to call `getSuperclass()` until a null value is returned, which means we have reached the base object. We'll be using this same loop to get all the implemented or extended interfaces (shown in Figure 11.7).

For each class in the hierarchy all of the implemented or extended interfaces are gathered. This is complicated by the fact that each interface may extend other interfaces as well; for this reason the `getInterfaces()` method is called recursively.

Next, we need to get the list of all the declared fields for the class; the code is shown in Figure 11.8.

Figure 11.6

Getting a list of superclasses.

```
/**
 * <p>Return a list of all of the super classes for the given
 * class
 *
 * @param c Class to check
 * @return List of super classes
 */
public java.util.Vector getSuperClasses(Class c)
  {
    java.util.Vector list = new java.util.Vector();

    // Get the first super class
    c = c.getSuperclass();

    // Loop while a class exists
    while (c != null) {

      // Add the super class name to the list
      list.addElement(c.getName());

      // Get the next super class
      c = c.getSuperclass();
    }
    return list;
  }
```

Figure 11.7

Getting a list of
implemented
interfaces.

```java
/**
 * <p>Returns a list containing all of the interfaces names
 * implemented by the given class. This includes not only
 * the interfaces implemented by the class, but all interfaces
 * implemented by any super classes as well
 *
 * @param c Class to check
 * @return List of implemented interfaces
 */
public java.util.Vector getInterfaces(Class c)
  {
    // Keep a hashtable of all of the implemented interfaces
    java.util.Hashtable list = new java.util.Hashtable();

    // Loop while a class exists
    while (c != null) {

      // Get the interfaces for this class
      getInterfaces(c, list);

      // Get the next super class
      c = c.getSuperclass();
    }

    // Return a vector with the sorted list
    return sort(list);
  }

/**
 * <p>Get the interfaces implemented for the given
 * class. This routine will be called recursively
 *
 * @param c Class to check
 * @param list Hashtable containing the list of all of the
 * implemented interfaces. Do not allow duplicates.
 */
public void getInterfaces(Class c, java.util.Hashtable list)
  {
    // If the class given is an interface add it to the list
    if (c.isInterface()) {
      // Remove if duplicate
      list.remove(c.getName());
      list.put(c.getName(), c.getName());
    }

    // Get the interfaces implemented for the class
    Class interfaces[] = c.getInterfaces();

    // Loop for each interface
    for (int i = 0; i < interfaces.length; i++) {

      // Get the interfaces extended for this interface
      getInterfaces(interfaces[i], list);
    }
  }
```

Figure 11.8

Getting a list of declared fields.

```java
/**
 * <p>Returns a sorted list of declared fields for the
 * given class
 *
 * @param c Class to check
 * @return List of declared fields
 */
public java.util.Vector getFields(Class c)
{
    java.util.Hashtable list = new java.util.Hashtable();

    // Get the list of declared fields
    java.lang.reflect.Field f[] = c.getDeclaredFields();

    // Loop for each field
    for (int i = 0; i < f.length; i++) {

        // Get the name, type, and modifiers
        String name = f[i].getName();
        String type = f[i].getType().getName();
        String modifiers = getModifierString(f[i].getModifiers());

        // Save in hashtable; the key is the field name
        list.put(name, modifiers + " " + decodeType(type)
                + " " + name);
    }

    return sort(list);
}
```

Of note here is how the Java language modifier is retrieved from the field object and converted into a String. The getModifierString() method simply uses the static Modifier.toString() method to convert the integer value returned by getModifiers() into the Java language representation.

Figure 11.9 shows the code necessary for gathering all the declared methods for the class.

Nothing too difficult here; we're just getting the declared methods using the Reflection API and walking through the list picking out the information we are interested in. Figure 11.10 shows our application in action, displaying the contents of the java.io.DataOutputStream class.

Figure 11.9

Getting a list of
declared methods.

```
/**
 * <p>Returns the list of declared methods for the class
 *
 * @param c Class to check
 * @return List of declared methods
 */
public java.util.Vector getMethods(Class c)
  {
    java.util.Hashtable list = new java.util.Hashtable();

    // Get the list of declared methods
    java.lang.reflect.Method methods[] =
      c.getDeclaredMethods();

    // Loop for each method
    for (int i = 0; i < methods.length; i++) {

      // Get the name, type, modifiers, and parameter types
      String name = methods[i].getName();
      String type = methods[i].getReturnType().getName();
      String modifiers =
        getModifierString(methods[i].getModifiers());
      String params =
        getParameterString(methods[i].getParameterTypes());

      // Save in the Hashtable; the key is the method name and
      // parameter list
      list.put(name + " " + params, modifiers + " " +
               decodeType(type) + " " + name + "(" + params + ")");
    }
    return sort(list);
  }
```

Writing ServletGen

Now that you are an expert in using the Reflection API, it's time to put
it to real use by helping to generate automatically the client and server
code necessary for HTTP tunneling. We have already taken an in-depth
look at the client and server code and how it is very repetitive; we'll be
using the Reflection API on the server object's interface to determine
the methods that need to be tunneled and then generate the appropriate Java source code.

Starting with a Template I have found that when generating source
code it is quite nice to start with some type of template. This template is
a regular text file; it can be edited as necessary and contains special tags
that direct the code generator to insert certain code snippets in specific

Figure 11.10

ShowClass
output using
java.io.DataOutput-
Stream.

```
java javaservlets.reflect.ShowClass java.io.DataOutputStream

public synchronized java.io.DataOutputStream
 extends:
  java.io.FilterOutputStream
   java.io.OutputStream
    java.lang.Object
 implements:
  java.io.DataOutput
 Fields:
  protected int written
 Constructors:
  public java.io.DataOutputStream(java.io.OutputStream)
 Methods:
  public void flush()
  public final int size()
  public synchronized void write(byte[], int, int)
  public synchronized void write(int)
  public final void writeBoolean(boolean)
  public final void writeByte(int)
  public final void writeBytes(java.lang.String)
  public final void writeChar(int)
  public final void writeChars(java.lang.String)
  public final void writeDouble(double)
  public final void writeFloat(float)
  public final void writeInt(int)
  public final void writeLong(long)
  public final void writeShort(int)
  public final void writeUTF(java.lang.String)
```

locations. Not only does this reduce the amount of hard-coded information in the code generator, but it greatly improves maintainability and readability.

Figure 11.11 shows the client proxy template we'll be using. We'll actually be using four different templates (client and server for "lite" and regular tunneling), but since they are all almost identical I'll be focusing on just one.

Notice the "#" characters that start each line? The code generator will replace each of these with the appropriate tab character. Some people prefer a "real" tab ("\t"), while others prefer to use some number of spaces. You can customize the code generator to use what you prefer; the default is spaces, since that's what I prefer.

You will also notice a number of special tags (starting and ending with "%"). These tags are code generator directives which control what type of code gets inserted into the source file. Table 11.2 lists all the valid tags and which type of code will be inserted in their place.

Figure 11.11

Client proxy
template.

```
/*
 * @(#)%CLIENT_NAME%
 *
 * This source code was created by %GENERATOR_NAME%
 * on %TIMESTAMP%
 *
 * This software is provided WITHOUT WARRANTY either expressed or
 * implied.
 *
 */

%PACKAGE_STATEMENT%

import java.io.*;
import javaservlets.tunnel.client.*;

/**
  * <p>This class implements the client for tunneling
  * calls to the %OBJECT_NAME% object.
  */

public class %CLIENT_NAME%
#extends %SUPER_CLASS%
#implements %INTERFACE_NAME%
{

#/**
#  * <p>Constructs a new %CLIENT_NAME% for the
#  * given URL. This will create a new %OBJECT_NAME%
#  * object on the server as well.
#  */
#public %CLIENT_NAME%(String url)
##throws TunnelException, IOException
#{
##// Append the remote server name
##url += "%SERVER_NAME%";

##// Set the URL
##_setURL(new java.net.URL(url));

##// Initialize the client and server
##_initialize();
#}

#%METHODS%

}
```

Writing the Base Code Generator   Before going too much further, let's take a look at the basic flow of our new code generator.

1. Open the template file.

2. Create a temporary buffer to hold the generated source code.

3. Read each line from the template file and search for tags.

TABLE 11.2

Code
Generator Tags

Tag	Description
CLIENT_NAME	The name of the client proxy.
GENERATOR_NAME	The name of the code generator used to create the source code.
INTERFACE_NAME	The name of the interface to be implemented.
METHODS	Insertion point for the code generated for each method.
OBJECT_NAME	The name of the server object that is receiving the tunneled method calls.
PACKAGE_STATEMENT	The "package" statement if the generated class is part of a package. If the generated class is not in a package then nothing is generated.
SERVER_NAME	The name of the server-side stub.
SUPER_CLASS	The name of the superclass that this class extends.
TIMESTAMP	The date and time that the code generation took place.

4. If a tag is found, generate the appropriate code.

5. When the end of file is reached for the template file, the temporary buffer containing the source code will be written to disk.

As usual, I prefer to start with a base class to provide common functionality, especially since we'll be creating four generators. This base class, BaseCodeGen, will open and read the template file, process tags, and write the final source file to disk; Figure 11.12 shows the main processing routine containing these steps.

Figure 11.12

Main processing
routine of
BaseCodeGen.

```
/**
 * <p>Generates the source file.
 */
public void generate()
  throws java.io.IOException
  {
    // Attempt to open the template file
    java.io.BufferedReader in = openTemplate();

    // The target output file
    java.io.PrintWriter outFile = null;

    // Create a new in-memory output stream that will hold
```

```
// the contents of the generated file. We will not create
// the output file until all processing has completed.
java.io.ByteArrayOutputStream baos =
  new java.io.ByteArrayOutputStream();
java.io.PrintWriter out = new java.io.PrintWriter(baos);

try {

  // Process the template file. Read each line until
  // the end of file
  String line;

  while (true) {

    // Read the next line
    line = in.readLine();

    // readLine returns null if EOF
    if (line == null) {
      break;
    }

    // Strip off any indentation characters
    int numIndent = 0;
    while ((line.length() > 0) &&
           line.startsWith(m_indentPattern)) {
      numIndent++;
      line = line.substring(m_indentPattern.length());
    }

    // Process any embedded tags
    process(line, numIndent, out);
  }

  // Flush the output stream
  out.flush();

  // Processing is complete. Write the generated source
  // code.
  String fileName = stripPackage(getObjectName());
  fileName = getTargetName(fileName) + ".java";
  System.out.println("Writing " + fileName);
  java.io.FileOutputStream fos =
    new java.io.FileOutputStream(fileName);
  outFile = new java.io.PrintWriter(fos);

  // Turn our buffered output stream into an input stream
  java.io.ByteArrayInputStream bais =
    new java.io.ByteArrayInputStream(baos.toByteArray());
  java.io.InputStreamReader isr =
    new java.io.InputStreamReader(bais);
  java.io.BufferedReader br =
    new java.io.BufferedReader(isr);

  // Read the contents of our buffer and dump it to the
  // output file
  while (true) {
```

```
      // Read the next line
      line = br.readLine();

      // readLine returns null when EOF is reached
      if (line == null) {
        break;
      }

      // Output the line
      outFile.println(line);
    }

  }
  finally {
    // Always close properly
    if (in != null) {
      in.close();
    }
    if (outFile != null) {
      outFile.close();
    }
  }
}
```

Each line read out of the template file is provided to the process()
method, which will search for tags, process any tags that are found, and
output the line to the in-memory buffer. The process() and proc-
essTag() methods are shown in Figure 11.13.

Figure 11.13

Processing
template lines and
tags.

```
/**
 * <p>Processes the given line. This involves scanning the line
 * for any embedded tags. If no tags exist the line will be
 * printed to the output stream.
 *
 * @param line Line from the template file
 * @param numIndent Number of indentations (tabs)
 * @param out Print writer
 */
protected void process(String line, int numIndent,
                       java.io.PrintWriter out)
  throws java.io.IOException
  {
    // Look for tags until all have been processed
    while (line != null) {

      // Search for the tag pattern
      int begPos = line.indexOf(m_tagPattern);

      // If no tag pattern exists, exit
      if (begPos < 0) {
        break;
      }

      // We have a starting tag pattern; look for an ending
      // tag pattern
```

```
      int endPos = line.indexOf(m_tagPattern, begPos + 1);

      // No ending tag pattern, exit
      if (endPos < 0) {
        break;
      }

      // Get the tag name
      String tag = line.substring(begPos + 1, endPos);

      // Process the tag
      line = processTag(line, tag, begPos, numIndent, out);
    }

    // If the line is not null it must be written to the
    // output stream
    if (line != null) {
      out.println(indent(numIndent) + line);
    }
  }
}

/**
 * <p>Process the tag for the given line. This method may be
 * overridden; just be sure to call super.processTag().
 *
 * @param line Line from the template file
 * @param tag Tag name
 * @param pos Starting position of the tag in the line
 * @param numIndent Number of indentations (tabs)
 * @param out Print writer
 * @return Line after tag replacement or null if the replacement
 * was written directly to the output stream
 */
protected String processTag(String line, String tag, int pos,
                            int numIndent,
                            java.io.PrintWriter out)
  throws java.io.IOException
{
  // Replacement code for the tag
  String code = null;

  if (tag.equals("GENERATOR_NAME")) {
    code = getClass().getName();
  }
  else if (tag.equals("TIMESTAMP")) {
    code = new java.util.Date().toString();
  }
  else if (tag.equals("CLIENT_NAME")) {
    String objectName = getObjectName();

    // Strip off the package name
    objectName = stripPackage(objectName);

    // Get the name of the client
    code = getClientName(objectName);
  }
  else if (tag.equals("SERVER_NAME")) {
    String objectName = getObjectName();
```

```
        // Strip off the package name
        objectName = stripPackage(objectName);

        // Get the name of the server
        code = getServerName(objectName);
    }
    else if (tag.equals("PACKAGE_STATEMENT")) {
        // Assume that the code is going in the same package
        // as the interface
        String p = getPackageName(getInterfaceName());

        // No package. Do not output a line
        if (p.length() == 0) {
            line = null;
        }
        else {
            code = "package " + p + ";";
        }
    }
    else if (tag.equals("OBJECT_NAME")) {
        code = getObjectName();
    }
    else if (tag.equals("SUPER_CLASS")) {
        code = getSuperclass();
    }
    else if (tag.equals("INTERFACE_NAME")) {
        code = getInterfaceName();
    }
    else if (tag.equals("METHODS")) {

        // Process the interface methods
        processMethods(numIndent, out);

        // All code was written directly to the output stream
        line = null;
    }
    else {
        // Unknown tag
        System.out.println("WARNING: Unknown tag '" + tag + "'");
        code = "<UNKNOWN TAG " + tag + ">";
    }

    // If a code replacement was created, replace it in the
    // line
    if (code != null) {
        line = line.substring(0, pos) + code +
            line.substring(pos + tag.length() + 2);
    }
    return line;
}
```

Note how the tags are processed; most are handled by making abstract method calls to gather additional information. These abstract method calls must be implemented by the final code generator (which we will look at later). The one exception is the methods tag, which makes

Figure 11.14

Processing the
methods tag.

```
/**
 * <p>Process the METHOD tag. This involves reflecting upon
 * the interface and generating proxy code for each method
 *
 * @param numIndent Number of indentations (tabs)
 * @param out Print writer
 */
protected void processMethods(int numIndent,
                                    java.io.PrintWriter out)
    throws java.io.IOException
    {
        // Get the interface class
        Class c = getInterfaceClass();

        // Get all of the methods for the interface
        java.lang.reflect.Method methods[] = c.getMethods();

        // Loop for each method in the interface
        for (int i = 0; i < methods.length; i++) {

            // Only generate code for public methods
            int modifiers = methods[i].getModifiers();
            if (!java.lang.reflect.Modifier.isPublic(modifiers)) {
                continue;
            }

            // Generate the code for the method
            codeMethod(methods[i], numIndent, out);
        }
    }
```

use of the Reflection API to get all the methods for the server object's interface (see Figure 11.14).

Note that the code generator requires an interface that defines the server object. All the methods in the interface are discovered using the Reflection API, and each method is then used to generate the appropriate code.

Writing the Code Generator   Now that the base code generator class is complete, we can focus on writing the final implementation for each of the client proxy and server stub code generators. There are a number of abstract methods that must be implemented, the most interesting of which is the codeMethod() routine. The codeMethod() routine is the heart of the code generator, generating the repetitive code necessary for each method call. Figure 11.15 shows the codeMethod() routine for the HTTP tunneling client.

Figure 11.15

Generating code for each method.

```java
/**
 * <p>Generates the code for the given method
 *
 * @param m Method to generate
 * @param numIndent Number of indentations (tabs)
 * @param out Print writer
 */
public void codeMethod(java.lang.reflect.Method m,
                       int numIndent,
                       java.io.PrintWriter out)
    throws java.io.IOException
{
    String line;
    String tab = indent(numIndent);
    boolean throwsClassNotFoundException = false;

    // Get the method return type
    Class ret = m.getReturnType();
    String retName = decodeType(ret.getName());

    // Validate the return type to ensure we can marshal it
    if (!validateType(ret)) {
        throw new java.io.IOException("Invalid return data type " +
                                      retName);
    }

    // Get the method parameters
    Class params[] = m.getParameterTypes();

    // Get the exceptions thrown by the method
    Class exceptions[] = m.getExceptionTypes();

    // Generate the method signature
    line = "public " +
        retName + " " +
        m.getName() + "(";

    // Loop for each parameter
    for (int i = 0; i < params.length; i++) {

        // Validate the parameter type to ensure we can marshal it
        if (!validateType(params[i])) {
            throw new java.io.IOException("Invalid parameter " +
                                          "data type " + retName);
        }

        // Insert a comma if necessary
        if (i > 0) {
            line += ", ";
        }

        // Call the parameters p0, p1, etc.
        line += decodeType(params[i].getName() + " p" + i);
    }

    // Add the ending paren
    line += ")";
```

```
        // Write out the method signature
        out.println(tab + line);

        // Take care of any exceptions thrown by the method
        if (exceptions.length > 0) {
          line = "throws ";
          for (int i = 0; i < exceptions.length; i++) {

            // Insert a comma if necessary
            if (i > 0) {
              line += ", ";
            }
            line += exceptions[i].getName();
          }
          out.println(tab + indent(1) + line);
        }

        // Start the method body
        numIndent++;
        tab = indent(numIndent);
        out.println(tab + "{");
        numIndent++;
        tab = indent(numIndent);

        // Generate the default return value
        if (!retName.equals("void")) {
          line = retName + " retValue = ";

          // Determine the default value
          if (retName.equals("boolean")) {
            line += "false;";
          }
          else if (retName.equals("char") ||
                   retName.equals("byte") ||
                   retName.equals("short") ||
                   retName.equals("int") ||
                   retName.equals("long") ||
                   retName.equals("float") ||
                   retName.equals("double")) {
            line += "0;";
          }
          else {
            line += "null;";
          }
          out.println(tab + line);
        }

        out.println(tab + "try {");
        numIndent++;
        tab = indent(numIndent);

        out.println(tab + "// Create an internal buffer");
        out.println(tab + "ByteArrayOutputStream baos = " +
                    "new ByteArrayOutputStream();");
        out.println("");
        out.println(tab + "// Create an object stream to write " +
                    "the request");
        out.println(tab + "ObjectOutputStream out =");
```

```
    out.println(tab + indent(1) + "(ObjectOutputStream) "+
                "_createHeader(baos, " + m_methodNum + ");");

// Write the parameters
for (int i = 0; i < params.length; i++) {
  String param = "p" + i;
  String paramType = decodeType(params[i].getName());

  // Convert scalars to the proper object
  if (paramType.equals("boolean")) {
    param = "new Boolean(" + param + ")";
  }
  else if (paramType.equals("byte")) {
    param = "new Byte(" + param + ")";
  }
  else if (paramType.equals("char")) {
    param = "new Character(" + param + ")";
  }
  else if (paramType.equals("short")) {
    param = "new Short(" + param + ")";
  }
  else if (paramType.equals("int")) {
    param = "new Integer(" + param + ")";
  }
  else if (paramType.equals("long")) {
    param = "new Long(" + param + ")";
  }
  else if (paramType.equals("float")) {
    param = "new Float(" + param + ")";
  }
  else if (paramType.equals("double")) {
    param = "new Double(" + param + ")";
  }

  out.println(tab + "out.writeObject(" + param + ");");
}

// Invoke the method
out.println("");
out.println(tab + "// Invoke the method");
out.println(tab + "ObjectInputStream in = ");
out.println(tab + indent(1) + "(ObjectInputStream) " +
            "_invokeMethod(baos.toByteArray());");

// Get the return value if necessary
if (!retName.equals("void")) {
  out.println("");
  out.println(tab + "// Get the return value");
  out.println(tab + "Object retObject = in.readObject();");
  if (retName.equals("boolean")) {
    out.println(tab + "retValue = " +
                "((Boolean) retObject).booleanValue();");
  }
  else if (retName.equals("byte")) {
    out.println(tab + "retValue = " +
                "((Byte) retObject).byteValue();");
  }
```

```
    else if (retName.equals("char")) {
      out.println(tab + "retValue = " +
                  "((Character) retObject).charValue();");
    }
    else if (retName.equals("short")) {
      out.println(tab + "retValue = " +
                  "((Short) retObject).shortValue();");
    }
    else if (retName.equals("int")) {
      out.println(tab + "retValue = " +
                  "((Integer) retObject).intValue();");
    }
    else if (retName.equals("long")) {
      out.println(tab + "retValue = " +
                  "((Long) retObject).longValue();");
    }
    else if (retName.equals("float")) {
      out.println(tab + "retValue = " +
                  "((Float) retObject).floatValue();");
    }
    else if (retName.equals("double")) {
      out.println(tab + "retValue = " +
                  "((Double) retObject).doubleValue();");
    }
    else {
      out.println(tab + "retValue = (" +
                  retName + ") retObject;");
    }
    throwsClassNotFoundException = true;
}

// Wrap up
out.println(tab + "out.close();");
out.println(tab + "in.close();");

// End the try block
numIndent--;
out.println(indent(numIndent) + "}");
out.println(indent(numIndent) +
            "catch (java.io.IOException ex) {");
out.println(indent(numIndent + 1) + "ex.printStackTrace();");
out.println(indent(numIndent) + "}");

if (throwsClassNotFoundException) {
  out.println(indent(numIndent) +
              "catch (ClassNotFoundException ex) {");
  out.println(indent(numIndent + 1) + "ex.printStackTrace();");
  out.println(indent(numIndent) + "}");
}

out.println(indent(numIndent) +
            "catch (TunnelException ex) {");
out.println(indent(numIndent + 1) + "ex.printStackTrace();");
out.println(indent(numIndent) + "}");

// Write the return value
if (!retName.equals("void")) {
  out.println(indent(numIndent) + "return retValue;");
}
```

```
    // End the method body
    numIndent--;
    out.println(indent(numIndent) + "}");
    out.println("");

    // Increment the method number
    m_methodNum++;
}
```

Let's break down what's going on in this method.

1. The return type is validated to ensure that it can be marshaled properly.

2. The method signature is created. This includes any language modifiers, return type, method name, parameter types, and exceptions. Each parameter type is validated to ensure that it can be marshaled properly.

3. The method body is created. Refer to Figure 11.2, which illustrates how the method will look after being generated.

Validating the data types to ensure they can be marshaled properly differs depending upon which type of HTTP tunneling is being used. "Lite" tunneling, which can be used with JDK 1.0.2, uses DataInputStream and DataOutputStream to marshal data; thus, only the scalars and the string object can be used. Regular tunneling uses ObjectInputStream and ObjectOutputStream to marshal data and requires that the object being used implements java.io.Serializable.

The last thing to do after each of the code generators have been implemented is to create an application that ties them all together. This application, ServletGen, accepts command-line arguments and invokes the proper code generators. The complete code listing is shown in Figure 11.16.

Figure 11.16

The ServletGen application.

```
package javaservlets.CodeGen;

/**
 * <p>This application will invoke the proper code generator
 * depending upon the command line options given:
 *
 *    -i   Interface name
 *    -c   Class name
 *    -l   (option) Lite version
 *
 * All generated source will be created in the current directory.
 */

public class ServletGen
{
  public static void main(String args[])
```

```java
{
  // Get the interface name
  String interfaceName = getArg(args, "-i");

  // Get the class name
  String className = getArg(args, "-c");

  // Get the optional 'lite' arg
  boolean lite = argExists(args, "-l");

  // Make sure the required parameters were given
  if ((interfaceName == null) ||
      (className == null)) {
    System.out.println("\nServletGen usage:\n");
    System.out.println("ServletGen -i<interface> -c<class> " +
                       "[-l]");
    return;
  }

  try {

    // Generate the appropriate code
    if (lite) {

      // Generate the lite client
      ServletGenLiteClient client = new ServletGenLiteClient();
      client.setInterfaceName(interfaceName);
      client.setObjectName(className);
      System.out.println("Generating servlet client proxy");
      client.generate();

      // Generate the server
      ServletGenLiteServer server = new ServletGenLiteServer();
      server.setInterfaceName(interfaceName);
      server.setObjectName(className);
      System.out.println("Generating servlet server stub");
      server.generate();
    }
    else {

      // Generate the client
      ServletGenClient client = new ServletGenClient();
      client.setInterfaceName(interfaceName);
      client.setObjectName(className);
      System.out.println("Generating servlet client proxy");
      client.generate();

      // Generate the server
      ServletGenServer server = new ServletGenServer();
      server.setInterfaceName(interfaceName);
      server.setObjectName(className);
      System.out.println("Generating servlet server stub");
      server.generate();

    }
  }
  catch (Exception ex) {
    ex.printStackTrace();
  }
}
```

```
/**
 * <p>Find the given argument switch.
 *
 * @param args Array of command line arguments
 * @param s Switch to find
 * @return Value of the argument or null if not found
 */
public static String getArg(String args[], String s)
{
   String arg = null;

   if (args != null) {
     // Find the switch in the array
     for (int i = 0; i < args.length; i++) {

        // Does the switch match?
        if (args[i].startsWith(s)) {
          if (args[i].length() > s.length()) {

            // Get the value
            arg = args[i].substring(s.length());
            break;
          }
        }
     }
   }

   return arg;
}

/**
 * <p>Determines if the given argument switch exists.
 *
 * @param args Array of command line arguments
 * @param s Switch to find
 * @return true if the switch exists
 */
public static boolean argExists(String args[], String s)
{
   boolean rc = false;

   if (args != null) {
     // Find the switch in the array
     for (int i = 0; i < args.length; i++) {

        // Does the switch match?
        if (args[i].startsWith(s)) {
          rc = true;
          break;
        }
     }
   }

   return rc;
}
}
```

Tunneling Example Revisited: RemoteMathLite

In Chapter 10, we developed a very basic math object. We started by defining the interface for the object (Figure 11.17) and then implementing the interface (Figure 11.18). Once complete, a client proxy and server-side stub were handwritten to enable "lite" HTTP tunneled method calls to the math object residing on the server.

Now comes the exciting part! Instead of writing the client proxy and server stub by hand, let's use our new code generator to do all the work for us (the Java command has been split into two lines to improve readability).

```
java javaservlets.CodeGen.ServletGen
                    -ijavaservlets.CodeGen.MathInterface
                    -cjavaservlets.CodeGen.Math -1
Generating servlet client proxy
Writing RemoteMathLiteClient.java
Generating servlet server stub
Writing RemoteMathLiteServer.java
```

Figure 11.17

MathInterface.java.

```
package javaservlets.CodeGen;

/**
 * <p>This interface defines the methods available for
 * performing math
 */

public interface MathInterface
{
  /**
   * <p>Adds two numbers
   */
  int add(int a, int b);

  /**
   * <p>Subtracts two numbers
   */
  int subtract(int a, int b);

  /**
   * <p>Multiplies two numbers
   */
  int multiply(int a, int b);

}
```

In a matter of seconds ServletGen has used the Reflection API to discover all the methods in the specified interface (javaservlets.Code-Gen.MathInterface) and generated both the client proxy and server stub for "lite" HTTP tunneling (specified by the –l switch). Figure 11.19 shows the RemoteMathLiteClient code, and Figure 11.20 shows the RemoteMathLiteServer code. Remember: Both these source files were completely machine generated.

Figure 11.18

Math.java.

```
package javaservlets.CodeGen;

/**
 * <p>This class performs simple math functions in order to
 * illustrate remote method tunneling.
 */

public class Math implements MathInterface
{
  /**
   * <p>Adds two numbers
   */
  public int add(int a, int b)
    {
      return (a + b);
    }

  /**
   * <p>Subtracts two numbers
   */
  public int subtract(int a, int b)
    {
      return (a - b);
    }

  /**
   * <p>Multiplies two numbers
   */
  public int multiply(int a, int b)
    {
      return (a * b);
    }

}
```

Figure 11.19

Generated
RemoteMathLite-
Client.java.

```
/*
 * @(#)RemoteMathLiteClient
 *
 * Generated by javaservlets.CodeGen.ServletGenLiteClient
 * on Mon May 04 23:11:57 EDT 1998
 *
 * This software is provided WITHOUT WARRANTY either expressed or
 * implied.
 *
 */

package javaservlets.CodeGen;

import java.io.*;
import javaservlets.tunnel.client.*;

/**
 * <p>This class implements the lite client for tunneling
 * calls to the javaservlets.CodeGen.Math object. 'Lite' clients use
 * simple data input and output streams and can be used
 * with JDK 1.0.2
 */

public class RemoteMathLiteClient
  extends javaservlets.tunnel.client.TunnelLiteClient
  implements javaservlets.CodeGen.MathInterface
{

  /**
   * <p>Constructs a new RemoteMathLiteClient for the
   * given URL. This will create a new javaservlets.CodeGen.Math
   * object on the server as well.
   */
  public RemoteMathLiteClient(String url)
    throws TunnelException, IOException
  {
    // Append the remote server name
    url += "RemoteMathLiteServer";

    // Set the URL
    _setURL(new java.net.URL(url));

    // Initialize the client and server
    _initialize();
  }

  public int add(int p0, int p1)
    {
      int retValue = 0;
      try {
        // Create an internal buffer
        ByteArrayOutputStream baos = new ByteArrayOutputStream();

        // Create a data stream to write the request
        DataOutputStream out =
          (DataOutputStream) _createHeader(baos, 0);
        out.writeInt(p0);
        out.writeInt(p1);
```

```
                        // Invoke the method
                        DataInputStream in =
                          (DataInputStream) _invokeMethod(baos.toByteArray());

                        // Get the return value
                        retValue = in.readInt();
                        out.close();
                        in.close();
                     }
                     catch (java.io.IOException ex) {
                        ex.printStackTrace();
                     }
                     catch (TunnelException ex) {
                        ex.printStackTrace();
                     }
                     return retValue;
                  }
             ...
```

Figure 11.20

Generated
RemoteMathLite-
Server.java.

```
/*
 * @(#)RemoteMathLiteServer
 *
 * Generated by javaservlets.CodeGen.ServletGenLiteServer
 * on Mon May 04 23:11:57 EDT 1998
 *
 * This software is provided WITHOUT WARRANTY either expressed or
 * implied.
 *
 */

package javaservlets.CodeGen;

import javax.servlet.*;
import javax.servlet.http.*;
import java.io.*;
import javaservlets.tunnel.server.*;

/**
  * <p>This class implements the lite server for tunneling
  * calls to the javaservlets.CodeGen.Math object.'Lite' servers
  * use simple data input and output streams and can be used
  * with JDK 1.0.2.
  */

public class RemoteMathLiteServer
   extends javaservlets.tunnel.server.TunnelLiteServer
{
  /**
    * <p>Creates a new instance of the server object.
    *
    * @return Instance of the server object
    */
  public Object _getNewInstance()
     throws ServletException
     {
       return new javaservlets.CodeGen.Math();
     }
```

```java
/**
 * <p>Invokes the method for the ordinal given. If the method
 * throws an exception it will be sent to the client.
 *
 * @param Object Server object
 * @param ordinal Method ordinal
 * @param in Input stream to read additional parameters
 * @param out Output stream to write return values
 */
public void _invokeMethod(Object serverObject, int ordinal,
    DataInput in, DataOutput out)
    throws Exception
{
  // Cast the server object
  javaservlets.CodeGen.Math o =
    (javaservlets.CodeGen.Math) serverObject;

  // Evaluate the ordinal
  switch (ordinal) {
  case 0: //add
    int p0_0 =
      ((DataInputStream) in).readInt();
    int p0_1 =
      ((DataInputStream) in).readInt();
    int r0 = o.add(p0_0, p0_1);
    ((DataOutputStream) out).writeInt(r0);
    break;
  case 1: //subtract
    int p1_0 =
      ((DataInputStream) in).readInt();
    int p1_1 =
      ((DataInputStream) in).readInt();
    int r1 = o.subtract(p1_0, p1_1);
    ((DataOutputStream) out).writeInt(r1);
    break;
  case 2: //multiply
    int p2_0 =
      ((DataInputStream) in).readInt();
    int p2_1 =
      ((DataInputStream) in).readInt();
    int r2 = o.multiply(p2_0, p2_1);
    ((DataOutputStream) out).writeInt(r2);
    break;
  default:
    throw new Exception("Invalid ordinal: " + ordinal);
  }
}
```

Tunneling Example Revisited: RemoteIndy

In Chapter 10, we also developed a simple object called Indy; which used JDBC; this object gathered information about the Indianapolis 500 winner for a given year and returned it to the client. The interface was defined (Figure 11.21), and the implementation was written (Figure 11.22).

Figure 11.21

IndyInterface.java.

```java
package javaservlets.CodeGen;

/**
 * <p>This interface defines the methods available for
 * performing queries on the Indianapolis 500 database
 */

public interface IndyInterface
{
  /**
    * <p>Connects to the database.
    *
    * @return True if the database connection was established
    */
  boolean connect();

  /**
    * <p>Closes the database connection
    */
  void close();

  /**
    * <p>Given the year return the corresponding Indianapolis
    * 500 record
    *
    * @param year Year of the race
    * @return Indy 500 record or null if not found
    */
  IndyRecord query(int year);

}
```

```
package javaservlets.CodeGen;

import java.sql.*;

/**
  * <p>Implements the IndyInterface to provide query capabilities
  * into the Indianapolis 500 database.
  */

public class Indy implements IndyInterface
{
  // The JDBC Connection
  Connection m_connection = null;

  // A prepared statement to use to query the database
  PreparedStatement m_ps = null;

  /**
    * <p>Connects to the database.
    *
    * @return True if the database connection was established
    */
  public boolean connect()
    {
      boolean rc = false;

      try {

        // Load the Bridge
        Class.forName("sun.jdbc.odbc.JdbcOdbcDriver").newInstance();

        // Connect to the Access database
        m_connection =
          DriverManager.getConnection("jdbc:odbc:MyAccessDataSource");

        // Go ahead and create a prepared statement
        m_ps = m_connection.prepareStatement
          ("SELECT Year, Driver, AvgSpeed from IndyWinners " +
          "WHERE Year = ?");

        rc = true;
      }
      catch (Exception ex) {
        ex.printStackTrace();
      }

      return rc;
    }

  /**
    * <p>Closes the database connection
    */
```

```java
public void close()
  {
    // Close the connection if it was opened
    if (m_connection != null) {
      try {
        m_connection.close();
      }
      catch (SQLException ex) {
        ex.printStackTrace();
      }
      m_connection = null;
    }
  }

/**
 * <p>Given the year return the corresponding Indianapolis
 * 500 record
 *
 * @param year Year of the race
 * @return Indy 500 record or null if not found
 */
public IndyRecord query(int year)
  {
    IndyRecord record = null;

    try {

      // Set the year parameter
      m_ps.setInt(1, year);

      // Execute the query
      ResultSet rs = m_ps.executeQuery();

      // Make sure a record exists
      if (rs.next()) {

        // Create a new IndyRecord object
        record = new IndyRecord();

        // Set the values
        record.year = rs.getInt(1);
        record.driver = rs.getString(2);
        record.speed = rs.getDouble(3);
      }
      rs.close();
    }
    catch (SQLException ex) {
      ex.printStackTrace();
      record = null;
    }

    return record;
  }

}
```

We then wrote a client proxy and server stub for HTTP tunneling by hand; now it's time to sit back, relax, and let your computer do the work for you.

```
java javaservlets.CodeGen.ServletGen
                    -ijavaservlets.CodeGen.IndyInterface
                    -cjavaservlets.CodeGen.Indy
Generating servlet client proxy
Writing RemoteIndyClient.java
Generating servlet server stub
Writing RemoteIndyServer.java
```

This time ServletGen has created the client proxy and server stub for regular HTTP tunneled method calls (using ObjectInputStream and ObjectOutputStream to marshal data). Figure 11.23 shows the RemoteIndyClient code, and Figure 11.24 shows the RemoteIndyServer code.

Figure 11.23

Generated RemoteIndy-Client.java.

```
/*
 * @(#)RemoteIndyClient
 *
 * Generated by javaservlets.CodeGen.ServletGenClient
 * on Mon May 04 23:31:58 EDT 1998
 *
 * This software is provided WITHOUT WARRANTY either expressed or
 * implied.
 *
 */

package javaservlets.CodeGen;

import java.io.*;
import javaservlets.tunnel.client.*;

/**
  * <p>This class implements the client for tunneling
  * calls to the javaservlets.CodeGen.Indy object.
  */

public class RemoteIndyClient
  extends javaservlets.tunnel.client.TunnelClient
  implements javaservlets.CodeGen.IndyInterface
{

  /**
    * <p>Constructs a new RemoteIndyClient for the
    * given URL. This will create a new javaservlets.CodeGen.Indy
    * object on the server as well.
    */
```

```
      public RemoteIndyClient(String url)
        throws TunnelException, IOException
      {
        // Append the remote server name
        url += "RemoteIndyServer";

        // Set the URL
        _setURL(new java.net.URL(url));

        // Initialize the client and server
        _initialize();
      }

  ...

  public javaservlets.CodeGen.IndyRecord query(int p0)
      {
        javaservlets.CodeGen.IndyRecord retValue = null;
        try {
          // Create an internal buffer
          ByteArrayOutputStream baos = new ByteArrayOutputStream();

          // Create an object stream to write the request
          ObjectOutputStream out =
            (ObjectOutputStream) _createHeader(baos, 2);
          out.writeObject(new Integer(p0));

          // Invoke the method
          ObjectInputStream in =
            (ObjectInputStream) _invokeMethod(baos.toByteArray());

          // Get the return value
          Object retObject = in.readObject();
          retValue = (javaservlets.CodeGen.IndyRecord) retObject;
          out.close();
          in.close();
        }
        catch (java.io.IOException ex) {
          ex.printStackTrace();
        }
        catch (ClassNotFoundException ex) {
          ex.printStackTrace();
        }
        catch (TunnelException ex) {
          ex.printStackTrace();
        }
        return retValue;
      }

  }
```

Figure 11.24

Generated
RemoteIndy-
Server.java.

```
/*
 * @(#)RemoteIndyServer
 *
 * Generated by javaservlets.CodeGen.ServletGenServer
 * on Mon May 04 23:31:59 EDT 1998
 *
 * This software is provided WITHOUT WARRANTY either expressed or
 * implied.
 *
 */

package javaservlets.CodeGen;

import javax.servlet.*;
import javax.servlet.http.*;
import java.io.*;
import javaservlets.tunnel.server.*;

/**
  * <p>This class implements the server for tunneling
  * calls to the javaservlets.CodeGen.Indy object.
  */

public class RemoteIndyServer
  extends javaservlets.tunnel.server.TunnelServer
{
  /**
    * <p>Creates a new instance of the server object.
    *
    * @return Instance of the server object
    */
  public Object _getNewInstance()
    throws ServletException
    {
      return new javaservlets.CodeGen.Indy();
    }

  /**
    * <p>Invokes the method for the ordinal given. If the method
    * throws an exception it will be sent to the client.
    *
    * @param Object Server object
    * @param ordinal Method ordinal
    * @param in Input stream to read additional parameters
    * @param out Output stream to write return values
    */
  public void _invokeMethod(Object serverObject, int ordinal,
      DataInput in, DataOutput out)
      throws Exception
    {
      // Cast the server object
      javaservlets.CodeGen.Indy o =
        (javaservlets.CodeGen.Indy) serverObject;

      // Evaluate the ordinal
      switch (ordinal) {
```

```
        case 0: //connect
          boolean r0 = o.connect();
          ((ObjectOutputStream) out).writeObject(new Boolean(r0));
          break;
        case 1: //close
          o.close();
          break;
        case 2: //query
          int p2_0 =
            ((Integer) read(in)).intValue();
          javaservlets.CodeGen.IndyRecord r2 = o.query(p2_0);
          ((ObjectOutputStream) out).writeObject(r2);
          break;
        default:
          throw new Exception("Invalid ordinal: " + ordinal);
      }
    }

  /**
   * <p>Helper method to read an object from the input stream
   *
   * @param in Input stream
   * @return The next object read from the input stream
   */
  protected Object read(DataInput in)
    throws Exception
  {
    return ((ObjectInputStream) in).readObject();
  }
}
```

Summary

In this chapter, we have moved to the next level of Java programming: using the built-in features of Java to automatically create other Java classes; the foundation that allows this to happen is the Reflection API. The Reflection API is a series of methods and classes that provide information about the internal structure of classes. We used this powerful API to develop a code generator to create the client proxy and server-side stub necessary for tunneling method calls over HTTP.

Coming up next, we'll take a small break from servlet programming and develop an application that will ease the distribution of applets. We'll do this by automatically creating an archive containing all the class file dependencies for any applet.

# CHAPTER 12

Easing the Distribution Process: Automatic JAR File Creation

I n this chapter, we're going to take a little break from servlet programming and look at how to make the distribution of your applets much easier. One of the hardest steps in distributing an applet is not only proper packaging, either in a compressed ZIP or JAR file, but knowing exactly what to include in the package. We'll solve both of these problems by developing a class file dependency checker and add the ability to archive any dependencies into a ZIP or JAR file.

Discovering Class File Dependencies

To discover all the dependencies for a given class file, we'll actually be examining the internal class structure as defined by the Java virtual machine. The Java virtual machine specification describes a class file as follows: A stream of 8-bit bytes. All 16-bit, 32-bit, and 64-bit quantities are constructed by reading in two, four, and eight consecutive 8-bit bytes, respectively. Multibyte data items are always stored in big-endian order, where the high-order bytes come first. As we'll see, all class references are kept within the class file; all we need to do is find them. Table 12.1 shows the basic class file structure we will be examining.

A Closer Look at the Class File Structure

Let's take a closer look at each of the items in the class file structure. Once you understand how the class structure is tied together, it becomes quite easy to traverse the structure and pick out valuable information.

Magic   The magic item contains a magic number common to all Java class files. The value of the magic item is always 0xCAFEBABE.

Minor Version and Major Version   The values of the minor and major version items are the minor and major version numbers of the compiler that created the class file. For Sun's JDK versions 1.0.2 and 1.1, the minor version is 3 and the major version is 45. Only Sun can define the meaning of new version numbers.

TABLE 12.1

The Java Class
File Structure

Item	Length
Magic	4
Minor version	2
Major version	2
Constant pool count	2
Constant pool	varies
Access flags	2
This class	2
Super class	2
Interface count	2
Interfaces	2 · Interface count
Field count	2
Fields	varies
Method count	2
Methods	varies
Attribute count	2
Attributes	varies

Constant Pool Count   The constant pool count must be greater than zero. It defines the number of entries in the constant pool table. Note that the constant pool count includes the constant pool entry at index 0, but the entry is not included in the class file and is reserved for internal use by the Java virtual machine.

Constant Pool   The constant pool is a table of variable-length entries. Each of the entries from index 1 to the constant pool count is variable in length. The format of each entry is defined by a leading tag byte, as shown in Table 12.2.

CONSTANT_Utf8   The CONSTANT_Utf8 entry represents a constant string value. Utf8 strings are encoded so that character sequences that contain only nonnull ASCII characters can be represented using only

TABLE 12.2 Constant Pool Tag Values

Constant Type	Value
CONSTANT_Utf8	1
CONSTANT_Integer	3
CONSTANT_Float	4
CONSTANT_Long	5
CONSTANT_Double	6
CONSTANT_Class	7
CONSTANT_String	8
CONSTANT_Fieldref	9
CONSTANT_Methodref	10
CONSTANT_InterfaceMethodref	11
CONSTANT_NameAndType	12

one byte per character. Characters up to 16 bits can also be represented. Table 12.3 shows the structure for the CONSTANT_Utf8 entry.

CONSTANT_Integer The CONSTANT_Integer entry represents a four-byte integer constant. Table 12.4 shows the structure for the CONSTANT_Integer entry.

TABLE 12.3 CONSTANT_Utf8 Entry

Item	Length	Notes
Tag	1	CONSTANT_Utf8, value of 1
Length	2	The number of bytes in the following bytes array. Strings are not null terminated.
Bytes	Specified by length	The bytes of the string

TABLE 12.4   CONSTANT_Integer Entry

Item	Length	Notes
Tag	1	CONSTANT_Integer, value of 3
Bytes	4	The value of the int constant. The bytes are stored in big-endian order.

CONSTANT_Float   The CONSTANT_Float entry represents a four-byte float constant. Table 12.5 shows the structure for the CONSTANT_Float entry.

CONSTANT_Long   The CONSTANT_Long entry represents an eight-byte long constant. Table 12.6 shows the structure for the CONSTANT_Long entry.

The CONSTANT_Long entry, as well as the CONSTANT_Double entry, actually consumes two constant pool entries. The following constant pool entry must be considered invalid and must not be used.

CONSTANT_Double   The CONSTANT_Double entry represents an eight-byte double constant. Table 12.7 shows the structure for the CONSTANT_Double entry.

TABLE 12.5   CONSTANT_Float Entry

Item	Length	Notes
Tag	1	CONSTANT_Float, value of 4
Bytes	4	The value of the float constant. The value is stored in IEEE 754 floating-point single format bit layout.

TABLE 12.6   CONSTANT_Long Entry

Item	Length	Notes
Tag	1	CONSTANT_Long, value of 5
Bytes	8	The value of the long constant. The bytes are stored in big-endian order.

TABLE 12.7 CONSTANT_Double Entry

Item	Length	Notes
Tag	1	CONSTANT_Double, value of 6
Bytes	8	The value of the double constant. The value is stored in IEEE 754 floating-point double format bit layout.

The CONSTANT_Double entry consumes two constant pool entries; for more information, see CONSTANT_Long.

CONSTANT_Class The CONSTANT_Class entry represents a class or interface. The CONSTANT_Class entry contains an index pointer back into the constant pool to a CONSTANT_Utf8 entry. The string found at the indexed entry is the name of a class or interface. Table 12.8 shows the structure for the CONSTANT_Class entry.

CONSTANT_String The CONSTANT_String entry represents a string constant. The CONSTANT_String entry contains an index pointer back into the constant pool to a CONSTANT_Utf8 entry. Table 12.9 shows the structure for the CONSTANT_String entry.

CONSTANT_Fieldref The CONSTANT_Fieldref entry represents a field within the class. The CONSTANT_Fieldref entry contains an index pointer back into the constant pool to a CONSTANT_Class entry of the field declaration and an index pointer to a CONSTANT_NameAndType entry defining the field name and descriptor. Table 12.10 shows the structure for the CONSTANT_Fieldref entry.

TABLE 12.8 CONSTANT_Class Entry

Item	Length	Notes
Tag	1	CONSTANT_Class, value of 7
Name Index	2	Valid constant pool index. The entry at the index must be of type CONSTANT_Utf8 and represents a class or interface name.

TABLE 12.9 CONSTANT_String Entry

Item	Length	Notes
Tag	1	CONSTANT_String, value of 8
String Index	2	Valid constant pool index. The entry at the index must be of type CONSTANT_Utf8 and represents a string constant.

CONSTANT_Methodref The CONSTANT_Methodref entry represents a method within the class. The CONSTANT_Methodref entry contains an index pointer back into the constant pool to a CONSTANT_Class entry of the method declaration and an index pointer to a CONSTANT_NameAndType entry defining the method name and descriptor. Table 12.11 shows the structure for the CONSTANT_Methodref entry.

CONSTANT_InterfaceMethodref The CONSTANT_InterfaceMethodref entry represents a method defined in an interface. The CONSTANT_InterfaceMethodref entry contains an index pointer back into the constant pool to a CONSTANT_Class entry of the method declaration and an index pointer to a CONSTANT_NameAndType entry defining the method name and descriptor. Table 12.12 shows the structure for the CONSTANT_InterfaceMethodref entry.

TABLE 12.10 CONSTANT_Fieldref Entry

Item	Length	Notes
Tag	1	CONSTANT_Fieldref, value of 9
Class Index	2	Valid constant pool index. The entry at the index must be of type CONSTANT_Class and represents a class or interface declaration type.
Name and Type Index	2	Valid constant pool index. The entry at the index must be of type CONSTANT_NameAndType and represents the name and descriptor of the field.

TABLE 12.11   `CONSTANT_Methodref` Entry

Item	Length	Notes
Tag	1	`CONSTANT_Methodref`, value of 10
Class Index	2	Valid constant pool index. The entry at the index must be of type `CONSTANT_Class` and represents a class or interface declaration type.
Name and Type Index	2	Valid constant pool index. The entry at the index must be of type `CONSTANT_NameAndType` and represents the name and descriptor of the method.

TABLE 12.12   `CONSTANT_InterfaceMethodref` Entry

Item	Length	Notes
Tag	1	`CONSTANT_InterfaceMethodref`, value of 11
Class Index	2	Valid constant pool index. The entry at the index must be of type `CONSTANT_Class` and represents an interface declaration type.
Name and Type Index	2	Valid constant pool index. The entry at the index must be of type `CONSTANT_NameAndType` and represents the name and descriptor of the method.

CONSTANT_NameAndType   The `CONSTANT_NameAndType` entry represents a field or method name and type. Note that the class or interface that the field or method belongs to is not indicated. The `CONSTANT_Fieldref`, `CONSTANT_Methodref`, and `CONSTANT_InterfaceMethodref` entries are used to tie classes and interfaces to method names and types. Table 12.13 shows the structure for the `CONSTANT_NameAndType` entry.

Access Flags   The value of the access flags indicates the modifiers used for the class or interface declaration. Table 12.14 shows the access flag modifier values.

TABLE 12.13   CONSTANT_NameAndType Entry

Item	Lengt	Notes
Tag	1	CONSTANT_NameAndType, value of 12
Class Index	2	Valid constant pool index. The entry at the index must be of type CONSTANT_Utf8 and represents a valid Java method or field name.
Descriptor Index	2	Valid constant pool index. The entry at the index must be of type CONSTANT_Utf8 and represents a valid Java method or field descriptor.

TABLE 12.14   Class and Interface Modifier Flags

Flag	Value	Notes
ACC_PUBLIC	0x0001	Public class or interface
ACC_FINAL	0x0010	Final class; no subclasses are allowed.
ACC_SUPER	0x0020	Treat superclass methods special.
ACC_INTERFACE	0x0200	Interface
ACC_ABSTRACT	0x0400	Abstract class or interface; may not be instantiated.

This Class   The value of this class item must be a valid index into the constant pool. The entry at the index must be of type CONSTANT_Class and represents the class or interface defined by this class.

Superclass   The value of the superclass item must be a valid index into the constant pool. The entry at the index must be of type CONSTANT_Class and represents the superclass of this class. The only exception is java.lang.Object, whose superclass index is 0.

Interface Count   The interface count defines the number of entries in the interface table, which defines the direct superinterfaces of this class or interface.

Interface Table   The interface table contains an array of valid constant pool index pointers. Each interface table entry must reference a CONSTANT_Class entry and represents an interface that is a direct superinterface of this class or interface.

Field Count   The field count defines the number of entries in the field table, which defines each field of this class or interface.

Field Table   The field table contains an array of variable-length entries representing each field of this class or interface. The field table does not include fields that are inherited from a superclass or superinterface; it contains only those fields that are defined in the class or interface. Since we won't be using the field table, I'll leave it to the virtual machine specification to explain the contents of each field entry.

Method Count   The method count defines the number of entries in the method table, which defines each method of this class or interface.

Method Table   The method table contains an array of variable-length entries representing each method of this class or interface. The method table does not include methods that are inherited from a superclass or superinterface; it contains only those methods that are defined in the class or interface. As with the field table, we won't be using the method table, and I'll leave it up to the virtual machine specification to explain the contents.

Attribute Count   The attribute count defines the number of entries in the attribute table, which defines each attribute of this class or interface.

Attribute Table   The attribute table contains an array of variable-length entries representing each attribute of this class or interface. Attributes give additional information about the class file, such as the SourceFile, Exceptions, and LineNumberTable. Again, we won't be using the attribute table, so refer to the virtual machine specification for details.

An Algorithm for Discovering Dependencies

Now that we have a firm grasp of the contents of the class file, we can easily pick out the dependencies. We'll consider a dependency to be any class reference found in the constant pool. The following list is a basic algorithm for finding the class references.

1. Open and read the class file.
2. Get the number of entries in the constant pool.
3. Read through the constant pool, keeping a list of class file and string references. Note that a class file reference is actually an index back into the constant pool. The constant pool entry the index is pointing to is a string giving the name of the class or interface.
4. For each class file reference, find the corresponding string constant containing the class file name.
5. For each class file found, repeat steps 1 through 5.

In the following sections, we'll work through each of these steps and look at the corresponding Java code we'll be using in our dependency checker.

Opening and Reading a Class File

The first challenge in our dependency checker seems as if it would be a very simple process. All we need to do is open a class file; how hard could that be? You might be tempted to treat a class file as a resource and use the `ClassLoader.getSystemResourceAsStream()` method to return an input stream we could very easily read. Unfortunately, the ClassLoader prohibits class files from being read this way as a security measure; you wouldn't want someone to be able to read your class file directly from the Internet, would you?

Well, if you can't treat a class as a system resource, how about just opening the class as a file? This would work well if you could always guarantee that the class file could be found in your local file structure. But what about classes that are loaded from the CLASSPATH from a compressed ZIP or JAR file? This is a very common way to package and distribute classes—after all, that's what we're trying to do! In order to reliably open a class file, regardless of where it is physically located, we'll need to walk through the CLASSPATH and look for the class in either the directory or archive (ZIP or JAR) in each CLASSPATH element. Figure 12.1 lists the Java code that performs this process.

Figure 12.1

Opening and reading a class file from the current CLASSPATH.

```
/**
 * Given a class name, open it and return a buffer with
 * the contents. The class is loaded from
 * the current CLASSPATH setting
 */
protected byte[] openResource(String name)
   throws Exception
   {
     byte buf[] = null;

     // Get the defined classpath

     String classPath = System.getProperty("java.class.path");
     int beginIndex = 0;
     int endIndex = classPath.indexOf(";");

     // Walk through the classpath

     while (true) {
       String element = "";

       if (endIndex == -1) {
         // No ending semicolon
         element = classPath.substring(beginIndex);
       }
       else {
         element = classPath.substring(beginIndex, endIndex);
       }

       // We've got an element from the classpath. Look for
       // the resource here

       buf = openResource(name, element);

       // Got it! Exit the loop

       if (buf != null) {
         break;
       }
```

```
      if (endIndex == -1) {
        break;
      }
      beginIndex = endIndex + 1;
      endIndex = classPath.indexOf(";", beginIndex);
    }

    return buf;
  }

/**
  * Given a resource name and path, open the resource and
  * return a buffer with the contents. Returns null if
  * not found
  */

protected byte[] openResource(String name,
                                String path)
  throws Exception
  {
    byte buf[] = null;

    // If the path is a zip or jar file, look inside for the
    // resource

    String lPath = path.toLowerCase();
    if (lPath.endsWith(".zip") ||
        lPath.endsWith(".jar")) {

      buf = openResourceFromJar(name, path);
    }
    else {

      // Not a zip or jar file. Look for the resource as a file

      String fullName = path;

      // Put in the directory separator if necessary

      if (!path.endsWith("\\") &&
          !path.endsWith("/")) {
        fullName += "/";
      }
      fullName += name;

      java.io.File f = new java.io.File(fullName);

      // Check to make sure the file exists and it truely
      // is a file

      if (f.exists() &&
          f.isFile()) {

        // Create an input stream and read the file

        java.io.FileInputStream fi = new java.io.FileInputStream(f);
        long length = f.length();
        buf = new byte[(int) length];
```

```
          fi.read(buf);
          fi.close();
        }
      }

      return buf;
    }

/**
 * Given a resource name and jar file name, open the jar file
 * and return a buffer containing the contents. Returns null
 * if the jar file could not be found or the resource could
 * not be found
 */

protected byte[] openResourceFromJar(String name,
                                     String jarFile)
  throws Exception
  {
    byte buf[] = null;

    java.io.File f = new java.io.File(jarFile);
    java.util.zip.ZipFile zip = null;

    // Make sure the file exists before opening it

    if (f.exists() &&
        f.isFile()) {

      // Open the zip file

      zip = new java.util.zip.ZipFile(f);

      // Is the entry in the zip file?

      java.util.zip.ZipEntry entry = zip.getEntry(name);

      // If found, read the corresponding buffer for the entry

      if (entry != null) {
        java.io.InputStream in = zip.getInputStream(entry);

        // Get the number of bytes available

        int len = (int) entry.getSize();

        // Read the contents of the class
        buf = new byte[len];
        in.read(buf, 0, len);
        in.close();
      }
    }

    if (zip != null) {
      zip.close();
    }
    return buf;
  }
```

Reading the Number of Entries in the Constant Pool

Now that we have opened and read the contents of the class file, we can start processing the raw byte stream. The first step is reading the class header and determining the number of entries in the constant pool. Since the header of the class file is a fixed-length structure (refer to Table 12.1), we can perform some basic header verification and read the value directly, as shown in Figure 12.2.

Processing the Constant Pool

Next, we can process each entry in the constant pool. We'll skip most of the information in the constant pool; we are only interested in the

Figure 12.2

Processing the class file header.

```
// Create a DataInputStream using the buffer. This will
// make reading the buffer very easy

java.io.ByteArrayInputStream bais =
  new java.io.ByteArrayInputStream(buf);

java.io.DataInputStream in = new java.io.DataInputStream(bais);

// Read the magic number. It should be 0xCAFEBABE

int magic = in.readInt();
if (magic != 0xCAFEBABE) {
  throw new Exception("Invalid magic number in " + className);
}

// Validate the version numbers

short minor = in.readShort();
short major = in.readShort();
if ((minor != 3) &&
    (major != 45)) {
  // The VM specification defines 3 as the minor version
  // and 45 as the major version for 1.1
  throw new Exception("Invalid version number in " + className);
}

// Get the number of items in the constant pool

short count = in.readShort();
```

CONSTANT_Class (**Table 12.8**) and CONSTANT_Utf8 (**Table 12.3**) entries.
Figure 12.3 lists the Java code that processes the constant pool.

Figure 12.3

Processing the
constant pool.

```java
// We'll keep a vector containing an entry for each
// CONSTANT_Class tag in the constant pool. The value
// in the vector will be an Integer object containing
// the name index of the class name

java.util.Vector classInfo = new java.util.Vector();

// We'll also keep a HashTable containing an entry for
// each CONSTANT_String. The key will be the index
// of the entry (relative to 1), while the element
// will be the String value.

java.util.Hashtable utf8 = new java.util.Hashtable();

// Now walk through the constant pool looking for class
// constants. All other constants are ignored, but we
// still need to understand the format so that they
// can be skipped.

for (int i = 1; i < count; i++) {
  // Read the tag
  byte tag = in.readByte();

  switch (tag) {
  case 7:  // CONSTANT_Class
    // Save the constant pool index for the class name
    short nameIndex = in.readShort();
    classInfo.addElement(new Integer(nameIndex));
    break;
  case 9:  // CONSTANT_Fieldref
  case 10: // CONSTANT_Methodref
  case 11: // CONSTANT_InterfaceMethodref
    // Skip past the structure
    in.skipBytes(4);
    break;
  case 8:  // CONSTANT_String
    // Skip past the string index
    in.skipBytes(2);
    break;
  case 3:  // CONSTANT_Integer
  case 4:  // CONSTANT_Float
    // Skip past the data
    in.skipBytes(4);
    break;
  case 5:  // CONSTANT_Long
  case 6:  // CONSTANT_Double
    // Skip past the data
    in.skipBytes(8);

    // As dictated by the Java Virtual Machine specification,
    // CONSTANT_Long and CONSTANT_Double consume two
    // constant pool entries.
    i++;
```

```
      break;
  case 12: // CONSTANT_NameAndType
    // Skip past the structure
    in.skipBytes(4);
    break;
  case 1:  // CONSTANT_Utf8
    String s = in.readUTF();
    utf8.put(new Integer(i), s);
    break;
  default:
    System.out.println("WARNING: Unknown constant tag (" +
                        tag + "@" + i + " of " + count +
                        ") in " + className);
  }
}
```

Note that even though we are only using the CONSTANT_Class and CONSTANT_Utf8 entries, we still need to understand the format of the other entries so that they can be properly skipped. Of special note are the CONSTANT_Long and CONSTANT_Double entries, which consume two constant pool entries each; we have to make sure that we advance our pool counter appropriately.

Finding All the Class Names

In the previous section, we read the constant pool table and kept a list of all the CONSTANT_Class and CONSTANT_Utf8 entries. Remember that the CONSTANT_Class entry contains a valid constant pool index, which points to the class or index name. Since the order of the constant pool entries is not dictated by the virtual machine specification, we had to read all the entries before any further processing. Now that the entire constant pool has been read, we can go back though our list of CONSTANT_Class entries and find the corresponding CONSTANT_Utf8 entry. Figure 12.4 shows the Java code that performs this task.

Note that arrays of class names are treated specially and contain a Java array type descriptor—for example, the class name representing a one-dimensional array of class object:

```
Object[]
```

is represented as the Java array type descriptor:

```
[Ljava.lang.Object;
```

Figure 12.4

Finding the class or
interface names
from the constant
pool.

```java
// Now we can walk through our vector of class name
// index values and get the actual class name

for (int i = 0; i < classInfo.size(); i++) {
  Integer index = (Integer) classInfo.elementAt(i);
  String s = (String) utf8.get(index);

  // Look for arrays. Only process arrays of objects

  if (s.startsWith("[")) {
    // Strip off all of the array indicators
    while (s.startsWith("[")) {
      s = s.substring(1);
    }
    // Only use the array if it is an object. If it is,
    // the next character will be an 'L'

    if (!s.startsWith("L")) {
      continue;
    }

    // Strip off the leading 'L' and trailing ';'
    s = s.substring(1, s.length() - 1);
  }

  // Append the .class
  s += ".class";
  // Now we have the full class or interface name in 's'
}
```

Now we can perform additional processing with each class name we
found. For our purposes, we need to add each file to a new archive (a
compressed ZIP or JAR file). Also, for each new class name we find, we
need to recursively check it for class file dependencies. By doing so, we
will find all the dependencies for our original class. Let's back up a bit
and look at how we create a new ZIP or JAR file. Both archives have the
same format, except that a JAR (Java ARchive) file can optionally have
a manifest file, as defined by the JavaBeans specification, which lists all

Figure 12.5

Creating a new ZIP
or JAR file.

```java
// Attempt to create the archive if one was given

if (m_archive != null) {
  java.io.File f = new java.io.File(m_archive);
  java.io.FileOutputStream fo =
    new java.io.FileOutputStream(f);

  // A new file was created. Create our zip output stream

  m_archiveStream = new java.util.zip.ZipOutputStream(fo);
}
```

■■■■ ■■■■ ■■■■ ■■■■
Figure 12.6

Writing to a ZIP or
JAR file.

```
/*
 * Adds the given buffer to the archive with the given
 * name
 */
private void addToArchive(String name, byte buf[])
  throws Exception
  {
    // Create a zip entry

    java.util.zip.ZipEntry entry = new
        java.util.zip.ZipEntry(name);
    entry.setSize(buf.length);

    // Add the next entry

    m_archiveStream.putNextEntry(entry);

    // Write the contents out as well

    m_archiveStream.write(buf, 0, buf.length);
    m_archiveStream.closeEntry();
  }
```

the valid beans in the JAR. We'll just assume there will be no beans in the JAR, so we can omit creating a manifest. Figure 12.5 shows the Java code that creates a new ZIP or JAR file.

The java.util.zip.ZipOutputStream class makes it very easy to create a compressed archive file. As shown in Figure 12.6, all we need to do is create a new java.util.zip.ZipEntry object, representing a header in the archive, and then write the data.

■■■■   ■■■■   # Putting It All Together: The CreateArchive Application

Now that we've got all the routines necessary to find all the dependencies for a given class, let's put it together by writing CreateArchive—a simple application that will accept a list of class files to check and, optionally, the name of the archive to create. CreateArchive will use the RollCall class, which will read the class files and create the archive for us. We've been looking at parts of RollCall.java throughout the chapter. As always, you can find the complete source code on the accompanying CD-ROM.

Figure 12.7

The CreateArchive
application.

```
package javaservlets.rollcall;

/**
 * <p>This simple application will use the RollCall class to
 * find all of the class file dependency for a given set of
 * classes. If an archive file is specified it will be created
 * and all of the dependent files will be added.
 */

public class CreateArchive
{
  public static void main(String args[])
    {
      // Create a new object and process

      CreateArchive ca = new CreateArchive();
      ca.create(args);
    }

  public void create(String args[])
    {
      // Get a list of all of the class files to check. Any
      // arguments given without a switch '-' will be considered
      // a class file

      String files[] = getFiles(args);

      if (files == null) {
        System.out.println("No class files specified");
        showHelp();
      }

      // Get the archive to create, if given

      String archive = getArg(args, "-a");

      // Create a new RollCall object

      RollCall rollCall = new RollCall();

      try {

        // Set the class files to check

        rollCall.setClasses(files);

        // Set the archive to create

        rollCall.setArchive(archive);

        // Perform check and create archive, if necessary.

        rollCall.start();
      }
      catch (Exception ex) {
        ex.printStackTrace();
      }
    }
```

The CreateArchive application will take as its parameters one or more class files to check (without the .class extension) and, optionally, a "-a" switch specifiying the name of the archive to create. If no archive is specified, the dependencies will simply be displayed. Figure 12.7 shows the main Java routines that use the RollCall class.

One thing worth mentioning is that when we run CreateArchive, all the java.* classes will be filtered out. You shouldn't have a need to distribute these classes, so they are explicitly excluded (not to mention that your archive would be quite large if you included all the java.* classes used by even the simplest of classes).

Let's try it out. As a simple test, we'll run CreateArchive using itself as the input class file.

```
java javaservlets.rollcall.CreateArchive
      javaservlets.rollcall.CreateArchive
```

You should get the following output.

```
javaservlets.rollcall.CreateArchive.class
  javaservlets.rollcall.RollCall.class
```

You can also try running CreateArchive with the -a switch, specifying the archive file to create.

```
java javaservlets.rollcall.CreateArchive
      javaservlets.rollcall.CreateArchive -atemp.jar
```

You should get the following output.

```
Creating temp.jar
javaservlets.rollcall.CreateArchive.class
  javaservlets.rollcall.RollCall.class
temp.jar created.
```

Distributing an Applet

Now that we have our CreateArchive utility, which will find all the dependencies for a given set of class files, let's try it out. We're going to create a very simple applet that uses another very basic class that implements an interface. The net effect is that we will have three dependencies for our applet: a class, an interface, and the applet itself. We'll start by writing a simple class that implements an interface with

Figure 12.8

A simple interface
and class to test
CreateArchive.

```
public interface SimpleInterface
{
    String getString();
}


public class SimpleClass implements SimpleInterface
{
  public String getString()
    {
      return "I loaded all of my classes from an archive!";
    }
}
```

a method that returns a string value. Figure 12.8 shows the Java source for both the interface and class.

The applet we'll use to test CreateArchive is shown in Figure 12.9. All we need to do is create a simple TextField to hold the results of the method call into our simple class.

Let's go ahead and create an archive for our simple applet so that it can be easily distributed.

```
java javaservlets.rollcall.CreateArchive
       javaservlets.rollcall.test.SimpleApplet
       -aSimpleApplet.zip
```

You should get the following output.

```
Creating archive SimpleApplet.zip
javaservlets.rollcall.test.SimpleApplet.class
  javaservlets.rollcall.test.SimpleClass.class
    javaservlets.rollcall.test.SimpleInterface.class
SimpleApplet.zip created.
```

SimpleApplet.zip now contains all the class files necessary to execute our simple applet. Remember that there are no java.* files included, but these will be part of the virtual machine of the browser. Before we can use our applet, we need to create an HTML file that will load the applet properly, as shown in Figure 12.10.

Note the "archive=" option on the applet tag. This specifies the archive to use to search for the applet, which in our case is the SimpleApplet.zip file created by CreateArchive. Let's go ahead and try it out.

■■ ■■ ■■ ■■
Figure 12.9

A simple applet to
test CreateArchive.

```
public class SimpleApplet extends java.applet.Applet
{
  // Define our fields

  java.awt.TextField output = new java.awt.TextField();

  /*
   * <p>init is called when the applet is loaded
   */

  public void init()
    {
      // Add components

      add(output);

      // Use our simple class to get some data. Set the
      // results in the output text field.

      SimpleClass sc = new SimpleClass();
      output.setText(sc.getString());
    }
}
```

We'll use Netscape Navigator to execute our applet, but you can use any
Java 1.1–enabled browser. In order to make this a valid test, verify that
the simple applet class files are not on your CLASSPATH to ensure that
they are loaded from the archive. Place `SimpleApplet.zip` and `Sim-
pleApplet.html` in your Web server's WWW root directory. Figure
12.11 shows the SimpleApplet loaded from our archive.

■■ ■■ ■■ ■■
Figure 12.10

Simple-
Applet.html.

```
<html>
<head>
<title>SimpleApplet - Simple applet for testing archives</title>
</head>
<body>
<h1><center>SimpleApplet</center></h1>
<hr>

<applet code=javaservlets.rollcall.test.SimpleApplet
        width=400
        height=100
        archive=SimpleApplet.zip>
</applet>
<hr>
</body>
</html>
```

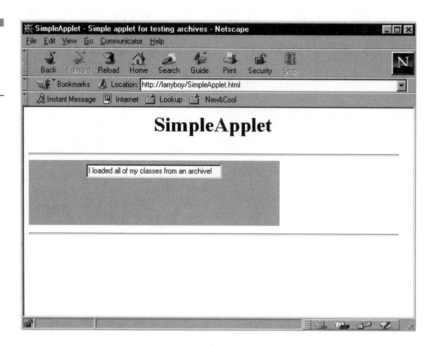

A Few Pitfalls

I don't want you to leave this chapter without being aware of a few pitfalls in our dependency checker.

- If the class you are trying to examine loads a class explicitly using `Class.forName("<class>")`, the dependency checker algorithm will not find the named class. This is because we are only looking for `CONSTANT_Class` constant; the named class in the `Class.forName()` method creates a `CONSTANT_Utf8` constant (for the named class). You could expand the dependency algorithm to treat each `CONSTANT_Utf8` constant as a possible class name and attempt to load each one.

- If the class you are trying to examine uses other system resources (such as audio or image files), the depepency checker will not find them. You could expand the dependency checker to examine each `CONSTANT_Utf8` constant for known file extensions (such as .wav, .giv, or .jpg) and include them as dependencies as well.

 ## Summary

In this chapter, we have seen how to develop a Java application not only to discover all the dependencies for a given class file but also to create an archive file (either a compressed ZIP or JAR), which can be used to distribute applets easily and quickly. In order to discover class file dependencies, we not only had to load the class file dependably, but we had to read it and process the raw byte stream. In order to process the byte stream, we needed to examine the class file format as defined by the Java virtual machine specification. It may have seemed complicated at first, but I hope that after seeing how to use the class structure you realize how simple it really is.

Coming up next, we'll get back into servlets by developing a JDBC driver, which can be deployed over the Internet. The JDBC driver we'll develop, SQLServlet, will use the HTTP tunneling techniques we explored in Chapters 9 and 10.

# CHAPTER 13

Three-Tier
JDBC Driver

I n Chapter 10, we looked at how to make remote method calls using HTTP tunneling; in this chapter we'll take that same concept one step further and create a JDBC driver that can easily be deployed over the Internet. The goal is to develop a pure Java JDBC driver that, when downloaded to the client, will connect back to a servlet process that will in turn use the JDBC driver of your choice on the server. All of the communication between the client and server will be done using HTTP tunneling.

JDBC Driver Types

JavaSoft has defined four different types (or classifications) of JDBC drivers. Before discussing the three-tier driver, let's recap these types.

1. Type 1: the JDBC-ODBC bridge—As we saw in Chapter 8, the JDBC-ODBC bridge is provided by JavaSoft as part of its JDK (starting with 1.1). The bridge is part of the sun.jdbc.odbc package and is not required to be ported by vendors that provide a Java virtual machine. Remember that the bridge uses native ODBC methods and has limitations in its use—the most severe of which is the inability to use the bridge from an applet.

2. Type 2: Java to native API—The Java to native API driver makes use of local native libraries provided by a vendor to communicate directly to the database.

3. Type 3: Java to proprietary network protocol—This type of JDBC driver is by far the most flexible. It is typically used in a three-tier situation and can be deployed over the Internet. Type 3 drivers are pure Java and communicate with some type of middle tier via a proprietary network protocol.

4. Type 4: Java to native database protocol—Type 4 JDBC drivers are pure Java drivers that communicate directly with the database engine via its native protocol.

What we will be developing is a type 3 JDBC driver; it will be a pure Java driver using HTTP tunneling (the proprietary network protocol) communicating with a series of servlet objects on the server (the middle tier). Figure 13.1 shows the individual components of a type 3 JDBC driver.

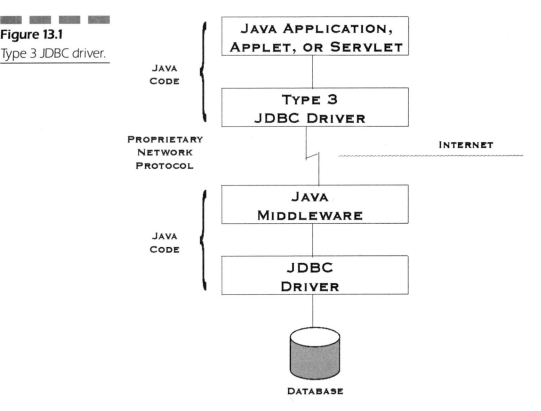

Figure 13.1

Type 3 JDBC driver.

The Challenge: A Lightweight JDBC Driver

Our task is to develop a lightweight type 3 JDBC driver that can easily be deployed over the Internet, even from behind a firewall. By lightweight, I mean that the driver should be as small as possible to keep download times to a minimum while providing a full-featured JDBC implementation. Remember that a type 3 JDBC driver has the following properties.

- All Java—The client-side JDBC implementation is 100 percent pure Java; this enables the driver to be deployed over the Internet without having to be concerned about preinstalling or configuring software on the client.

- Communicates with the server via a proprietary network protocol—The communication between the client and the server is typically done with TCP/IP or (in our case) HTTP.

- Uses a server-side application to process client requests—A server process will typically reside on the Web server. This server process will receive each client request and in turn use a JDBC driver on the server to fulfill the request. You have probably guessed by now that our server process will involve a servlet.

Figure 13.2 shows the components of our type 3 JDBC driver, which will be named SQLServlet.

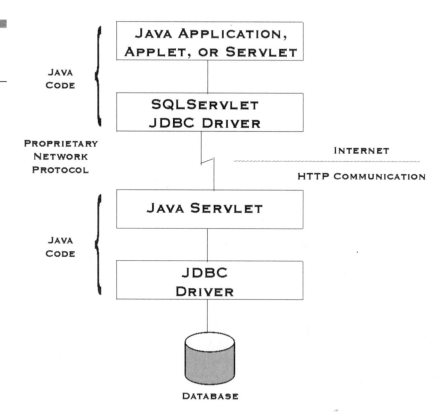

Figure 13.2

SQLServlet JDBC driver.

JDBC Hurdles

Before getting started on the SQLServlet JDBC driver, you need to be aware of some hurdles.

- Remote method calls—We've got to somehow capture a JDBC method call on the client, instruct the server to make the same method call on a server-side JDBC driver, and return the results. Chapter 10 covered how to make remote method calls using HTTP tunneling, which is the process we will be using for SQLServlet.

- Marshaling query results—The implementation of HTTP tunneling in Chapter 10 covered how to marshal data using Java serialization; this might seem like the answer to all our marshaling woes. Unfortunately most of the classes in the JDBC specification (specifically ResultSet) are not serializable; this means that we cannot rely on Java to marshal these objects for us automatically. This might seem odd at first, but note that a result set may contain hundreds or thousands of rows of data; you wouldn't want to have to transmit all these data to the client unconditionally. What we'll need to do is create our own way to marshal result data.

- Performance—While using HTTP tunneling gives us a reliable way to make remote method calls, it also comes with a performance penalty. Remember that HTTP is a connectionless protocol; the client must reestablish a connection with each new request. In order to get adequate performance with our JDBC driver, we will have to be very smart about using data caching and combining method calls in order to reduce the number of times that we need to actually make a remote method request. Reducing the number of times that we need to "hit the wire" will result in a huge boost in performance.

- Tedium—Speaking from experience (I've developed seven different JDBC drivers), there is a certain amount of tedium involved, especially when it comes to implementing the DatabaseMetaData interface, which has over 130 methods.

Writing SQLServlet

If you refer back to Figure 13.2, you will notice that the SQLServlet JDBC driver is comprised of both server-side and client-side implementation. The client-side implementation will take a standard JDBC call and, using HTTP tunneling, invoke a method on the server via a servlet; the servlet will then invoke the appropriate JDBC method on the target database and return the results.

Remember that the complete source code for SQLServlet can be found on the accompanying CD-ROM.

Implementing the JDBC API

The JDBC specification provides a series of Java interfaces that must be implemented by the driver developer. A JDBC application is written using these interfaces, not a specific driver implementation. Because all JDBC drivers must implement the same interfaces, they are interchangeable; the client can be written without regard to the underlying database (in theory, at least).

Figure 13.3 shows all the interfaces and relationships defined by the JDBC API. We'll cover each the major interfaces and discuss the implications for the SQLServlet driver. Note that this section is meant to enhance the JDBC specification, not to replace it.

Driver   The driver interface is the entry point for all JDBC drivers. From here a connection to the database can be established in order to perform work. This class is, by design, very small; the intent is that JDBC drivers can be preregistered with the system, enabling the Driver-Manager to select an appropriate driver given only a URL. The only way to determine which driver can service a particular URL is to instantiate the driver object for each JDBC driver and call the `acceptsURL()` method. To keep the amount of time required to find an appropriate JDBC driver to a minimum, each driver object should be as small as possible so it can be loaded quickly.

So how do you preregister a driver? It is the responsibility of every JDBC driver to register itself with the DriverManager during instantia-

Figure 13.3

The JDBC
interfaces.

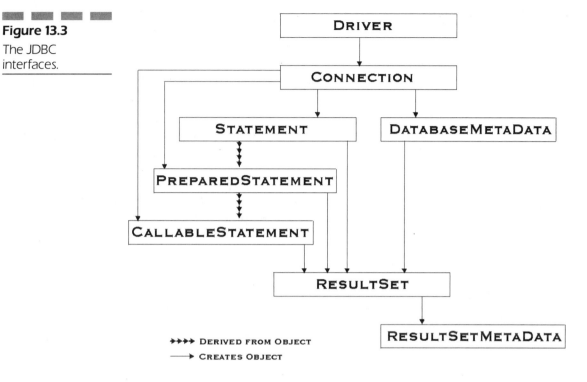

Figure 13.4

Registering with
the DriverManager.

tion. This can be done in either the default constructor or a static constructor. Figure 13.4 shows the code for registering the SQLServlet JDBC driver in the default constructor.

```
/**
 * <p>Default constructor. This constructor will register
 * the SQLServlet driver with the JDBC DriverManager.
 */
public Driver()
  throws java.sql.SQLException
  {
    if (isTracing()) {
      trace("Attempting to register");
    }

    // Attempt to register this driver with the JDBC
    // DriverManager. If it fails an exception will be thrown
    java.sql.DriverManager.registerDriver(this);
  }
```

Figure 13.5

Registering the
SQLServlet driver.

```
// Register the SQLServlet driver
javaservlets.SQLServlet.Driver d =
           new javaservlets.SQLServlet.Driver();

// Alternate way to register a JDBC driver
String driverName = "javaservlets.SQLServlet.Driver";
Class.forName(driverName).newInstance();
```

The SQLServlet driver can then be registered with the DriverManager by simply creating a new instance of the driver object, as shown in Figure 13.5.

As I mentioned a moment ago, the `acceptsURL()` method is used by the DriverManager to determine whether a driver can support a given URL. The general format for a JDBC URL is:

```
jdbc:subprotocol:subname
```

where:

jdbc specifies that a JDBC driver will be used.

subprotocol is the particular database connectivity mechanism supported (note that this mechanism may be supported by multiple drivers).

subname is additional connection information defined by the JDBC driver.

The URL supported by our SQLServlet driver has the format:

```
jdbc:SQLServlet:<code base>@<driver name>:<connection URL>
```

where:

jdbc specifies that a JDBC driver will be used.

SQLServlet is the subprotocol that specifies the connectivity mechanism.

<code base> is the server location the applet was downloaded from.

<driver name> is the name of the JDBC driver to register on the server.

<connection URL> is the full connection URL to be used on the server.

Most of the driver interface is quite simple to implement and can be done almost exclusively on the client. Where we need to communicate

■■■ ■■■ ■■■ ■■■
Figure 13.6

DriverInterface.java
code listing.

```
package javaservlets.SQLServlet.server;

/**
 * <p>This is the server-side driver object used by SQLServlet.
 */

public interface DriverInterface
{
  /**
   * <p>Attempt to establish a connection to the given
   * URL.
   *
   * @param driverName Optional JDBC driver name to register
   * @param url The URL of the database to connect to
   * @param info A list of arbitrary String tag/value pairs as
   * connection arguments; normally at least a "user" and
   * "password" property will be included
   * @return A database connection handle
   */
  int connect(String driverName,
              String url,
              java.util.Properties info)
     throws java.sql.SQLException;

}
```

with the server is in creating a new database connection. As we saw in Chapter 10, all server-side services should be defined using an interface. Figure 13.6 shows the driver interface that defines the methods available to the client.

So, given a JDBC driver name, a JDBC connection URL, and an optional list of connection properties, a call to the connect method will create a new JDBC connection on the server and return a reference handle. Why return a handle instead of a connection object? Simple: the connection object is not serializable and thus cannot be marshaled using Java serialization (which is how our HTTP tunneling protocol for JDK 1.1 functions). Instead, we'll use a handle to reference the server-side connection object and look up the object whenever we need to use it. Figure 13.7 shows the server-side connect method, which attempts to establish a database connection and returns the connection handle.

Note that the connection handles are stored in a public static vector, which can easily be accessed by all the objects on the server. A side benefit of centralizing all the connection objects is that you can write some type of database monitoring application that can keep track of the number of connections, how long the connection has been established, and so forth.

Before being able to make a remote method call to create a new database connection on the server, we first need to instantiate the client-side

Figure 13.7

Server-side
connect method.

```java
/**
 * <p>Attempt to establish a connection to the given
 * URL.
 *
 * @param driverName Optional JDBC driver name to register
 * @param url The URL of the database to connect to
 * @param info A list of arbitrary String tag/value pairs as
 * connection arguments; normally at least a "user" and
 * "password" property will be included
 * @return A database connection handle
 */
public int connect(String driverName,
                   String url,
                   java.util.Properties info)
  throws java.sql.SQLException
{
  int handle = 0;

  // If a driver was given, register it
  if ((driverName != null) && (driverName.length() > 0)) {

    try {

      // Create a new instance of the driver so that it
      // will register itself
      Class.forName(driverName).newInstance();

    }
    catch (Exception ex) {

      // Print the error and convert to an SQLException
      ex.printStackTrace();
      throw new java.sql.SQLException("Unable to register " +
                                      driverName);
    }

    // Ask the DriverManager to create a connection. An
    // exception will be thrown if a connection cannot
    // be made
    java.sql.Connection con =
      java.sql.DriverManager.getConnection(url, info);

    // Got a connection?
    if (con != null) {
      handle = addConnection(con);
    }
  }

  return handle;
}
```

proxy. The proxy will, in turn, create a new server-side object, which will communicate directly with the database. All this is done using HTTP tunneling, which we explored in great detail in Chapter 10. Figure 13.8 shows the code needed to create the driver proxy on the client.

▬ ▬ ▬ ▬

Figure 13.8

Instantiating the
Driver client-side
proxy.

```java
/**
 * <p>Creates a new DriverObject. For testing purposes if the
 * code base is null a local version is created.
 *
 * @return A DriverObject instance
 */
protected DriverInterface newDriverObject()
  throws java.sql.SQLException
{
  DriverInterface di = null;

  if (isTracing()) {
    trace("Creating new DriverObject");
  }

  try {
    if (getCodeBase() == null) {

      // Attempt to create a new local version of the driver
      // object
      di = (DriverInterface) Class.forName(
        "javaservlets.SQLServlet.server.DriverObject")
        .newInstance();
    }
    else {

      // Create a new driver object proxy
      di = (DriverInterface)
        new RemoteDriverObjectClient(getCodeBase());
    }
  }
  catch (Exception ex) {

    // Convert all exceptions into a SQLException
    throw new java.sql.SQLException(ex.getMessage());
  }

  return di;
}
```

There are a few things to note about this code. First, if the code base
in the connection URL is empty (not given), the server-side object will be
used directly. This is a great way to enable local testing without having
to use a Web server. This also emphasizes the beauty of using interface-
based programming; the actual implementation (in our case remote objects via HTTP or local objects) can be changed without having to modify the calling application. Second, notice that when a new instance of
the local object is created, `Class.forName().newInstance()` is being
used. This is an important detail, since we will be using the CreateArchive utility (Chapter 12) to create a distribution archive for the application (applet). By using `Class.forName()`, the object will not be
considered a class dependency and thus will not be included in the ar-

chive. Third, note the use of the `isTracing()` and `trace()` methods; these methods will determine if a print stream is currently active in the JDBC DriverManager and print debugging information to the print stream if one exists.

Where did this driver proxy come from? If you remember, in Chapter 11 we developed a code generation tool, which automatically created the client-side proxies and server-side stubs necessary to perform HTTP tunneling. The following code shows the arguments used to generate the tunneling code for the Driver object (the command has been split over several lines to improve readability).

```
java javaservlets.CodeGen.ServletGen
        -ijavaservlets.SQLServlet.server.DriverInterface
        -cjavaservlets.SQLServlet.server.DriverObject
```

The "–i" switch specifies the interface, and the "–c" switch specifies the server-side class that will be used. The command will generate two Java source files.

1. RemoteDriverObjectClient.java—This is the client-side proxy for HTTP tunneling. This class implements the DriverInterface interface.

2. RemoteDriverObjectServer.java—This is the server-side stub that the client proxy will communicate with. This is also a Java servlet and must be added to your Web server configuration.

To recap, the general process flow for establishing a remote database connection is as follows.

1. Register the SQLServlet JDBC driver. This is done by instantiating a new driver object. Once registered, the JDBC DriverManager will load the SQLServlet driver to service a `getConnection()` request for a given URL.

2. In the `getConnection()` method a new client-side proxy will be instantiated. The proxy will invoke the generated servlet, which will, in turn, create a new driver object on the server. The client and server object will communicate via HTTP tunneling.

3. The `getConnection()` method will be invoked on the client-side proxy (as defined in DriverInterface). The arguments will be marshaled to the server-side object, where the "real" method will be invoked.

4. Once a database connection has been established on the server, the connection object will be placed in a table and a handle to the connection will be returned to the client. The client can use this handle to reference the connection.

All the objects we will be creating for the SQLServlet JDBC driver will follow the same basic process flow.

Connection   The connection interface represents a session with the data source. Using this interface you can create statement objects to execute SQL statements and gather additional information about the database via the DatabaseMetaData interface (covered in the next section).

Remember that when the driver created a new connection object it actually created a connection object on the server and was given a handle to the new object. The driver must then use the connection handle to reference the actual connection object on the server. Before this can be done, we must first define the services the server-side connection object will provide, shown in Figure 13.9.

Figure 13.9

ConnectionInterface.java code listing.

```
package javaservlets.SQLServlet.server;

/**
 * <p>This is the server-side connection object used by SQLServlet.
 */
public interface ConnectionInterface
{
  /**
   * <p>Sets the connection handle
   *
   * @param handle Connection handle
   */
  void setHandle(int handle);

  /**
   * <p>Creates a new Statement object
   */
  int createStatement() throws java.sql.SQLException;

  /**
   * <p>Returns the native SQL string as known by the driver
   *
   * @param sql Input SQL statement
   * @return The converted SQL statement
   */
  String getNativeSQL(String sql) throws java.sql.SQLException;

  /**
   * <p>Closes and frees the connection
   */
```

```
void close() throws java.sql.SQLException;

/**
 * <p>Gets the DatabaseMetaData
 *
 * @return Data cache containing static meta data information
 */
DBMD getMetaData() throws java.sql.SQLException;

/**
 * <p>Sets the auto-commit mode
 *
 * @param autoCommit true to turn on auto-commit mode
 */
void setAutoCommit(boolean autoCommit) throws java.sql.SQLException;

/**
 * <p>Gets the auto-commit mode
 *
 * @return true if auto-commit mode is on
 */
boolean getAutoCommit() throws java.sql.SQLException;

/**
 * <p>Commits the current transaction
 */
void commit() throws java.sql.SQLException;

/**
 * <p>Rolls back (cancels) the current transaction
 */
void rollback() throws java.sql.SQLException;

/**
 * <p>Sets the read-only flag for the database. Note that
 * this is only a suggestion to the database and may have
 * no effect
 *
 * @param readOnly true if the database should be read-only
 */
void setReadOnly(boolean readOnly) throws java.sql.SQLException;

/**
 * <p>Gets the read-only flag
 *
 * @return true if the database is read-only
 */
boolean isReadOnly() throws java.sql.SQLException;

/**
 * <p>Sets the database catalog name
 *
 * @param catalog Catalog name
 */
void setCatalog(String catalog) throws java.sql.SQLException;

/**
 * <p>Gets the current database catalog name
 *
```

```
   * @return The current catalog
   */
  String getCatalog() throws java.sql.SQLException;

  /**
   * <p>Attempts to set the current transaction isolation level
   *
   * @param level Transaction isolation level
   */
  void setTransactionIsolation(int level)
    throws java.sql.SQLException;

  /**
   * <p>Gets the current transaction isolation level
   *
   * @return The current transaction isolation level
   */
  int getTransactionIsolation() throws java.sql.SQLException;

  /**
   * <p>Get any warnings for the connection
   *
   * @return The first warning in a possible chain of warnings
   */
  java.sql.SQLWarning getWarnings() throws java.sql.SQLException;

  /**
   * <p>Clears warnings
   */
  void clearWarnings() throws java.sql.SQLException;
}
```

Most of the methods defined in the connection interface are simply pass-through methods that correlate directly to JDBC API methods. Notice that, as with creating a new connection, the createStatement() method returns a handle to the server-side statement object (which is not serializable).

Figure 13.10 shows the code for creating the client-side connection proxy. Notice that after the proxy is created, the connection handle is set on the object so that the server can bind to the "real" connection object.

The createStatement() method works in a manner similar to the getConnection() method on the driver object; a statement object is created on the server and a handle to the Statement is returned to the client. What is even more interesting is the getMetaData() method and how we can cache data on the client to improve performance. Since most of the DatabaseMetaData information is static during the lifetime of the database connection, we can gather all this information on the server and send it to the client in a single transmission. We need to cre-

Figure 13.10

Instantiating type
Connection client-
side proxy.

```java
/**
 * <p>Creates a new ConnectionObject. For testing purposes if the
 * code base is null a local version is created.
 *
 * @return A ConnectionObject instance
 */
protected ConnectionInterface newConnectionObject()
  throws java.sql.SQLException
{
  ConnectionInterface ci = null;

  if (isTracing()) {
    trace("Creating new ConnectionObject");
  }

  try {
    if (getCodeBase() == null) {

      // Attempt to create a new local version of the connection
      // object
      ci = (ConnectionInterface) Class.forName(
        "javaservlets.SQLServlet.server.ConnectionObject")
        .newInstance();
    }
    else {

      // Create a new connection object proxy
      ci = (ConnectionInterface)
        new RemoteConnectionObjectClient(getCodeBase());
    }
  }
  catch (Exception ex) {

    // Convert all exceptions into a SQLException
    throw new java.sql.SQLException(ex.getMessage());
  }

  // Set the handle on the connection
  ci.setHandle(m_handle);

  return ci;
}
```

ate a serializable object to encapsulate all this static information. This object, called DBMD, is shown in Figure 13.11.

This object will be instantiated on the server, the public properties will be set using the results of server-side DatabaseMetaData method calls, and it will be returned to the client in a single transmission, where all these properties can be referenced directly. Since we're using the relatively slow HTTP protocol, it is critically important to cache data wherever possible.

Figure 13.11

DBMD.java partial code listing.

```
package javaservlets.SQLServlet.server;

/**
 * <p>This class represents the DatabaseMetaData for a Connection.
 * Only static meta data (data that will not changed for the
 * lifetime of a connection) will be stored here.
 */

public class DBMD
  implements java.io.Serializable
{
  // Our DatabaseMetaData object on the server. By defining the
  // object as transient it will not be serialized when written
  // to the client
  transient public java.sql.DatabaseMetaData m_dbmd;

  // Server-side connection handle
  public int m_handle;

  public DBMD(java.sql.DatabaseMetaData dbmd, int handle)
    {
      m_dbmd = dbmd;
      m_handle = handle;
    }

  // Can all the procedures returned by getProcedures be called
  // be the current user?
  public boolean proceduresAreCallable;

  // Can all of the tables returned by getTables have data
  // selected?
  public boolean tablesAreSelectable;

  // The url for the database
  public String url;

  // The current user name
  public String userName;

  (continued...)
}
```

Figure 13.12 shows the server-side `getMetaData()` method for the connection object. Notice that the first order of business is to find the proper connection object for the handle that was supplied by the client. The connection object is actually stored in a connection holder object, which stores other information as well (such as a DatabaseMetaData cache and statement objects). After finding the connection, we check to see if we have already created a metadata cache; if not, a new cache is created using the results from the "real" DatabaseMetaData object. The

```
/**
 * <p>Gets the DatabaseMetaData
 *
 * @return Data cache containing static meta data information
 */
public DBMD getMetaData() throws java.sql.SQLException
{
    // Find the ConnectionHolder for the connection handle
    ConnectionHolder holder = getHolder();

    // Get the cached data
    DBMD dbmd = holder.getDatabaseMetaData();

    if (dbmd == null) {

        // No data cache yet; create a new DatabaseMetaData object
        java.sql.DatabaseMetaData metadata =
          holder.getConnection().getMetaData();

        // Create a new data cache
        dbmd = new DBMD(metadata, m_handle);

        // Now get all of the static values and place them into
        // the data cache
        dbmd.proceduresAreCallable =
          metadata.allProceduresAreCallable();
        dbmd.tablesAreSelectable =
          metadata.allTablesAreSelectable();
        dbmd.url = metadata.getURL();
        dbmd.userName = metadata.getUserName();
        (continued...)
        // Cache the data
        holder.setDatabaseMetaData(dbmd);
    }
    return dbmd;
}
```

metadata cache is then returned to the client (remember that the DBMD object is serializable so that it can be marshaled).

The rest of the server-side connection object is basically a one-to-one mapping between the JDBC API method and the connection interface method. Figure 13.13 shows an example of how this is done.

As with the driver object, we need to generate the client-side proxies and server-side stubs so that the method calls can be tunneled.

```
java javaservlets.CodeGen.ServletGen
      -ijavaservlets.SQLServlet.server.ConnectionInterface
      -cjavaservlets.SQLServlet.server.ConnectionObject
```

```
/**
 * <p>Sets the read-only flag for the database. Note that
 * this is only a suggestion to the database and may have
 * no effect
 *
 * @param readOnly true if the database should be read-only
 */
public void setReadOnly(boolean readOnly)
  throws java.sql.SQLException
  {
    // Find the ConnectionHolder for the connection handle
    ConnectionHolder holder = getHolder();

    // Set the read-only flag
    holder.getConnection().setReadOnly(readOnly);
  }

/**
 * <p>Gets the read-only flag
 *
 * @return true if the database is read-only
 */
public boolean isReadOnly() throws java.sql.SQLException
  {
    // Find the ConnectionHolder for the connection handle
    ConnectionHolder holder = getHolder();

    // Get the read-only flag
    return holder.getConnection().isReadOnly();
  }
```

Remember that the resulting RemoteConnectionObjectServer object
is a servlet that must be configured in your Web server.

DatabaseMetaData   With over 130 methods the DatabaseMetaData
interface is the undisputed heavyweight of the JDBC API. It supplies information about which database options are supported, as well as supplying catalog information such as tables, columns, procedures, and so
on.

As we saw previously, when we discussed connections, most of the
DatabaseMetaData are cached and returned to the client encapsulated
in the DBMD object. Because of this, the interface that describes the
server-side methods is quite manageable. The only methods we need to
define are those that have even the smallest possibility of returning dynamic information—in other words, information that can be modified
on the server by another user (or even you). Figure 13.14 shows the complete code listing for the DatabaseMetaDataInterface interface.

Figure 13.14

DatabaseMeta-
DataInterface.java
code listing.

```java
package javaservlets.SQLServlet.server;

/**
 * <p>This is the server-side DatabaseMetaData object used by
 * SQLServlet.
 */

public interface DatabaseMetaDataInterface
{
  /**
   * <p>Sets the connection handles
   *
   * @param conHandle Connection handle
   */
  void setHandle(int conHandle);

  /**
   * <p>Is the database read-only?
   *
   * @return true if the database is read-only
   */
  boolean isReadOnly() throws java.sql.SQLException;

  /**
   * <p>Is CONVERT between the given SQL types supported?
   *
   * @param fromType The SQL type to convert from
   * @param toType The SQL type to convert to
   * @return true if the conversion is supported
   */
  boolean supportsConvert(int fromType, int toType)
    throws java.sql.SQLException;

  /**
   * <p>Does the database support the given transaction isolation
   * level?
   *
   * @param level The transaction isolation level
   * @return true if the isolation level is supported
   */
  boolean supportsTransactionIsolationLevel(int level)
    throws java.sql.SQLException;

  /**
   *  Get a description of tables available in a catalog.
   *
   * Only table descriptions matching the catalog, schema, table
   * name and type criteria are returned.  They are ordered by
   * TABLE_TYPE, TABLE_SCHEM and TABLE_NAME.
   *
   * @param catalog Catalog name or null for all
   * @param schemaPattern Schema name or null for all
   * @param tableNamePattern A table name pattern
   * @param types List of table types to include
   * @return ResultSet handle
   */
  int getTables(String catalog, String schemaPattern,
                String tableNamePattern, String types[])
    throws java.sql.SQLException;
```

```
/**
 * <p>Get the schema names available in this database.  The
 * results are ordered by schema name.
 *
 * @returns ResultSet handle
 */
int getSchemas() throws java.sql.SQLException;

/**
 * <p>Get a description of stored procedures available in a
 * catalog.
 *
 * @param catalog Catalog name or null for all
 * @param schemaPattern Schema name pattern or null for all
 * @param procedureNamePattern Procedure name pattern or null for
 * all
 * @return ResultSet handle
 */
int getProcedures(String catalog, String schemaPattern,
                  String procedureNamePattern)
    throws java.sql.SQLException;

/**
 * <p>Get a description of a catalog's stored procedure parameters
 * and result columns.
 *
 * @param catalog Catalog name or null for all
 * @param schemaPattern Schema name pattern or null for all
 * @param procedureNamePattern Procedure name pattern or null for
 * all
 * @param columnNamePattern Column name pattern or null for all
 * @return ResultSet handle
 */
int getProcedureColumns(String catalog,
                        String schemaPattern,
                        String procedureNamePattern,
                        String columnNamePattern)
    throws java.sql.SQLException;

/**
 * <p>Get the catalog names available in this database.  The
 * results are ordered by catalog name.
 *
 * @return ResultSet handle
 */
int getCatalogs() throws java.sql.SQLException;

/**
 * <p>Get the table types available in this database.  The results
 * are ordered by table type.
 *
 * @return ResultSet handle
 */
int getTableTypes() throws java.sql.SQLException;

/**
 * <p>Get a description of table columns available in a catalog.
 *
 * @param catalog Catalog name or null for all
```

```
   * @param schemaPattern Schema name or null for all
   * @param tableNamePattern A table name pattern
   * @param columnNamePattern A column name pattern
   * @return ResultSet handle
   */
int getColumns(String catalog, String schemaPattern,
               String tableNamePattern, String columnNamePattern)
   throws java.sql.SQLException;


/**
   * <p>Get a description of the access rights for a table's columns.
   *
   * @param catalog Catalog name or null for all
   * @param schemaPattern Schema name or null for all
   * @param tableNamePattern A table name pattern
   * @param columnNamePattern A column name pattern
   * @return ResultSet handle
   */
int getColumnPrivileges(String catalog,
                        String schema,
                        String table,
                        String columnNamePattern)
   throws java.sql.SQLException;


/**
   * <p>Get a description of the access rights for each table
   * available in a catalog.
   *
   * @param catalog Catalog name or null for all
   * @param schemaPattern Schema name or null for all
   * @param tableNamePattern A table name pattern
   * @return ResultSet handle
   */
int getTablePrivileges(String catalog, String schemaPattern,
                       String tableNamePattern)
   throws java.sql.SQLException;


/**
   * <p>Get a description of a table's optimal set of columns that
   * uniquely identifies a row. They are ordered by SCOPE.
   *
   * @param catalog Catalog name or null for all
   * @param schema Schema name or null for all
   * @param table Table name
   * @param scope The scope if interest
   * @param nullable Include columns that are nullable?
   * @return ResultSet handle
   */
int getBestRowIdentifier(String catalog, String schema,
                         String table, int scope,
                         boolean nullable)
   throws java.sql.SQLException;


/**
   * <p>Get a description of a table's columns that are automatically
   * updated when any value in a row is updated.
   *
   * @param catalog Catalog name or null for all
   * @param schema Schema name or null for all
```

```
    * @param table Table name
    * @return ResultSet handle
    */
int getVersionColumns(String catalog, String schema, String table)
   throws java.sql.SQLException;

/**
   * <p>Get a description of a table's primary key columns.  They
   * are ordered by COLUMN_NAME.
   *
   * @param catalog Catalog name or null for all
   * @param schema Schema name or null for all
   * @param table Table name
   * @return ResultSet handle
   */
int getPrimaryKeys(String catalog, String schema, String table)
   throws java.sql.SQLException;

/**
   * <p>Get a description of the primary key columns that are
   * referenced by a table's foreign key columns (the primary keys
   * imported by a table).  They are ordered by PKTABLE_CAT,
   * PKTABLE_SCHEM, PKTABLE_NAME, and KEY_SEQ.
   *
   * @param catalog Catalog name or null for all
   * @param schema Schema name or null for all
   * @param table Table name
   * @return ResultSet handle
   */
int getImportedKeys(String catalog, String schema, String table)
   throws java.sql.SQLException;

/**
   * <p>Get a description of a foreign key columns that reference a
   * table's primary key columns (the foreign keys exported by a
   * table).  They are ordered by FKTABLE_CAT, FKTABLE_SCHEM,
   * FKTABLE_NAME, and KEY_SEQ.
   *
   * Column definitions, parameters, and return value are the
   * same as getImportedKeys.
   */
int getExportedKeys(String catalog, String schema, String table)
   throws java.sql.SQLException;

/**
   * <p>Get a description of the foreign key columns in the foreign
   * key table that reference the primary key columns of the
   * primary key table (describe how one table imports another's
   * key.) This should normally return a single foreign key/primary
   * key pair (most tables only import a foreign key from a table
   * once.)  They are ordered by FKTABLE_CAT, FKTABLE_SCHEM,
   * FKTABLE_NAME, and KEY_SEQ.
   *
   * Column definitions are the same as getImportedKeys.
   */
int getCrossReference(String primaryCatalog,
                      String primarySchema,
                      String primaryTable,
                      String foreignCatalog,
```

```
                        String foreignSchema,
                        String foreignTable)
    throws java.sql.SQLException;

  /**
    * <p>Get a description of all the standard SQL types supported by
    * this database. They are ordered by DATA_TYPE and then by how
    * closely the data type maps to the corresponding JDBC SQL type.
    *
    * @return ResultSet handle
    */
  int getTypeInfo() throws java.sql.SQLException;

  /**
    * <p>Get a description of a table's indices and statistics.
    * They are ordered by NON_UNIQUE, TYPE, INDEX_NAME, and
    * ORDINAL_POSITION.
    *
    * @param catalog Catalog name or null for all
    * @param schema Schema name or null for all
    * @param table Table name
    * @param unique when true, returns only unique indices
    * @param approximate when true, results are allowed to reflect
    * approximate (or out of data) values
    * @return ResultSet handle
    */
  int getIndexInfo(String catalog, String schema, String table,
                   boolean unique, boolean approximate)
    throws java.sql.SQLException;

}
```

Creating the DatabaseMetaData object on the client follows the same pattern we have already seen with the driver and connection objects: The client proxy is instantiated and will then create the "real" object on the server, which will then return a handle to the object. The server implementation also follows the pattern we've already covered (see Figure 13.15). First, the connection holder object is located using the handle supplied by the client. The connection holder contains a reference to the "real" DatabaseMetaData object, which we can then use to invoke the proper method. Next, we invoke the method, and, if the return object is not serializable, the return object is stored and the handle to the object is returned to the client. We'll cover how result set objects are handled later in the chapter.

Once again, the client-side proxies and server-side stubs must be generated and the resulting servlet must be configured in your Web server.

Statement   The statement interface contains methods to execute SQL statements directly against the database. These methods will return the

■■■ ■■ ■■ ■■
Figure 13.15

Server-side
getTables()
method.

```
/**
 *   Get a description of tables available in a catalog.
 *
 * Only table descriptions matching the catalog, schema, table
 * name and type criteria are returned.  They are ordered by
 * TABLE_TYPE, TABLE_SCHEM and TABLE_NAME.
 *
 * @param catalog Catalog name or null for all
 * @param schemaPattern Schema name or null for all
 * @param tableNamePattern A table name pattern
 * @param types List of table types to include
 * @return ResultSet handle
 */
public int getTables(String catalog, String schemaPattern,
                        String tableNamePattern, String types[])
  throws java.sql.SQLException
  {
     // Find the ConnectionHolder for the connection handle
     ConnectionHolder holder = getHolder();

     java.sql.ResultSet rs =
       holder.getMetaData().getTables(catalog, schemaPattern,
                                        tableNamePattern, types);

     // Create a dummy statement object
     StatementHolder stmtHolder = holder.addDummyStatement();
     return stmtHolder.setResultSet(rs);
  }
```

results of the SQL statement whether it be a result set containing rows of data (from a SELECT statement) or a count of the number of rows affected (from an UPDATE, INSERT, or DELETE statement).

Our statement object is, for the most part, a simple one-to-one mapping from the client to the server. The interface that defines the server-side services (shown in Figure 13.16) is almost an exact duplicate of the JDBC statement interface.

■■■ ■■ ■■ ■■
Figure 13.16

StatementInter-
face.java code
listing.

```
package javaservlets.SQLServlet.server;

/**
 * <p>This is the server-side statement object used by SQLServlet.
 */

public interface StatementInterface
{
  /**
    * <p>Sets the connection and statement handles
    *
    * @param conHandle Connection handle
    * @param stmtHandle Statement handle
    */
  void setHandle(int conHandle, int stmtHandle);
```

```
/**
 * <p>Executes the given query
 *
 * @param sql SQL statement to execute
 * @return Handle to the remote result set
 */
int executeQuery(String sql) throws java.sql.SQLException;

/**
 * <p>Closes the statement
 */
void close() throws java.sql.SQLException;

/**
 * <p>Executes the given INSERT, UPDATE, or DELETE statement
 *
 * @param sql SQL statement to execute
 * @return The number of rows affected
 */
int executeUpdate(String sql) throws java.sql.SQLException;

/**
 * <p>Sets the maximum field size
 *
 * @param size Maximum field size
 */
void setMaxFieldSize(int size) throws java.sql.SQLException;

/**
 * <p>Gets the maximum field size
 *
 * @return The maximum field size
 */
int getMaxFieldSize() throws java.sql.SQLException;

/**
 * <p>Sets the maximum number of rows a ResultSet can contain
 *
 * @param size The maximum number of rows
 */
void setMaxRows(int size) throws java.sql.SQLException;

/**
 * <p>Gets the maximum number of rows a ResultSet can contain
 *
 * @return The maximum number of rows
 */
int getMaxRows() throws java.sql.SQLException;

/**
 * <p>Sets the flag indicating whether to perform escape
 * processing
 *
 * @param enable true to enable escape processing
 */
void setEscapeProcessing(boolean enable)
  throws java.sql.SQLException;
```

```
/**
 * <p>Sets the query timeout
 *
 * @param seconds The number of seconds to wait until the
 * statement is timed out
 */
void setQueryTimeout(int seconds) throws java.sql.SQLException;

/**
 * <p>Gets the query timeout
 *
 * @return The number of seconds to wait until the statement
 * is timed out
 */
int getQueryTimeout() throws java.sql.SQLException;

/**
 * <p>Cancel can be used by one thread to cancel a statement that
 * is being executed by another thread.
 */
void cancel() throws java.sql.SQLException;

/**
 * <p>Get any warnings for the statement
 *
 * @return The first warning in a possible chain of warnings
 */
java.sql.SQLWarning getWarnings() throws java.sql.SQLException;

/**
 * <p>Clears warnings
 */
void clearWarnings() throws java.sql.SQLException;

/**
 * <p>Sets the cursor name to be used for executing statements
 *
 * @param name The new cursor name
 */
void setCursorName(String name) throws java.sql.SQLException;

/**
 * <p>Executes the given SQL statement
 *
 * @param sql SQL statement to execute
 * @return true if the first result is a ResultSet
 */
boolean execute(String sql) throws java.sql.SQLException;

/**
 * <p>Gets the next result as a ResultSet
 *
 * @return Handle to the remote result set
 */
int getResultSet() throws java.sql.SQLException;
```

```
/**
 * <p>Gets the next result as a row count
 *
 * @return The current row count
 */
int getUpdateCount() throws java.sql.SQLException;

/**
 * <p>Moves to the next result in a series of SQL statement
 * results.
 *
 * @return true if the next result is a ResultSet; false if
 * is a row count
 */
boolean getMoreResults() throws java.sql.SQLException;
}
```

Let's take a closer look at the getResultSet() method, which will return the results of a query (see Figure 13.17). The getResultSet() method is invoked on the client-side proxy (which implements StatementInterface), which returns a handle to a result set object. The handle is then used to create a new result set on the client using (of course) the result set proxy.

ResultSet   The result set interface provides methods to access data generated by a table query. This includes a series of get methods, which retrieve data in any one of the JDBC SQL type formats, either by column number or column name.

Figure 13.17

Calling the getResultSet() remote method

```
/**
 * <p>Returns the current result as a ResultSet.   It
 * should only be called once per result.
 *
 * @return The current result as a ResultSet or null if it is
 * a row count
 */
public java.sql.ResultSet getResultSet()
  throws java.sql.SQLException
  {
    // Execute the query on the server
    int rsHandle = m_statement.getResultSet();

    // Create a new ResultSet object
    java.sql.ResultSet rs = null;
    if (rsHandle != 0) {
      rs = new ResultSet(m_conHandle, rsHandle, getCodeBase());
    }
    return rs;
  }
```

Our implementation of the result set interface must be very effi-cient; for this reason we'll be reading a configurable number of rows at a time and caching them on the client. Figure 13.18 shows the interface that defines the server-side services for the result set.

Figure 13.18

ResultSetInter-face.java code listing.

```java
package javaservlets.SQLServlet.server;

/**
 * <p>This is the server-side ResultSet object used by SQLServlet.
 */
public interface ResultSetInterface
{
  /**
    * <p>Sets the connection and ResultSet handles
    *
    * @param conHandle Connection handle
    * @param rsHandle Statement handle
    */
  void setHandle(int conHandle, int rsHandle);

  /**
    * <p>Closes the ResultSet
    */
  void close() throws java.sql.SQLException;

  /**
    * <p>Get all of the ResultSetMetaData information. All of the
    * information will be gathered and returned at once so that
    * it can be cached on the client
    *
    * @return The ResultSetMetaData information
    */
  RSMD getMetaData() throws java.sql.SQLException;

  /**
    * <p>Read the next chunk of rows. The ResultSetObject knows
    * how many rows to read.
    *
    * @return ResultSetData object containing information about
    * the read request and the data that was read.
    */
  ResultSetData read() throws java.sql.SQLException;

  /**
    * <p>Get the name of the SQL cursor used by this ResultSet.
    *
    * @return The ResultSet's SQL cursor name
    */
  String getCursorName() throws java.sql.SQLException;

}
```

Figure 13.19

SQLServlet.cfg.

```
#SQLServlet.cfg
ResultSetCache=10
```

Figure 13.19

SQLServlet.cfg.

Of note here is the `read()` method, which will read a predetermined number of rows from the server and return all the data back to the client in a single transmission. Just how is the number of rows to read determined? The server contains a configuration file, SQLServlet.cfg, which specifies the number of rows to read. The configuration file is shown in Figure 13.19. The configuration file is read each time a new connection object is created on the server by using the java.util.Properties `load()` method.

You may also notice that the `read()` method returns a ResultSetData object. This serializable object contains all the column data for every row read from the database. This is done by keeping a vector, which has an element for each row that contains another vector. The second vector contains an element that holds the data for each column. Along with the data for each row we also need to keep the SQLWarning chain for each row. Figure 13.20 shows the code for the ResultSetData object.

Figure 13.20

ResultSetData.java code listing.

```java
package javaservlets.SQLServlet.server;

/**
 * <p>This class holds the data read from a ResultSet. The ResultSet
 * can have multiple rows read and returned.
 */

public class ResultSetData
  implements java.io.Serializable
{
  // true if EOF was reached while reading
  public boolean eofFound = false;

  // A Vector containing the results of the read. Each element
  // in the vector is another vector that holds each row's data
  public java.util.Vector readData = new java.util.Vector();

  // A Vector containing the warnings for each row read.
  public java.util.Vector warnings = new java.util.Vector();

  /**
   * <p>Returns the current size of the cache
   *
   * @return The number of rows in the cache
   */
  public int getSize()
    {
      int size = 0;
```

```
      // Make sure we have read a cache
      if (readData != null) {
        size = readData.size();
      }
      return size;
    }

/**
  * <p>Determines if another cache should be read
  *
  * @return true if another cache should be read
  */
public boolean more()
  {
      boolean moreData = true;

      // If we have read a cache determine if we reached eof on
      // the server
      if (readData != null) {
        moreData = !eofFound;
      }
      return moreData;
    }

/**
  * <p>Returns the row of data for the given element
  *
  * @param ptr Element pointer
  * @return The Vector containing the row data
  */
public java.util.Vector getRow(int ptr)
    throws java.sql.SQLException
    {
      if ((ptr < 0) ||
          (ptr >= getSize())) {
        throw new java.sql.SQLException("Invalid row pointer");
      }
      return (java.util.Vector) readData.elementAt(ptr);
    }

/**
  * <p>Returns the warnings for the current row
  *
  * @param ptr Element pointer
  * @return The warning object(s) if any
  */
public java.sql.SQLWarning getWarnings(int ptr)
    throws java.sql.SQLException
    {
      if ((ptr < 0) ||
          (ptr >= getSize())) {
        throw new java.sql.SQLException("Invalid row pointer");
      }
      return (java.sql.SQLWarning) warnings.elementAt(ptr);
    }

  }
```

The server-side code used to populate the ResultSetData object is shown in Figure 13.21. Note that we need to keep a flag indicating whether the end of the result set has been reached. Also, take a look at how each column is read and stored in its native SQL format, whether it be character, binary, numeric, or timestamp data. The SQL data type is retrieved from the ResultSetMetaData, which we'll cover shortly.

Figure 13.21

Reading a result set on the server.

```
/**
 * <p>Read the next chunk of rows. The ResultSetObject knows
 * how many rows to read.
 *
 * @return ResultSetData object containing information about
 * the read request and the data that was read.
 */
public ResultSetData read() throws java.sql.SQLException
  {
    // Get the ResultSet object
    java.sql.ResultSet rs = getResultSet();

    // Create a new ResultSetData object
    ResultSetData rsd = new ResultSetData();

    // Loop for the size of the cache
    for (int i = 0; i < m_cacheSize; i++) {
      // Get the next row
      boolean valid = rs.next();

      // If we have hit end of file set the flag on the
      // ResultSetData object and exit
      if (!valid) {
        rsd.eofFound = true;
        break;
      }

      // We have a valid row. Create a new Vector for the
      // row and add it to the ResultSetData
      rsd.readData.addElement(formatRow(rs));

      // Save any warnings for the row
      rsd.warnings.addElement(rs.getWarnings());
    }

    return rsd;
  }

/**
 * <p>Formats the current row into a Vector that will be
 * returned to the client
 *
 * @param rs ResultSet object
 * @return A Vector holding the row data
 */
protected java.util.Vector formatRow(java.sql.ResultSet rs)
  throws java.sql.SQLException
  {
```

```java
// Create a new Vector to hold the data
java.util.Vector row = new java.util.Vector();

// Get the meta data
RSMD rsmd = getMetaData();

// Loop for each column
for (int col = 1; col <= rsmd.columnCount; col++) {

  Object o = null;
  int sqlType = rsmd.getColumn(col).columnType;

  // Evaluate the column type
  switch(sqlType) {

  case java.sql.Types.CHAR:
  case java.sql.Types.VARCHAR:
    // Character data
    o = rs.getString(col);
    break;

  case java.sql.Types.NUMERIC:
  case java.sql.Types.DECIMAL:
    // Exact numeric values
    o = rs.getBigDecimal(col, rsmd.getColumn(col).scale);
    break;

  case java.sql.Types.BIT:
    // Boolean value
    o = new Boolean(rs.getBoolean(col));
    break;

  case java.sql.Types.TINYINT:
    // Byte value
    o = new Byte(rs.getByte(col));
    break;

  case java.sql.Types.SMALLINT:
    // Short value
    o = new Short(rs.getShort(col));
    break;

  case java.sql.Types.INTEGER:
    // Integer value
    o = new Integer(rs.getInt(col));
    break;

  case java.sql.Types.BIGINT:
    // Long value
    o = new Long(rs.getLong(col));
    break;

  case java.sql.Types.REAL:
  case java.sql.Types.FLOAT:
    // Approximate values
    o = new Float(rs.getFloat(col));
    break;

  case java.sql.Types.DOUBLE:
```

```
        // Approximate double value
        o = new Double(rs.getDouble(col));
        break;

    case java.sql.Types.DATE:
      // Date value
      o = rs.getDate(col);
      break;

    case java.sql.Types.TIME:
      // Time value
      o = rs.getTime(col);
      break;

    case java.sql.Types.TIMESTAMP:
      // Timestamp (date and time) value
      o = rs.getTimestamp(col);
      break;

    case java.sql.Types.BINARY:
    case java.sql.Types.VARBINARY:
    case java.sql.Types.LONGVARBINARY:
    case java.sql.Types.LONGVARCHAR:
      // Binary or long data. Get as a byte stream
      o = rs.getBytes(col);
      break;

    default:
      // Unknown/Unsupported data type. Attempt to get the
      // data as a String
      o = rs.getString(col);
      break;
    }

    // Create a new ColumnData object
    ColumnData colData = new ColumnData();

    // Check to see if the column was null
    if (rs.wasNull()) {
      o = null;
      colData.isNull = true;
    }

    // Set the column data
    colData.data = o;

    // Add it to the row
    row.addElement(colData);
  }

  return row;
}
```

The column data are not stored directly in the vector but in a holder object cleverly named "ColumnData," which is then stored in the vector.

The reason for this extra object is so that we can store a NULL value flag with each column of data.

OK, we've created the result set proxy on the client, which then created the "real" result set object on the server. A SQL query has been submitted, and a cache of row data has been read and returned by to the client. Now what? We've got to process the data cache on the client and return the column data in the format requested by the application. The first thing we need to do is implement the result set `next()` method, which will move the cursor to the next row. If there are no more rows of data in the cache, we'll have to issue a read request from the server (see Figure 13.22).

Notice how a pointer for the current position within the cache is being used; when this pointer exceeds the size of the cache, a new read will be invoked (unless end-of-file was reached during the last read). Also, note how the SQLWarnings for each row are being retrieved from the cache and set on the object.

Next we need to implement each of the result set `getXXX` methods (`getString`, `getChar`, `getInt`, etc.). The basic flow of each `get` method will be to determine the native type of the column; if the application requested the data in the same format, simply return it to the application. Otherwise, some level of data coercion must take place; we'll just do the best we can. Figure 13.23 shows the code for attempting to get a double value for a given column.

We always get the value of the column as an object and then determine its native Java type. Once this is known we can attempt to convert the value to the requested SQL type.

As before, the client-side proxies and server-side stubs for the result set must be generated, and the resulting servlet must be configured in your Web server.

ResultSetMetaData The ResultSetMetaData interface contains methods that describe all the columns in a result set, as well as the number of columns present in the result set. As with the DatabaseMetaData, we'll cache all the static information on the server and return it to the client all at once. Fortunately, all the ResultSetMetaData are static for a given result set, so we can simply gather all the data from within the result set object on the server and return these data to the client. Figure 13.24 shows the serializable object used to hold the metadata for each column, and Figure 13.25 shows the object used to store all the metadata plus the number of columns in the result set.

Figure 13.22

The result set
next () method.

```
/**
 * <p>A ResultSet is initially positioned before its first row;
 * the first call to next makes the first row the current row;
 * the second call makes the second row the current row, etc.
 *
 * If an input stream from the previous row is open it is
 * implicitly closed. The ResultSet's warning chain is cleared
 * when a new row is read.
 *
 * @return true if the new current row is valid; false if there
 *   are no more rows
 */
public boolean next()
  throws java.sql.SQLException
  {
    // Clear the last row
    m_row = null;

    // Read the initial ResultSetData object if necessary
    if (m_data == null) {
      m_data = m_resultSet.read();
      m_dataPtr = 0;
    }

    // Determine if we have used all of the rows in the
    // current cache
    if (m_dataPtr >= m_data.getSize()) {

      // No more data in the cache. If we need to read more data
      // do so; otherwize return false to indicate eof
      if (m_data.more()) {

        // Read another cache
        m_data = m_resultSet.read();
        m_dataPtr = 0;

        // Make sure we didn't hit eof on the first read
        if ((m_data.getSize() == 0) &&
            !m_data.more()) {
          return false;
        }
      }
      else {
        return false;
      }
    }

    // Get the current row
    m_row = m_data.getRow(m_dataPtr);

    // Get the warnings for the current row
    m_warnings = m_data.getWarnings(m_dataPtr);

    // Increment the row pointer
    m_dataPtr++;

    return true;
  }
```

■■■ ■■■ ■■■ ■■■
Figure 13.23
The result set
getDouble()
method.

```
/**
 * <p>Get the value of a column in the current row as a Java
 * double.
 *
 * @param columnIndex The index of the column relative to 1
 * @return The column value
 */
public double getDouble(int columnIndex)
  throws java.sql.SQLException
  {
    double value = 0;

    // Get the object data
    Object o = getObject(columnIndex);

    // Check for a null value
    if (o == null) {
      return 0;
    }

    // Get the value
    if (o instanceof Float) {
      value = ((Float) o).doubleValue();
    }
    else if (o instanceof Double) {
      value = ((Double) o).doubleValue();
    }
    else if (o instanceof java.math.BigDecimal) {
      value = ((java.math.BigDecimal) o).doubleValue();
    }
    else if (o instanceof String) {
      value = (Float.valueOf((String) o)).doubleValue();
    }
    else {
      value = (double) getLong(columnIndex);
    }

    return value;
  }
```

■■■ ■■■ ■■■ ■■■
Figure 13.24
RSMDColumn.java
code listing.

```
package javaservlets.SQLServlet.server;

/**
 * <p>This class represents a single column's ResultSetMetaData
 */
public class RSMDColumn
  implements java.io.Serializable
{
  // The name of the catalog that contains this column
  public String catalogName;

  // The maximum display width for this column
  public int columnDisplaySize;

  // The preferred display name for this column
  public String columnLabel;
```

```
    // The name of this column as known by the database
    public String columnName;

    // The SQL data type of this column
    public int columnType;

    // The SQL data type name
    public String columnTypeName;

    // The precision of this column
    public int precision;

    // The scale of this column
    public int scale;

    // The name of the schema that contains this column
    public String schemaName;

    // The name of the table that contains this column
    public String tableName;

    // true if this column is automatically numbered by the database
    public boolean autoIncrement;

    // true if the column contents are case sensitive
    public boolean caseSensitive;

    // true if this column represents currency
    public boolean currency;

    // true if this column can definitely be written to
    public boolean definitelyWritable;

    // Does this column accepts null values
    public int nullable;

    // true if this column is read-only
    public boolean readOnly;

    // true if this column can be used in a WHERE clause
    public boolean searchable;

    // true if this column contains a signed number
    public boolean signed;

    // true if this column may be written to
    public boolean writable;
}
```

Since all the data are cached in a serializable object, there is no need to create a client proxy or server-side stub.

Figure 13.25

RSMD.java code listing.

```
package javaservlets.SQLServlet.server;

/**
 * <p>This class represents the ResultSetMetaData for a ResultSet
 */
public class RSMD
  implements java.io.Serializable
{
  // The number of columns in the ResultSet
  public int columnCount;

  // A vector of RSMDColumn objects; one for each column in the
  // ResultSet
  public java.util.Vector columns = new java.util.Vector();

  /**
   * <p>Returns the RSMDColumn object for the given column index
   * (relative to 1)
   */
  public RSMDColumn getColumn(int index)
    throws java.sql.SQLException
    {
      if ((index < 1) ||
          (index > columns.size())) {
        throw new java.sql.SQLException("Invalid column number");
      }

      // Get the column
      RSMDColumn col = (RSMDColumn) columns.elementAt(index - 1);

      return col;
    }
}
```

What Did We Leave Out?   While the SQLServlet JDBC driver is quite functional, there are several areas that may need to be addressed, depending on your needs.

- Prepared statements—The JDBC prepared statement interface is not implemented. If you wish to use a prepared SQL statement, you will need to implement the prepared statement interface in the same manner as the statement interface.

- Callable statements—The JDBC callable statement interface is not implemented. If you wish to invoke stored procedures with in/out parameters, you will need to implement the callable statement interface.

- Data encryption—If you are highly sensitive to the privacy of the data being transmitted, you may want to use some type of data encryption algorithm to encode results before they are returned to the client.

- Data compression—If you are working with large sets of data, you may want to consider compressing the data before they are transmitted. Remember that we are dealing with a potentially slow network connection; the time necessary to compress/decompress the data may be significantly less than transmitting these data without modification.

- Faster communication protocols—You may find that HTTP is just not fast enough to suit your needs. The underlying architecture of the driver makes it possible to use Java Remote Method Invocation (RMI) without too much trouble; RMI uses serialization similar to our HTTP tunneling scheme. I'll leave that as an exercise for you.

SQLServlet Example: SimpleQueryApplet

Now that we've covered the SQLServlet JDBC driver, it's time to give it a test drive. To do this we'll create an applet, called SimpleQueryApplet, which will do the following.

- Use the SQLServlet driver to establish a connection with the specified JDBC driver on the server.

- Accept a SQL statement from the user and execute it on the server.

- Display the results of the SQL statement.

Writing the Applet

Let's take a look at some of the more important aspects of writing SimpleQueryApplet. The first part of any applet is the `init()` routine, which is called when the applet is initialized. It is here that we can create GUI components, add them to the applet frame, and establish a connection with the SQLServlet driver. These steps are shown in Figure 13.26.

Figure 13.26

SimpleQuery-
Applet init()
method.

```
package javaservlets.SQLServlet;

import java.applet.*;
import java.awt.*;
import java.awt.event.*;

/**
 * <p>This is a simple SQL query applet that uses the SQLServlet
 * JDBC driver to query a database and process the results
 */

public class SimpleQueryApplet
  extends Applet
  implements ActionListener
{
  // Create the applet components
  TextField user = new TextField(40);
  TextField password = new TextField(40);
  TextField driver = new TextField(40);
  TextField url = new TextField(40);
  TextField sql = new TextField(40);
  TextArea  results = new TextArea(8, 70);

  Button connect = new Button("");
  Button execute = new Button("Execute Query");

  // The database connection
  java.sql.Connection m_con = null;

  /**
   * <p>Initialize the applet
   */
  public void init()
    {
      // Don't allow the results to be edited
      results.setEditable(false);

      // Add listeners
      connect.addActionListener(this);
      execute.addActionListener(this);

      // Setup the UI
      GridBagLayout gridBag = new GridBagLayout();
      GridBagConstraints gbc = new GridBagConstraints();

      // Set the layout manager
      setLayout(gridBag);

      // Setup the contraints
      gbc.weightx = 1.0;
      gbc.weighty = 1.0;
      gbc.anchor = gbc.CENTER;
      gbc.fill = gbc.NONE;
      gbc.gridwidth = gbc.REMAINDER;

      // Add the components to the applet frame
      add(new Label("JDBC Driver Name:"));
      gridBag.setConstraints(driver, gbc);
      add(driver);
```

```
        add(new Label("Connection URL:"));
        gridBag.setConstraints(url, gbc);
        add(url);

        add(new Label("User Name:"));
        gridBag.setConstraints(user, gbc);
        add(user);

        add(new Label("Password:"));
        gridBag.setConstraints(password, gbc);
        password.setEchoChar('*');
        add(password);

        gridBag.setConstraints(connect, gbc);
        add(connect);

        add(new Label("SQL Statement:"));
        gridBag.setConstraints(sql, gbc);
        add(sql);

        gridBag.setConstraints(execute, gbc);
        add(execute);

        Label l = new Label("---- Results ----");
        gridBag.setConstraints(l, gbc);
        add(l);

        gridBag.setConstraints(results, gbc);
        add(results);

        // Setup the components for connecting to the database
        setForConnect();

        // Attempt to create an instance of the SQLServlet JDBC
        // driver. This will cause the driver to register itself
        // with the JDBC DriverManager
        try {
          javaservlets.SQLServlet.Driver d =
            new javaservlets.SQLServlet.Driver();
        }
        catch (java.sql.SQLException ex) {
          ex.printStackTrace();
        }
    }
```

The flip side of initializing the applet is properly destroying the applet. The `destroy()` method is invoked when the applet terminates and is the perfect place to terminate a database connection (shown in Figure 13.27).

Finally, we need to look at the event handler for the applet, which is where all the action takes place. If you looked closely at Figure 13.26, you would have noticed that the applet implements the action listener interface (in the java.awt.event package). This interface has a single method,

Figure 13.27

SimpleQueryApplet
destroy()
method.

```
/**
 * <p>Called when the applet is destroyed
 */
public void destroy()
    {
      disconnect();
    }

/**
 * <p>Disconnect from the database if necessary
 */
protected void disconnect()
    {
      if (m_con != null) {
        try {
          m_con.close();
          m_con = null;
        }
        catch (java.sql.SQLException ex) {
          // Ignore any close errors
        }
      }
    }
```

actionPerformed(), which will be invoked whenever an action event
occurs on a component that has an action listener object registered; this
is done by calling addActionListener() on the component. Figure
13.28 shows the actionPerformed() method, which will be invoked if
the Connect or Execute buttons are pressed.

Figure 13.28

SimpleQuery-
Applet action-
Performed()
method.

```
/**
 * <p>Process an action
 */
public void actionPerformed(ActionEvent event)
    {
      Object o = event.getSource();

      // Figure out which component caused the event
      if (o == connect) {

        // If we are already connected, disconnect
        if (m_con != null) {
          disconnect();
          setForConnect();
          results.setText("");
        }
        else {

          // The 'connect' button was pressed. Attempt to
          // connect to the database
          results.setText("");

          // Format the complete URL
```

```
        String fullURL = "jdbc:SQLServlet:" + getCodeBase() +
          "servlet/@" + driver.getText() + ":" + url.getText();

        results.append("Attempting to connect to:\n" +
                       fullURL + "\n");

        try {

          // Record how long it takes to connect
          long start = System.currentTimeMillis();

          // Attempt to connect to the remote database
          m_con =
            java.sql.DriverManager.getConnection(fullURL,
                       user.getText(), password.getText());

          results.append("Connection ready in " +
                         (System.currentTimeMillis() - start) +
                         "ms\n");
          setForConnected();
        }
        catch (java.sql.SQLException ex) {
          results.append("Connection failed: " +
                         ex.getMessage() + "\n");
        }
      }
    }
    else if (o == execute) {

      // Execute the given SQL statement
      results.setText("");

      // The Statement object
      java.sql.Statement stmt = null;

      try {
        // Create a new statement object
        results.append("Creating new Statement\n");
        long start = System.currentTimeMillis();

        stmt = m_con.createStatement();
        results.append("Created in " +
                       (System.currentTimeMillis() - start) +
                       "ms\n");

        results.append("Executing " + sql.getText() + "\n");
        start = System.currentTimeMillis();

        // Execute the query. Since we don't know what type
        // of query is being executed we'll have to determine
        // whether we need to display a row count or display
        // the results of a query
        boolean hasResultSet = stmt.execute(sql.getText());
        results.append("Executed in " +
                       (System.currentTimeMillis() - start) +
                       "ms\n\n");

        // Determine what type of results were returned
        if (hasResultSet) {
```

```java
      // Get the ResultSet for the query
      java.sql.ResultSet rs = stmt.getResultSet();

      // Dump the column headings
      java.sql.ResultSetMetaData md = rs.getMetaData();

      String line = "";
      for (int i = 1; i <= md.getColumnCount(); i++) {

        // Comma separate if necessary
        if (i > 1) line += ", ";

        // Get the column name and add to the list
        line += md.getColumnName(i);
      }
      results.append(line + "\n");

      // Dump the data. Only allow the first 20 rows to
      // be displayed
      int rowCount = 0;
      while (rs.next() && (rowCount < 20)) {
        rowCount++;
        line = "";
        for (int i = 1; i <= md.getColumnCount(); i++) {

          // Comma separate if necessary
          if (i > 1) line += ", ";

          // Get the column data and add to the list
          line += rs.getString(i);
        }
        results.append(line + "\n");
      }
    }
    else {
      // Display a row count
      results.append("" + stmt.getUpdateCount() +
                     " rows affected\n");
    }

  }
  catch (java.sql.SQLException ex) {
    results.append("Failed: " + ex.getMessage() + "\n");
  }
  finally {
    // Always close the statement
    if (stmt != null) {
      try {
        stmt.close();
        stmt = null;
      }
      catch (java.sql.SQLException ex) {
        // Ignore close errors
      }
    }
  }
 }
}
```

Note the process that takes place when the Connect button is pressed. If a connection has already been established, it will be closed. After that the connection URL is assembled, and the SQLServlet driver is used to establish a new connection on the server.

If the Execute button is pressed, the SQL statement is retrieved from the user and sent to the server for processing. Once the results are returned to the client, they are formatted and displayed.

Configuring the Server

Don't forget that the SQLServlet JDBC driver consists of a series of servlets that must be configured in your Web server. Table 13.1 lists the servlet aliases that must be configured before using the driver.

Creating a Distribution Archive

Let's put what we covered in Chapter 12 to good use by creating a distribution ZIP file for SimpleQueryApplet. Creating a single ZIP file containing all the required class files using the CreateArchive utility is much easier than having to worry about moving all the class files into a Web server download directory. There's not much else to do other than

TABLE 13.1

Servlet Aliases for the SQLServlet JDBC Driver

Alias	Class Name
RemoteDriverObjectServer	javaservlets.SQLServlet.server.RemoteDriverObjectServer
RemoteConnectionObjectServer	javaservlets.SQLServlet.server.RemoteConnectionObjectServer
RemoteDatabaseMetaDataObject-Server	javaservlets.SQLServlet.server.RemoteDatabaseMetaData-ObjectServer
RemoteStatementObjectServer	javaservlets.SQLServlet.server.RemoteStatementObjectServer
RemoteResultSetObjectServer	javaservlets.SQLServlet.server.RemoteResultSetObjectServer

Figure 13.29

Using the
CreateArchive
utility.

```
java javaservlets.rollcall.CreateArchive
    javaservlets.SQLServlet.SimpleQueryApplet
    -aSimpleQueryApplet.zip

Creating archive SimpleQueryApplet.zip
javaservlets.SQLServlet.SimpleQueryApplet.class
  javaservlets.SQLServlet.Driver.class
    javaservlets.SQLServlet.BaseObject.class
    javaservlets.SQLServlet.Connection.class
      javaservlets.SQLServlet.DatabaseMetaData.class
        javaservlets.SQLServlet.ResultSet.class
          javaservlets.SQLServlet.ResultSetMetaData.class
            javaservlets.SQLServlet.server.RSMD.class
              javaservlets.SQLServlet.server.RSMDColumn.class
          javaservlets.SQLServlet.server.ColumnData.class

javaservlets.SQLServlet.server.RemoteResultSetObjectClient.class
          javaservlets.SQLServlet.server.ResultSetData.class
          javaservlets.SQLServlet.server.ResultSetInterface.class
          javaservlets.tunnel.client.BaseTunnelClient.class
            javaservlets.tunnel.client.TunnelException.class
          javaservlets.tunnel.client.TunnelClient.class
      javaservlets.SQLServlet.server.DBMD.class
      javaservlets.SQLServlet.server.DatabaseMetaDataInterface.class

javaservlets.SQLServlet.server.RemoteDatabaseMetaDataObjectClient.class
      javaservlets.SQLServlet.Statement.class

javaservlets.SQLServlet.server.RemoteStatementObjectClient.class
        javaservlets.SQLServlet.server.StatementInterface.class
      javaservlets.SQLServlet.server.ConnectionInterface.class

javaservlets.SQLServlet.server.RemoteConnectionObjectClient.class
    javaservlets.SQLServlet.server.DriverInterface.class
    javaservlets.SQLServlet.server.RemoteDriverObjectClient.class

SimpleQueryApplet.zip created.
```

to invoke the CreateArchive application and watch it work; the results
are shown in Figure 13.29.

Writing the HTML to Load the Applet

The HTML necessary to load the applet is shown in Figure 13.30. Note
the ARCHIVE tag, which specifies the ZIP file we just created. The
SimpleQueryApplet.zip file must be placed in the same directory as the
HTML.

Figure 13.30

SimpleQuery.html listing.

```
<HTML>
<HEAD>
<TITLE>Simple Query</TITLE>
</HEAD>
<BODY>
<h3>Simple applet that makes remote JDBC method calls
using HTTP tunneling.</h3>
<center>
<HR>
<APPLET WIDTH=450
        HEIGHT=350
        NAME="SimpleQueryApplet"
        CODE=javaservlets.SQLServlet.SimpleQueryApplet
        ARCHIVE=SimpleQueryApplet.zip></APPLET>
</center>
</BODY>
</HTML>
```

Figure 13.31

The completed applet.

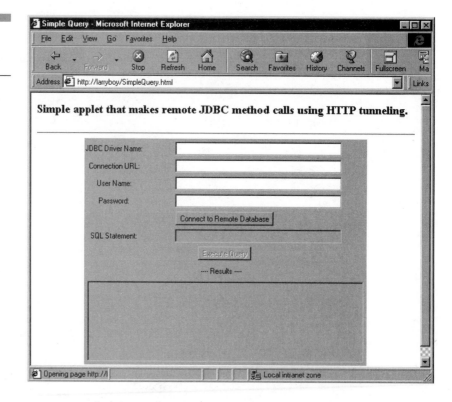

See It In Action

Figure 13.31 shows the completed applet after it has been loaded in a Web browser.

We can now enter the JDBC driver name to use on the server, as well as the connection URL, user name, and password. After this information has been entered, pressing the Connect button will attempt to establish a new database connection on the server. Figure 13.32 shows the applet after successfully connecting to our sample access database.

The applet is now ready to process SQL statements. Figure 13.33 shows the results of executing a SELECT statement on the employee table.

Note that the database connection will be properly terminated when the applet is destroyed. This will prevent resources from being wasted on the server.

Figure 13.32

A successful database connection.

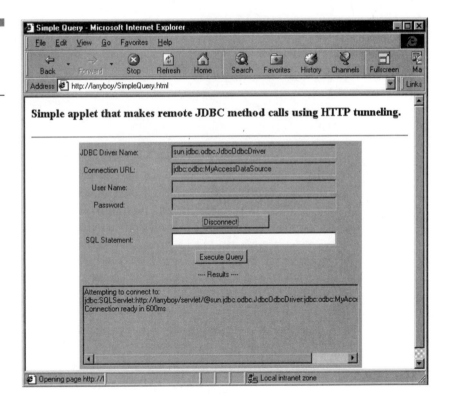

Figure 13.33

Results of the
SELECT statement.

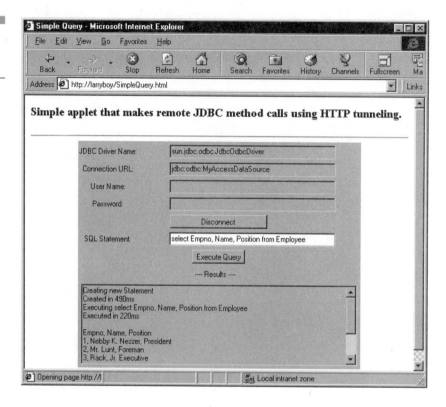

Summary

This chapter has served well as an example of how to tie together several of the technologies we have discussed throughout this book. We've explored how to use HTTP tunneling and the automatic generation of proxies and servlets to create a three-tier JDBC driver; this same methodology can be used to develop just about any kind of distributed application. We also developed a simple applet to exercise our new JDBC driver and saw how to create a ZIP file with all the applet class dependencies; this ZIP file greatly simplified the distribution process.

Coming up next, we'll examine how to use Java's Remote Method Invocation (RMI) from within a servlet to communicate to other Java servers.

# CHAPTER 14

Using Servlets
and RMI

I n this chapter, we're going to focus on using the Java Remote Invocation Interface (RMI) from within the servlet environment. RMI enables Java applications to seamlessly make method calls on objects residing in a different virtual machine; this may be on the same host or, more likely, on a different host.

The Challenge: Accessing Other Java Servers

Servlets are a great way to utilize Java on the Web server; but what if you need to access another server running Java in the network? The answer, of course, is to use RMI. RMI allows you to expose the functionality of a Java object on a given server to any other Java process; whether it be on the same host or a remote host (see Figure 14.1).

If you are well versed in distributed object technology, you may wonder about using other technologies, such as Common Object Request Broker Architecture (CORBA). CORBA exists to solve this same problem but with a much wider scope; it also supports mixing distributed objects written in different languages. Since we will be using Java on the client (our servlet) and on the server we obviously don't care about using objects written in other languages. Also, CORBA requires that you use

Figure 14.1

Servlets and RMI.

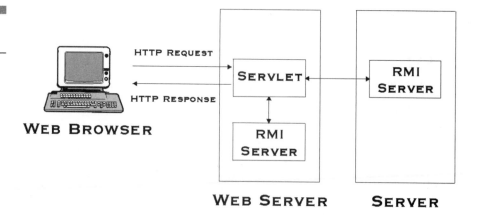

some type of Object Request Broker (ORB) to service object requests on the network. ORBs are available only from third parties (such as VisiBroker from Inprise); everything you need to use RMI comes as part of the standard JDK and is freely distributable.

RMI Overview

RMI is an API developed by JavaSoft that allows objects to be used in a remote manner; by this I mean that you can use a Java object from a different virtual machine. Java has always supported the use of sockets, which are very flexible and work quite well for general communication. However, sockets require that the client and server implement some type of protocol to marshal data (similar to the HTTP tunneling scheme we developed in Chapter 10); while this is not difficult, it would be nice if the underlying system handled this automatically. Enter RMI, which has a distributed object technology built into the very core of Java. RMI takes care of the issues surrounding data marshaling (using serialization) and allows you to write and use objects in a remote manner without necessarily being aware that they are, indeed, remote.

Let's take a look at the original goals of RMI as defined in the specification.

- Support seamless remote invocation on objects in different Java virtual machines
- Support callbacks from servers to clients
- Integrate the distributed object model into the Java language in a natural way while retaining most of the Java language's object semantics
- Make writing reliable distributed applications as simple as possible
- Preserve the safety provided by the Java run time environment

Of these goals the most important are to make RMI simple to use and to provide a very natural extension to the language. To illustrate how well these goals have been accomplished let's dive right in and develop a servlet that uses RMI.

RMI Example: CustomerInfo

The CustomerInfo servlet will use RMI to connect to a remote server and execute a database query to gather customer information. After requesting an instance of the remote object, the servlet will not know, or care, that methods are being executed in a different virtual machine. This certainly satisfies the goal of making RMI very natural to use. Just how does the servlet interact with the remote object? The answer is a standard Java interface.

Define the Remote Interface

Similar to the way that server-side services were defined for our HTTP tunneling process, RMI requires that an interface be created to define the methods that will be invoked on the remote host. There are a few requirements when defining the remote interface.

- The interface must be declared as public.

- The interface must extend the RMI base interface java.rmi.Remote. The java.rmi.Remote interface does not define any methods; it serves simply as an indication that the object will be used remotely.

- Each method defined in the interface must throw java.rmi.RemoteException (plus any other exceptions thrown by the method).

The CustomerInfo object only contains a single method, which will return all the information gathered by the server. The interface is shown in Figure 14.2.

Notice that all the interface requirements previously defined are met; CustomerInterface is declared as public, it extends java.rmi.Remote; and all the methods throw java.rmi.RemoteException. Also note that the return value of the method is an object named CustomerData. This serializable object will contain all of the customer information; it is created on the server and a copy of the object is serialized over the RMI connection and recreated on the client, where it can by used directly. Figure 14.3 shows the CustomerData class.

Figure 14.2

CustomerInter-
face.java code
listing.

```
package javaservlets.rmi.server;

/**
 * <p>This interface defines the remote methods available for
 * the Customer object.
 */

public interface CustomerInterface
  extends java.rmi.Remote
{

  /**
   * <p>Retrieves the customer data for the given customer ID
   * number. If the customer is not found a null value will be
   * returned.
   *
   * @param id Customer ID number
   * @return CustomerData object containing all of the customer
   * data or null if not found
   */
  CustomerData getCustomerData(String id)
    throws java.rmi.RemoteException, java.sql.SQLException;
}
```

Figure 14.3

CustomerData.java
code listing.

```
package javaservlets.rmi.server;

/**
 * <p>This class holds the data for a customer
 */

public class CustomerData
  implements java.io.Serializable
{
  // The customer ID number
  public String id;

  // The customer name
  public String name;

  // The current customer balance
  public java.math.BigDecimal balance;
}
```

Write the Server Implementation

Now that the remote interface has been defined, you can implement each of the methods. Figure 14.4 shows the customer code.

Figure 14.4

Customer.java code
listing.

```java
package javaservlets.rmi.server;

/**
 * <p>The server implementation for CustomerInterface. This
 * object will be instantiated remotely via RMI.
 */

public class Customer
    extends java.rmi.server.UnicastRemoteObject
    implements CustomerInterface
{
    // Database connection
    java.sql.Connection m_con;

    // Prepared Statement
    java.sql.PreparedStatement m_ps;

    // JDBC driver to register
    static String m_driver = "sun.jdbc.odbc.JdbcOdbcDriver";

    // Connection URL
    static String m_url = "jdbc:odbc:MyAccessDataSource";

    /**
     * <p>Default constructor.
     *
     * @param con JDBC Connection to use for the query
     */
    public Customer(java.sql.Connection con)
        throws java.rmi.RemoteException, java.sql.SQLException
        {
            super();
            m_con = con;

            // Create a prepared statement for us to use
            String sql = "SELECT Custno, Name, Balance from Customer " +
                "WHERE Custno = ?";

            m_ps = con.prepareStatement(sql);
        }

    /**
     * <p>Retrieves the customer data for the given customer ID
     * number. If the customer is not found a null value will be
     * returned.
     *
     * @param id Customer ID number
     * @return CustomerData object containing all of the customer
     * data or null if not found
     */
    public CustomerData getCustomerData(String id)
        throws java.rmi.RemoteException, java.sql.SQLException
        {
            CustomerData data = null;

            System.out.println("Customer query for " + id);

            // Set the customer ID
            m_ps.setInt(1, Integer.parseInt(id));
```

```java
        // Execute the query
        java.sql.ResultSet rs = m_ps.executeQuery();

        // Get the results. If there are no results available,
        // return null to the client
        if (rs.next()) {

            // A row exists. Create a new CustomerData object and
            // fill it in
            data = new CustomerData();
            data.id = rs.getString(1);
            data.name = rs.getString(2);
            data.balance = rs.getBigDecimal(3, 2);
        }

        // Close the ResultSet
        rs.close();

        return data;
    }

    /**
     * <p>Main entry point for the remote object. This method
     * will bootstrap the object and register it with the
     * RMI registry.
     */
    public static void main(String args[])
    {
        // Install the default RMI security manager
        System.setSecurityManager(new java.rmi.RMISecurityManager());

        try {

            // Register the JDBC driver
            Class.forName(m_driver).newInstance();

            System.out.println("Opening database connection");

            // Create a new JDBC connection
            java.sql.Connection con =
              java.sql.DriverManager.getConnection(m_url);

            // Create a new instance of the server object
            Customer cust = new Customer(con);

            // Bind the object to the RMI registry. If the object is
            // already bound it will be replaced
            java.rmi.Naming.rebind("/Customer", cust);

            System.out.println("Customer server object ready.");
        }
        catch (Exception ex) {

            // Display any errors
            ex.printStackTrace();
        }
    }
}
```

Notice that the main() method (which is the entry point for the application) installs a new security manager. You might think that you don't need to worry about any security issues since you are isolated inside your own virtual machine. However, when using RMI you may have to load classes from clients across the network. The RMISecurity-Manager will ensure that you aren't downloading anything from the client that would violate the safety of the system. If you do not set a security manager when the application is started, the RMI will load only classes from local files in the current CLASSPATH.

You will also see that we are binding the application into the RMI namespace so that the object will be known externally. The RMI system provides a URL-based registry (known as rmiregistry), which allows you to bind an application to a specific URL in the format:

```
//[<host name>[:<port number>]]/<object name>
```

where:

<host name> will default to the current host if omitted.

<port number> will default to 1099 if omitted. If a port number is given, the rmiregistry process must use the same port as well.

<object name> is the name of the remote object as known externally. The name does not need to correspond to the actual object name.

One other requirement when implementing the server object is to define a constructor. The constructor must throw java.rmi.RemoteException; this is due to the fact that RMI will be attempting to export the remote object during its construction, and a failure may occur if communication resources are not available.

Generate the Stubs and Skeletons

Before the object can be used remotely, you need to execute the RMI compiler. The compiler, rmic, will take the full class name and generate two new classes: a stub and a skeleton. The stub is used by the client (although you will not be aware of it) to marshal all the method parameters to the server. The skeleton is used by the server to unmarshal the method request and invoke the actual method. After the method is invoked, the skeleton will marshal the return value back to the client, where the stub will unmarshal it and return the data to the caller.

The format of the rmic command is:

```
rmic [-d <root directory>] <server class>
```

where:

<root directory> is the root directory of your package. If you are not running rmic from the root directory, you need to specify it with the "–d" switch so that rmic will know where to place the generated class files.

<server class> is the full class name of the server implementation.

To generate the stub and skeleton for the customer object, use the following command from the same directory as the class file:

```
rmic -d ../../.. javaservlets.rmi.server.Customer
```

This will generate the following files.

- Customer_stub.class—The client-side stub for marshaling method requests
- Customer_skel.class—The server-side skeleton for unmarshaling method requests

Write the Client Using the Remote Object

In our case the client to the remote object is actually a servlet. The servlet itself is very similar to the ones we have developed before with the following exceptions.

- The remote object is resolved by using the Naming.lookup() service. The external name of the remote object is given and it is looked up on the target host in the rmiregistry.
- All remote method calls can throw a remote exception.

Figure 14.5 shows the code listing for the CustomerInfo servlet. This servlet will connect to a remote Java host, make a method call to gather all the information for the specified customer, and format an HTML page which displays all this information.

```
package javaservlets.rmi;

import javax.servlet.*;
import javax.servlet.http.*;
import javaservlets.rmi.server.*;

/**
 * <p>This is a simple servlet that will return customer
 * information. Note that this servlet implements the
 * SingleThreadModel interface which will force the Web browser
 * to synchronize all requests
 */

public class CustomerInfo
    extends HttpServlet
    implements SingleThreadModel
{
  /**
     * <p>Performs the HTTP POST operation
     *
     * @param req The request from the client
     * @param resp The response from the servlet
     */

  public void doPost(HttpServletRequest req,
                     HttpServletResponse resp)
    throws ServletException, java.io.IOException
    {

      // Create a PrintWriter to write the response
      java.io.PrintWriter out =
        new java.io.PrintWriter(resp.getOutputStream());

      // Set the content type of the response
      resp.setContentType("text/html");

      // Print the HTML header
      out.println("<html>");
      out.println("<head>");
      out.println("<title>Customer Balance Information</title>");
      out.println("</head>");

      // Get the Customer id
      String id = null;
      String values[] = req.getParameterValues("CustomerID");
      if (values != null) {
        id = values[0];
      }

      // The target host. Change to 'rmi://yourhost/' when the
      // server runs on a remote machine
      String host = "";

      try {

        // Attempt to bind to the remote host and get the
        // instance of the Customer object
        CustomerInterface cust = (CustomerInterface)
          java.rmi.Naming.lookup(host + "Customer");
```

```
            // We have an instance of the remote object. Get the
            // customer information
            CustomerData data = cust.getCustomerData(id);

            // Format the HTML
            out.println("The current balance for " + data.name +
                        " is $" + data.balance);
        }
        catch (Exception ex) {

            // Turn exceptions into a servlet exception
            ex.printStackTrace();
            throw new ServletException(ex.getMessage());
        }

        // Wrap up
        out.println("</html>");
        out.flush();
        out.close();
    }
```

You may have noticed that the CustomerInfo servlet also implements the SingleThreadModel interface. This interface does not define any methods; instead, it serves as a marker indicating that the servlet is not thread-safe and all requests should be synchronized. The Web server is responsible for ensuring that no two client sessions are using the object at the same time. This is important since our simple RMI example only has one instance of the server object in the remote virtual machine, and we are using a database which may not be thread-safe.

Bootstrap the Server

Before using the remote object, it needs to be loaded and registered with the system. As previously mentioned, the name-to-remote object mapping is done via the rmiregistry; this is an application provided by Java-Soft that must be running on the server. To do this you must start the rmiregistry application.

(Win95/NT)	start rmiregistry
(Unix)	rmiregistry &

This will start a new RMI naming service that resides on the default port 1099. If any requests are made on the port, rmiregistry will look up the specified object name and, if found, return an instance handle back to the client. How does a remote object get bound to the naming service? If you remember when the server object was implemented, we created a `main()` method, which bound an external name with the actual remote object instance:

```
java.rmi.Naming.rebind("/Customer", cust);
```

Thus, executing the remote object (which is a Java application) will cause it to be instantiated and bound with rmiregistry.

```
java javaservlets.rmi.server.Customer
Opening database connection
Customer server object ready
```

The customer object is now bound to the external name of "/Customer" and is ready for use.

Writing the HTML to Execute the Servlet

We'll invoke the servlet by creating a simple HTML form, which prompts for a customer ID (see Figure 14.6). Once the customer ID is given, the user can press the Perform Query button, which will invoke the servlet.

Figure 14.6

CustomerInfo.html listing.

```
<html>
<head>
<title>Customer Balance Inquiry</title>
</head>
<body>
<h1><center>Customer Balance Inquiry</center></h1>
<hr><br>

<form method=POST action="http://larryboy/servlet/CustomerInfo">
<center>
Customer ID:<input type=text name=CustomerID size=10><br>
<br>
<input type=submit value="Perform Query">
</center>
</form>

</body>
</html>
```

See It In Action

After adding the CustomerInfo servlet to the Web server configuration and placing the HTML file in your document directory, it's time to try it out (don't forget that the servlet uses an RMI stub as well). Figure 14.7 shows the page after it is first loaded, and Figure 14.8 shows the results of a query.

There's quite a bit happening behind the scenes to bring you the customer information.

- An HTML POST is generated when the user submits the query request. The customer ID is embedded with the request and sent to the Web server.

Figure 14.7

CustomerInfo web page.

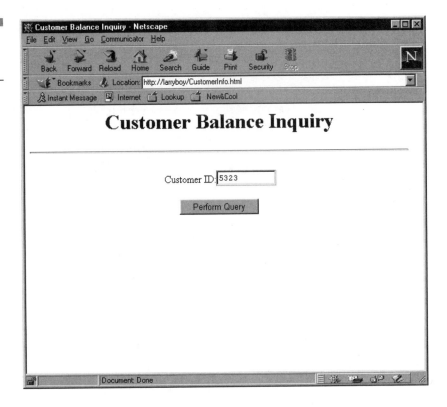

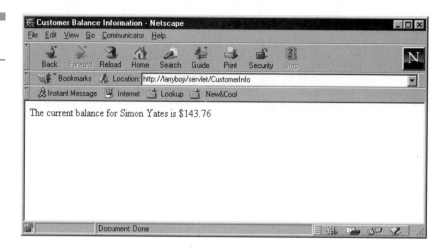

- The Web server recognizes that it is a servlet request and the CustomerInfo servlet is invoked.

- The CustomerInfo servlet will perform an RMI naming lookup in an attempt to load a remote customer object.

- The rmiregistry process, which was started earlier and is listening on port 1099, receives the naming lookup request and locates the customer object. The customer object had to be loaded on the server so that it could bind itself in the registry.

- A handle to the remote customer object is returned to the servlet.

- The servlet makes method calls on the customer interface. The method call is passed to the stub, which marshals the method request to the server. The server contains a skeleton, which unmarshals the method request and invokes the "real" method on the customer object. The server-side implementation is invoked, and the customer database is queried. The results are placed into a customer data object, which the skeleton marshals back to the client. The stub is responsible for unmarshaling the return value and returning the data back to the caller.

That was a long way to go to service the query request. But I think you will agree that JavaSoft made using distributed objects with RMI quite easy (especially by providing tools such as rmic and rmiregistry). Did JavaSoft meet all their goals when designing RMI? I think so, and once you've worked with other distributed object technologies (such as

CORBA) I'll bet you'll want to stick with RMI if you can use Java on both the client and the server.

Converting a Servlet into an RMI Server

While I won't cover the details of how to modify a servlet to become an RMI (or CORBA) server object, the fine folks at Inprise (formerly Borland) and Live Software have created a series of white papers that describe how to do this. You'll find the papers at http://www.inprise.com/jbuilder/papers/jb2servlet/jb2servlet2.html. While the papers detail how to convert servlets using JBuilder, you can adapt this information for any development environment.

Making RMI Even Easier

If you think back to Chapter 11, we developed a series of Java code generators that took an arbitrary interface and its implementation and generated the client proxy and server-side stub. Without too much imagination you should be able to adapt this same process to RMI. Instead of a servlet hosting the object let a generic RMI server object be the host.

Summary

In this chapter, we took a whirlwind look at RMI and how to use distributed objects from within a servlet. We defined the server-side methods that will be used via a standard Java interface and then created the implementation. We also saw how to bind the server object with the rmiregistry so that the object could be used externally. A simple servlet was developed to look up the remote object and, if found, make remote method calls. I hope you realize how easy it is to perform distributed computing using Java, RMI, and servlets.

APPENDIX

This appendix describes each class in the Java servlet API. The classes are given in alphabetical order, and an illustration of the class hierarchy, a description, a method summary, and a detailed method description are given for each class.

javax.servlet.http
Cookie

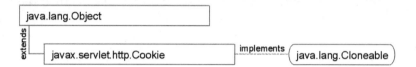

```
package javax.servlet.http;
public class Cookie
    extends Object
    implements Cloneable
```

The Cookie class represents data used for session management with HTTP and HTTPS protocols. Cookies are used by clients (specifically Web browsers) to hold small amounts of data to persist state in a client session.

Cookies are named and have a single value. Current Web browsers differ in their use of cookies, so the servlet writer should not depend upon them too heavily.

Summary

clone()	Returns a copy of this object
getComment()	Returns a comment describing this cookie or null if none
getDomain()	Returns the domain of this cookie
getMaxAge()	Returns the maximum age of this cookie

`getName()`	Returns the name of this cookie
`getPath()`	Returns the prefix of all URLs for which this cookie is intended
`getSecure()`	Returns the value of the secure flag
`getValue()`	Returns the value of this cookie
`getVersion()`	Returns the version of this cookie
`setComment(String)`	Sets the comment describing the cookie's purpose
`setDomain(String)`	Sets the domain of this cookie
`setMaxAge(int)`	Sets the maximum age of this cookie
`setPath(String)`	This cookie should only be presented for requests beginning with the given URL
`setSecure(boolean)`	If true, the cookie should only be sent using a secure protocol (such as HTTPS)
`setValue(String)`	Sets the value of this cookie
`setVersion(int)`	Sets the version of the protocol used by this cookie

Constructors

Cookie

```
public Cookie(String name, String value)
```

This creates a new `Cookie` object with the given cookie name and initial value. Note that names starting with the $ character are reserved and should not be used.

Methods

clone

```
public Object clone()
```

This returns a copy of this object.

getComment

```
public String getComment()
```

This returns a string describing the purpose of this cookie or null if no description has been defined.

getDomain

```
public String getDomain()
```

This returns the domain of this cookie. A domain name begins with a dot (such as .sun.com) and only hosts with that domain name should be able to see the cookie.

getMaxAge

```
public int getMaxAge()
```

This returns the maximum number of seconds before the cookie expires. Negative values indicate that the cookie will be destroyed when the browser exits.

getName

```
public String getName()
```

This returns the name of the cookie. The name may not be changed after the cookie has been created.

getPath

```
public String getPath()
```

This returns the prefix of all URLs for which this cookie is intended.

getSecure

```
public boolean getSecure()
```

This returns the value of the secure flag.

getValue

```
public String getValue()
```

This returns the current value of this cookie.

getVersion

```
public int getVersion()
```

This returns the version of this cookie. Version 0 indicates the original version as specified by Netscape. Version 1 complies with the current standardization request, RFC 2109.

setComment

```
public void setComment(String purpose)
```

This sets the descriptive purpose of this cookie. The purpose will be used to describe the cookie to the user.

setDomain

```
public void setDomain(String pattern)
```

This sets the domain name that the cookie will be presented to. A domain name starts with a dot (such as .sun.com); a cookie should only be presented to hosts within this domain (such as www.sun.com).

setMaxAge

```
public void setMaxAge(int seconds)
```

This sets the maximum age of this cookie in seconds, after which the cookie will expire. A negative value indicates the default behavior: The cookie is not stored persistently and will be deleted when the browser exists. A zero value deletes the cookie.

setPath

```
public void setPath(String url)
```

This cookie should be presented only with requests that start with the given URL. URLs in the same location as the one that set the cookie (and any subdirectories) will be able to see the cookie.

setSecure

```
public void setSecure(boolean value)
```

This indicates whether the cookie should only be sent using a secure protocol, such as HTTPS.

setValue

```
public void setValue(String value)
```

This sets the value of this cookie. Note that values with special characters (whitespace, [,], =, comma, ", /, \, ?, @, :, and ;) should be avoided. Empty values may not behave the same way in all browsers.

setVersion

```
public void setVersion(int version)
```

This sets the version of the cookie protocol. Since, at the time of writing, the standards are still being finalized, consider version 1 to be experimental; do not use anything but version 0 on production sites.

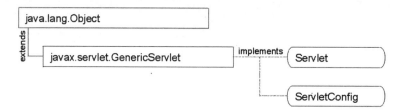

package javax.servlet;

public abstract class GenericServlet

    extends Object

    implements Servlet, ServletConfig

The `GenericServlet` abstract class is intended to make writing servlets easier. It provides simple implementations of `init()` and `destroy()`, as well as all the methods in the `ServletConfig` interface. A servlet writer must override only the service method, which is abstract.

Summary

`destroy()`	Called when the servlet is destroyed
`GenericServlet()`	Constructs a new `GenericServlet` object
`getInitParameter(String)`	Returns the string value of a named initialization parameter
`getInitParameterNames()`	Returns an enumeration of the initialization parameter names
`getServletConfig()`	Returns a `servletConfig` object for the servlet

`getServletContext()`	Returns a `servletContext` object for the servlet
`getServletInfo()`	Returns a string containing information about the servlet
`init(ServletConfig)`	Called when the servlet is initialized
`log(String)`	Writes a message to the servlet log file
`service(ServletRequest, ServletResponse)`	Called to service a client request

Constructors

GenericServlet

```
protected GenericServlet()
```

This is the default constructor for the `GenericServlet` class. The constructor does no work.

Methods

destroy

```
public void destroy()
```

This method is called once when the servlet is destroyed by a service. The servlet writer should use the `destroy()` method to clean up any resources being used by the servlet, such as a database connection.

getInitParameter

```
public String getInitParameter(String name)
```

This returns a string value for the named initialization parameter; it returns null if the requested parameter does not exist. The parameter value is retrieved from the ServletConfig object, which was given during the init() call.

getInitParameterNames

```
public java.util.Enumeration getInitParameterNames()
```

This returns an enumeration containing the names of the servlet's initialization parameters; it returns an empty enumeration if there are no parameters. The parameter names are retrieved from the ServletConfig object, which was given during the init() call.

getServletConfig

```
public ServletConfig getServletConfig()
```

This returns the ServletConfig object that was provided for the init() method.

getServletContext

```
public ServletContext getServletContext()
```

This returns a ServletContext object, which contains information about the network in which the servlet is running. The ServletContext object is retrieved from the ServletConfig object, which was given during the init() call.

getServletInfo

```
public String getServletInfo()
```

This returns a string containing information about the servlet. This can include the author, version number, and a copyright statement. This method must be overridden by the servlet writer; null is returned by default.

init

```
public void init(ServletConfig config) throws ServletException
```

This method is called once when the servlet is first loaded by a service. It is guaranteed to complete before any service requests are accepted by the servlet. If a fatal initialization error occurs, an UnavailableException should be thrown; do not call the System.exit() method. The servlet writer should use the init() method to perform any necessary servlet initialization, such as creating a database connection.

The init() method stores the ServletConfig object that is passed; if this method is overridden by the servlet writer, super.init() must be called.

log

```
public void log(String message)
```

This writes the given message to the servlet log file, along with the class name of the servlet. The name of the servlet log file is defined by the specific server being used; it will normally be an event log.

GenericServlet

service

```
public abstract void service(ServletRequest req, ServletResponse
resp)
throws ServletException, java.io.IOException
```

This satisfies a single request from a client. The `ServletRequest` object contains parameters provided by the client. The `ServletRequest` object also contains an input stream, which can be used to retrieve data from the client. To return information to the client, the servlet writer can write data to the output stream of the `ServletResponse` object.

The servlet writer should be aware that servlets typically run inside multithreaded services that can handle multiple client requests simultaneously; it is the servlet writer's responsibility to synchronize access to shared resources (such as database connections).

javax.servlet.http
HttpServlet

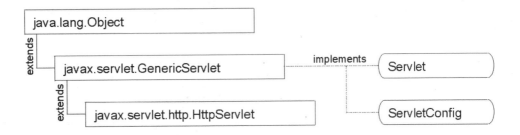

package javax.servlet.http;

public abstract class HttpServlet

    extends javax.servlet.GenericServlet

The HttpServlet class is provided to simplify writing servlets for HTTP. It extends the GenericServlet class and provides a framework for handling HTTP. Since this class is abstract, the servlet writer must override at least one method. The methods typically overridden are as follows.

- doGet() if HTTP GET requests are supported. The servlet writer should also consider overriding the getLastModified() method to support caching of the HTTP response data.

- doPost() if HTTP POST requests are supported

- doPut() if HTTP PUT requests are supported

- doDelete() if HTTP DELETE requests are supported

- init() if a costly initialization service must be performed, such as connecting to a database

- destroy() if the servlet needs to perform some type of resource cleanup, such as disconnecting from a database

- getServletInfo to provide information about the servlet

HttpServlet

Summary

doDelete(HttpServletRequest, HttpServletResponse)	Performs the HTTP DELETE operation
doGet(HttpServletRequest, HttpServletResponse)	Performs the HTTP GET operation
doOptions(HttpServletRequest, HttpServletResponse)	Performs the HTTP OPTIONS operation
doPost(HttpServletRequest, HttpServletResponse)	Performs the HTTP POST operation
doPut(HttpServletRequest, HttpServletResponse)	Performs the HTTP PUT operation
doTrace(HttpServletRequest, HttpServletResponse)	Performs the HTTP TRACE operation
getLastModified(HttpServletRequest)	Returns the time that the requested entry was last modified
HttpServlet()	Constructs a new HttpServlet object
service(HttpServletRequest, HttpServletResponse)	Performs a service with HTTP-specific parameters
service(ServletRequest, ServletResponse)	Implements Servlet.service() by calling the HTTP-specific service() method

Constructors

HttpServlet

```
protected HttpServlet()
```

This is the default constructor for the HttpServlet class. The constructor does no work.

Methods

doDelete

```
protected void doDelete(HttpServletRequest req, HttpServletResponse
resp)
throws ServletException, java.io.IOException
```

This performs the HTTP DELETE operation, if supported. The default implementation provided by the HttpServlet class returns an HTTP BAD_REQUEST error. The DELETE operation allows a client to request that a URI be removed from the server.

doGet

```
protected void doGet(HttpServletRequest req, HttpServletResponse
resp)
throws ServletException, java.io.IOException
```

This performs the HTTP GET operation, if supported. The default implementation provided by the HttpServlet class returns an HTTP BAD_REQUEST error. The servlet writer should also consider overriding the getLastModified() method to support caching of the HTTP response data.

doOptions

```
protected void doOptions(HttpServletRequest req,
HttpServletResponse resp)
throws ServletException, java.io.IOException
```

This performs the HTTP OPTIONS operation. The default implementation provided by the HttpServlet class determines what HTTP options are supported. This method does not need to be overridden unless the servlet implements new methods that are not supported by the HTTP/1.1 protocol.

doPost

```
protected void doPost(HttpServletRequest req, HttpServletResponse
resp)
throws ServletException, java.io.IOException
```

This performs the HTTP POST operation. The default implementation provided by the HttpServlet class returns an HTTP BAD_REQUEST error. Servlet writers should read data from the request (such as parameters), set headers in the response (such as content type, length, and encoding), and then write the response data using the output stream on the HttpServletResponse.

doPut

```
protected void doPut(HttpServletRequest req, HttpServletResponse
resp)
throws ServletException, java.io.IOException
```

This performs the HTTP PUT operation. The default implementation provided by the HttpServlet class returns an HTTP BAD_REQUEST error. The PUT operation is synonymous to sending a file via FTP.

doTrace

```
protected void doTrace(HttpServletRequest req, HttpServletResponse
resp)
throws ServletException, java.io.IOException
```

This performs the HTTP TRACE operation. The default implementation provided by the HttpServlet class returns a response with a message containing all the headers sent with the trace request.

getLastModified

```
protected long getLastModified(HttpServletRequest req)
```

This returns the time that the requested entity was last modified (in milliseconds). The default implementation provided by `HttpService` returns a negative number, indicating that the modification time is unknown and should not be used for conditional GET operations.

Servlets supporting the HTTP GET request should override this method to provide an accurate modification time for objects. This makes browser and proxy caches work much more efficiently by reducing the load on server and network resources.

service

```
protected void service(HttpServletRequest req, HttpServletResponse
resp)
throws ServletException, java.io.IOException
```

This performs an HTTP service. This service method is rarely overridden by servlet writers; `doGet()` and `doPost()` should be overridden instead.

service

```
protected void service(ServletRequest req, ServletResponse resp)
throws ServletException, java.io.IOException
```

This implements the `Servlet.service()` method by calling the HTTP-specific service method. This method is not normally overridden by the servlet writer.

javax.servlet.http
HttpServletRequest

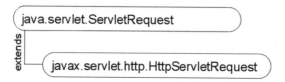

package javax.servlet.http;

public interface HttpServletRequest

    extends javax.servlet.ServletRequest

The `HttpServletRequest` interface represents an HTTP servlet request. Data from the client are provided to the servlet for use in the `do-Get()`, `doPost()`, `doPut()`, `doDelete()`, or `service()` method.

Summary

getAuthType()	Returns the authentication scheme of the request or null if none
getCookies()	Returns an array of cookies for the request
getDateHeader(String)	Returns the value of the given date header field or –1 if not found
getHeader(String)	Returns the value of the given header field or null if not found
getHeaderNames()	Returns an enumeration of header names for this request
getIntHeader(String)	Returns the integer value of the given header field or –1 if not found
getMethod()	Returns the method with which the request was made
getPathInfo()	Returns extra path information following the servlet path

getPathTranslated()	Returns extra path information translated to a physical path
getQueryString	Returns the query string part of the URI or null if none
getRemoteUser()	Returns the name of the user making this request or null if not known
getRequestedSessionId()	Gets the session ID specified for this request
getRequestURI()	Returns the request URI
getServletPath()	Returns the servlet being invoked
getSession(boolean)	Gets or creates the session associated with this request
isRequestedSessionIdFromCookie()	Returns true if the session ID for this request came from a cookie
isRequestedSessionIdFromUrl()	Returns true if the session ID for this request came as part of the URL
isRequestedSessionIdValid()	Returns true if the session ID for this request is valid in the current session context

Methods

getAuthType

```
public abstract String getAuthType()
```

This returns the HTTP authentication scheme of the request. It returns null if no authentication is present. This is analogous to the CGI AUTH_TYPE variable.

getCookies

```
public abstract Cookie[] getCookies()
```

This returns all the cookies found in this request as an array of cookie objects.

getDateHeader

```
public abstract long getDateHeader(String name)
```

This returns the value of the given date header field or –1 if the header field is not known. The header field given is not case sensitive.

getHeader

```
public abstract String getHeader(String name)
```

This returns the value of the given header field or null if the header field is not known. The header field given is not case sensitive.

getHeaderNames

```
public abstract java.util.Enumeration getHeaderNames()
```

This returns an enumeration of the header field names. It returns null if the header names cannot be accessed by the server.

getIntHeader

```
public abstract int getIntHeader(String name)
```

This returns the integer value of the given header field or –1 if the header field is not known. The header field given is not case sensitive.

getMethod

```
public abstract String getMethod()
```

This returns the method in which the client made the request. The returned value can be "GET," "HEAD," or "POST." This is analogous to the CGI REQUEST_METHOD variable.

getPathInfo

```
public abstract String getPathInfo()
```

This returns optional extra path information following the servlet path in the Uniform Resource Identifier (URI). It returns null if no path information is present. This is analogous to the CGI PATH_INFO variable.

getPathTranslated

```
public abstract String getPathTranslated()
```

This returns extra path information, which is translated into a physical path. It returns null if no extra path information is present. This is analogous to the CGI PATH_TRANSLATED variable.

getQueryString

```
public abstract String getQueryString()
```

This returns the query string part of the servlet URI (the information that follows the ?). It returns null if no query string is present. This is analogous to the CGI QUERY_STRING variable.

getRemoteUser

```
public abstract String getRemoteUser()
```

This returns the name of the user making the servlet request. It returns null if the user is not known. The format and whether the name will be sent with each HTTP request are browser dependent. This is analogous to the CGI REMOTE_USER variable.

getRequestedSessionId

```
public abstract String getRequestedSessionId()
```

This returns the session ID specified with this request.

getRequestURI

```
public abstract String getRequestURI()
```

This returns the URI of the request. One thing that sets a URI apart from a URL is that the URI spec allows for the possibility of encoding a forwarding address when a link moves.

getServletPath

```
public abstract String getServletPath()
```

This returns the part of the request URI that refers to the servlet being invoked. This is analogous to the CGI SCRIPT_NAME variable.

getSession

```
public abstract HttpSession getSession(boolean create)
```

This gets the current session associated with this request or, if create is true and a session does not exist, creates a new session for the request. To ensure that the session is properly maintained the servlet writer must call this method at least once before any output is written to the response.

isRequestedSessionIdFromCookie

```
public abstract boolean isRequestedSessionIdFromCookie()
```

This returns true if the session ID specified in this request was from a cookie.

isRequestedSessionIdFromUrl

```
public abstract boolean isRequestedSessionIdFromUrl()
```

This returns true if the session ID specified in this request originated as part of the URL.

isRequestedSessionIdValid

```
public abstract boolean isRequestedSessionIdValid()
```

This returns true if this request is associated with a session that is valid in the current context.

javax.servlet.http
HttpServletResponse

package javax.servlet.http;

public interface HttpServletResponse

    extends javax.servlet.ServletResponse

The `HttpServletResponse` interface represents an HTTP servlet response, allowing the servlet writer to return HTTP-specific header information and data back to the requesting client.

Variables

SC_ACCEPTED	Status code (202) indicating that a request was accepted for processing but was not completed
SC_BAD_GATEWAY	Status code (502) indicating that the HTTP server received an invalid response from a proxy or gateway server
SC_BAD_REQUEST	Status code (400) indicating that the request sent from the client was syntactically invalid
SC_CONFLICT	Status code (409) indicating that the request could not be completed due to a conflict with the current state of the resource
SC_CONTINUE	Status code (100) indicating that the client can continue
SC_CREATED	Status code (201) indicating that the request succeeded and created a new resource on the server

SC_FORBIDDEN	Status code (403) indicating that the server got the request but refused to service it
SC_GATEWAY_TIMEOUT	Status code (504) indicating that the server timed out while waiting for a response from a gateway or proxy server
SC_GONE	Status code (410) indicating that the resource requested is no longer available and no forwarding address is known
SC_HTTP_VERSION_NOT_SUPPORTED	Status code (505) indicating that the server does not support the HTTP version used in the request
SC_INTERNAL_SERVER_ERROR	Status code (500) indicating that an error occurred inside the HTTP service and the request cannot be serviced
SC_LENGTH_REQUIRED	Status code (411) indicating that the request requires a defined content length to be processed
SC_METHOD_NOT_ALLOWED	Status code (405) indicating that the method specified in the request line is not allowed
SC_MOVED_PERMANENTLY	Status code (301) indicating that the resource has been permanently moved to a new location and that future references should use a new Uniform Resource Identifier (URI)
SC_MOVED_TEMPORARILY	Status code (302) indicating that the resource has been temporarily moved to a new location but that future references should still use the original Uniform Resource Identifier (URI)
SC_MULTIPLE_CHOICES	Status code (300) indicating that the requested resource has multiple representations each with its own location
SC_NO_CONTENT	Status code (204) indicating that the request succeeded but there was no new information
SC_NON_AUTHORITATIVE_INFORMATION	Status code (203) indicating that the metainformation given by the client did not originate from the server
SC_NOT_ACCEPTABLE	Status code (406) indicating that the resource requested can only respond with content characteristics not acceptable to the request
SC_NOT_FOUND	Status code (404) indicating that the requested resource is not available

HttpServletResponse

SC_NOT_IMPLEMENTED	Status code (501) indicating that the HTTP service does not support the functionality necessary to service the request
SC_NOT_MODIFIED	Status code (304) indicating that a conditional GET operation determined that the requested resource was available but not modified
SC_OK	Status code (200) indicating that the request succeeded
SC_PARTIAL_CONTENT	Status code (206) indicating that the service fulfilled the partial GET request
SC_PAYMENT_REQUIRED	Status code (402) reserved for future use
SC_PRECONDITION_FAILED	Status code (412) indicating that the precondition given in one or more of the request header fields failed
SC_PROXY_AUTHENTICATION_REQUIRED	Status code (407) indicating that the client must authenticate itself
SC_REQUEST_ENTITY_TOO_LARGE	Status code (413) indicating that the request is too large and has been refused by the server
SC_REQUEST_TIMEOUT	Status code (408) indicating that the client took too long to produce a request to the server
SC_REQUEST_URI_TOO_LONG	Status code (414) indicating that the request URI is too large and has been refused by the server
SC_RESET_CONTENT	Status code (205) indicating that the client should reset the document view
SC_SEE_OTHER	Status code (303) indicating that the response can be found under a different URL
SC_SERVICE_UNAVAILABLE	Status code (503) indicating that the HTTP service is temporarily unavailable, perhaps due to being overloaded
SC_SWITCHING_PROTOCOLS	Status code (101) indicating that the server is switching protocols according to an upgrade header
SC_UNAUTHORIZED	Status code (401) indicating that the request requires HTTP authentication

SC_UNSUPPORTED_MEDIA_TYPE	Status code (415) indicating that the format of the request is being rejected by the server
SC_USE_PROXY	Status code (305) indicating that the requested resource must be accessed via a proxy

Summary

addCookie(Cookie)	Adds the given cookie to the response
containsHeader(String)	Returns true if the given field name is in the message header
encodeRedirectUrl(String)	Encodes the given URL for use in the sendRedirect method
encodeUrl(String)	Encodes the given URL by including the session ID
sendError(int)	Sends an error response with the given status code to the client
sendError(int, String)	Sends an error response with the given status code and message to the client
sendRedirect(String)	Sends a redirect response with the given URL to the client
setDateHeader(String, long)	Adds the given field to the response header with a date value
setHeader(String, String)	Adds the given field to the response header with a string value
setIntHeader(String, int)	Adds the given field to the response header with an int value
setStatus(int)	Sets the status code for the response
setStatus(int, String)	Sets the status code and message for the response

HttpServletResponse

Methods

addCookie

```
public abstract void addCookie(Cookie cookie)
```

This adds the given cookie to the response.

containsHeader

```
public abstract boolean containsHeader(String name)
```

This returns true if the given field is present in the response message header.

encodeRedirectUrl

```
public abstract encodeRedirectUrl(String url)
```

This encodes the given URL for use in the `sendRedirect` method.

encodeUrl

```
public abstract encodeUrl(String url)
```

This encodes the given URL by including the session ID if necessary. All URLs returned by a servlet should be encoded with this method.

sendError

```
public abstract void sendError(int code) throws java.io.IOException
```

This sends an error response to the client with the given status code. A default error message will be used.

sendError

```
public abstract void sendError(int code, String message) throws
java.io.IOException
```

This sends an error response to the client with the given status code and error message.

sendRedirect

```
public abstract void sendRedirect(String url) throws
java.io.IOException
```

This sends a redirect response to the client with the given URL. The URL must be absolute (i.e., http://larryboy/path/file.html).

setDateHeader

```
public abstract void setDateHeader(String name, long value)
```

This adds the given field to the response header with a date value. If the field value has already been set, it will be overwritten with the new value.

setHeader

```
public abstract void setHeader(String name, String value)
```

This adds the given field to the response header with a string value. If the field value has already been set, it will be overwritten with the new value.

setIntHeader

```
public abstract void setIntHeader(String name, int value)
```

This adds the given field to the response header with an integer value. If the field value has already been set, it will be overwritten with the new value.

setStatus

```
public abstract void setStatus(int code)
```

This sets the status code for the response. A default message will be used.

setStatus

```
public abstract void setStatus(int code, String message)
```

This sets the status code and message for the response.

java.servlet.http.HttpSession

package javax.servlet.http;

public interface HttpSession

The HttpSession interface is implemented by services to provide an association (or session) between an HTTP client (browser) and an HTTP server. This session will persist over multiple connections and/or requests during a given time period. Sessions are used to maintain state and user identity.

HttpSession defines methods that store data in the following ways.

■ Standard session properties, such as a session ID, and the context for the session.

■ Application layer data that are stored using a dictionary-like interface

Summary

getCreationTime()	Returns the time that this session was created
getId()	Returns the session ID
getLastAccessedTime()	Returns the last time that a client sent a request for this session
getSessionContext()	Returns the session context
getValue(String)	Returns the object bound to the given name in the session's application layer data
getValueNames()	Returns an array of the application layer data names

invalidate()	Invalidates the session and removes it from the session context
isNew()	Returns true if the context has been created by the server but not yet joined by a client
putValue(String, Object)	Binds the given data with the given name in the application layer data
removeValue(String)	Removes the data bound to the given name in the application layer data

Methods

getCreationTime

```
public abstract long getCreationTime()
```

This returns the creation time of this session in milliseconds.

getId

```
public abstract String getId()
```

This returns the session identifier assigned to this session. The identifier is a unique string that is created and maintained by HttpSessionContext.

getLastAccessedTime

```
public abstract long getLastAccessedTime()
```

This returns the last time a client sent a request using the identifier for this session in milliseconds. Application-level operations, such as setting or getting values, do not affect the access time.

getSessionContext

```
public abstract HttpSessionContext getSessionContext()
```

This returns the session context in which this session is bound.

getValue

```
public abstract Object getValue(String name)
```

This returns the object value of the given name in the session's application layer data or null if the name is not found.

getValueNames

```
public abstract String[] getValueNames()
```

This returns an array of string containing the names of all the application layer data objects for the session.

invalidate

```
public abstract void invalidate()
```

This invalidates this session and removes it from the context.

isNew

```
public abstract boolean isNew()
```

This returns true if this session is new. A session is considered to be new if it has been created by the server but not yet joined by a client.

putValue

```
public abstract void putValue(String name, Object value)
```

This binds the given object value into the session's application layer data with the given name. If a value already exists for the given name, it is replaced. Any values that implement the `HttpSessionBindingListener` interface will call its `valueBound()` method.

removeValue

```
public abstract void removeValue(String name)
```

This removes the object value bound to the given name in the session's application layer data. If the name does not exist, this method has no effect. If the value implements the `HttpSessionBindingListener` interface, the `valueUnbound()` method will be called.

javax.servlet.http
HttpSessionBindingEvent

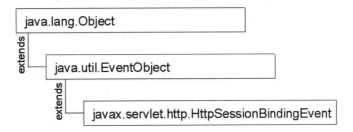

package javax.servlet.http;

public class HttpSessionBindingEvent

    extends Object

    implements java.util.EventObject

This event is provided to an `HttpSessionBindingListener` whenever the listener is bound to (`HttpSession.putValue`) or unbound from (`HttpSession.removeValue`) an `HttpSession` value.

Summary

`getName()`	Returns the name to which the object is being bound or unbound
`getSession()`	Returns the session into which the object is being bound or unbound

HttpSessionBindingEvent

Constructors

HttpSessionBindingEvent

```
public HttpSessionBindingEvent(HttpSession session, String name)
```

This creates a new HttpSessionBindingEvent object with the given session and object name.

Methods

getName

```
public String getName()
```

This returns the name of the object being bound or unbound.

getSession

```
public HttpSession getSession()
```

This returns the session of the object being bound or unbound.

package javax.servlet.http;

public interface HttpSessionBindingListener

    extends java.util.EventListener

Objects implement the HttpSessionBindingListener interface to be notified when they are bound to (HttpSession putValue) or unbound from (HttpSession.removeValue) an HttpSession.

Summary

valueBound(HttpSessionBindingEvent)	Notifies the listener that it is being bound into a session
valueUnbound(HttpSessionBindingEvent)	Notifies the listener that it is being unbound from a session

HttpSessionBindingListener

Methods

valueBound

```
public abstract void valueBound(HttpSessionBindingEvent event)
```

This notifies the listener that it is being bound to a session.

valueUnbound

```
public abstract void valueUnbound(HttpSessionBindingEvent event)
```

This notifies the listener that is it being unbound from a session.

javax.servlet.http
HttpSessionContext

java.servlet.http.HttpSessionContext

package javax.servlet.http;

public interface HttpSessionContext

The `HttpSessionContext` interface provides methods for listing session IDs and the `HttpSession` based on an ID. A context is a grouping of `HttpSessions`.

Summary

`getIds()`	Returns an enumeration of all the session IDs for this context
`getSession(String)`	Returns the session bound to the given session ID

Methods

getIds

```
public abstract java.util.Enumeration getIds()
```

This returns an enumeration of all the session IDs in this context.

getSession

```
public abstract HttpSession getSession(String id)
```

This returns the session bound to the given session ID or null if the ID does not refer to a valid session.

javax.servlet.http

HttpUtils

```
java.lang.Object
    extends
        javax.servlet.http.HttpUtils
```

package javax.servlet.http;

public class HttpUtils

    extends Object

The `HttpUtils` class contains a collection of static methods that are useful for HTTP servlet writers.

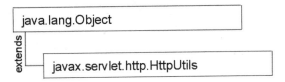

Summary

`getRequestURL(HttpServletRequest)`	Returns a `StringBuffer` containing the URL of the client
`parsePostData(int, ServletInputStream)`	Parses FORM data posted to the HTTP server
`parseQueryString(String)`	Parses a query string and returns a hash table of keys and values

HttpUtils

Constructors

HttpUtils

```
protected HttpUtils()
```

This is the default constructor for the HttpUtils class. The constructor does no work. Note that it is not necessary to instantiate HttpUtils, since all the methods are static.

Methods

getRequestURL

```
public static StringBuffer getRequestURL(HttpServletRequest req)
```

This reconstructs the URL used by the client to make the servlet request. Differences such as addressing schemes (HTTP, HTTPS) and default ports are accounted for, but no attempt is made to include query parameters. This method is useful for creating redirect messages and reporting errors.

parsePostData

```
public static java.util.Hashtable parsePostData(int length,
ServletInputStream in)
```

This parses form data; these data are posted to the HTTP server using the POST method and return a hash table containing key/value pairs. If a key appears multiple times, the values are stored as an array of strings.

parseQueryString

```
public static java.util.Hashtable parseQueryString(String query)
throws IllegalArgumentException
```

This parses the given query string and returns a hash table containing key/value pairs. The query string should be in the format "key=value&key=value"; the keys and values should be separated by an equal sign (=), and each key/value pair should be separated by an ampersand (&). Keys can appear in the query string multiple times; if so, the values are stored as an array of strings.

javax.servlet
Servlet

(javax.servlet.Servlet)

package javax.servlet;

public interface Servlet

The servlet interface is provided for servlet writers to develop servlets. All servlets implement this interface, either by subclassing Generic-Servlet or HttpServlet.

Summary

destroy()	Called when the servlet is destroyed
getServletConfig()	Returns a ServletConfig object, which contains initialization parameters and startup configuration for the servlet
getServletInfo()	Returns a string containing information about the servlet
init(ServletConfig)	Called when the servlet is first instantiated
service(ServletRequest, ServletResponse)	Fulfills a single request from a client

Methods

destroy

```
public abstract void destroy()
```

This is called once when the servlet is destroyed by the server. This gives the servlet writer an opportunity to clean up any allocated resources, such as a database connection.

getServletConfig

```
public abstract ServletConfig getServletConfig()
```

This returns the `ServletConfig` object used to initialize the servlet. The `ServletConfig` object contains initialization parameters and start configuration options.

getServletInfo

```
public abstract String getServletInfo()
```

This returns a string containing optional information about the servlet. This can include the author, version, and copyright statement.

init

```
public abstract void init(ServletConfig config) throws
ServletException
```

This is called once when the servlet is instantiated. This gives the servlet writer an opportunity to perform initialization tasks, such as establishing a database connection. The `init()` method is guaranteed to complete before any service requests are accepted by the servlet. If a fatal initialization error occurs, an `UnavailableException` should be thrown.

service

```
public abstract void service(ServletRequest req, ServletResponse
resp)
throws ServletException, java.io.IOException
```

This carries out a single request from a client. The `ServletRequest` object contains information about the service request, including parameters provided by the client. The `ServletResponse` object is used to return information to the client. Note that servlets usually run inside multithreaded servers that can handle multiple service requests simultaneously; it is the servlet writer's responsibility to synchronize access to all shared resources (such as database connections and instance variables).

javax.servlet

ServletConfig

> javax.servlet.ServletConfig

package javax.servlet;

public interface ServletConfig

The `ServletConfig` interface is implemented in order to pass configuration information to a servlet when it is first instantiated.

Summary

`getInitParameter(String)`	Returns a string containing the value of the given initialization parameter name or null if the parameter does not exist
`getInitParameterNames()`	Returns an enumeration of the initialization parameter names
`getServletContext()`	Returns the context for the servlet

Methods

getInitParameter

```
public abstract String getInitParameter(String name)
```

This returns a string containing the value of the given initialization parameter name or null if the parameter does not exist. Initialization parameters can only have a single string value and must be interpreted by the servlet writer.

getInitParameterNames

```
public abstract java.util.Enumeration getInitParameterNames()
```

This returns an enumeration of the initialization parameter names or an empty enumeration if there are no initialization parameters.

getServletContext

```
public abstract ServletContext getServletContext()
```

This returns the context for the servlet that provides information about the environment in which the servlet is running.

javax.servlet.ServletContext

package javax.servlet;

public interface ServletContext

The ServletContext interface provides servlets access to information about their environment and also provides a logging mechanism. This interface is implemented by individual services (such as HTTP).

Summary

getAttribute(String)	Returns the value of the given attribute name or null if the attribute does not exist
getMimeType(String)	Returns the mime type of the given file or null if not known
getRealPath(String)	Converts the given virtual path into a physical path
getServerInfo()	Returns the name and version of the current network service
getServlet(String)	Returns a servlet of the specified name or null if not found
getServletNames()	Returns an enumeration of servlet object names in this service
getServlets()	Returns an enumeration of the servlet objects in this service (deprecated)

ServletContext

log(Exception, String)	Writes the stacktrace and the given message to the servlet log file
log(String)	Writes the given message to the servlet log file

Methods

getAttribute

```
public abstract Object getAttribute(String name)
```

This returns the value of the given attribute or null if the attribute does not exist. This method provides access to additional information about the service. Attribute names should follow the same convention as package names.

getMimeType

```
public abstract String getMimeType(String file)
```

This returns the mime type of the given file or null if not known.

getRealPath

```
public abstract String getRealPath(String path)
```

This transforms the given virtual path, applying alias rules, and returns the corresponding physical path.

getServerInfo

```
public abstract String getServerInfo()
```

This returns information about the server in which the servlet is being invoked, such as name and version. For an HTTP service, this would be analogous to the CGI SERVER_SOFTWARE variable.

getServlet

```
public abstract Servlet getServlet(String name) throws
SerlvetException
```

This returns a servlet of the given name or null if not found. If a servlet is returned, it has already been initialized and is ready to receive requests.

getServletNames

```
public abstract java.util.Enumeration getServletNames()
```

This returns an enumeration of the servlet names in this server. Only servlets within the same namespace will be returned. The enumeration always includes the calling servlet.

getServlets

```
public abstract java.util.Enumeration getServlets()
*DEPRECATED* (Use getServletNames() with getServlet() instead)
```

This returns an enumeration of the servlet objects in this server. Only servlets that are accessible will be returned. The enumeration will contain the current servlet as well.

log

```
public abstract void log(Exception e, String message)
```

This writes the stacktrace from the given exception and the given message to the servlet log file. The name of the servlet log file is determined by the server; it is usually an event log.

log

```
public abstract void log(String message)
```

This writes the given message to the servlet log file. The name of the servlet log file is determined by the server; it is usually an event log.

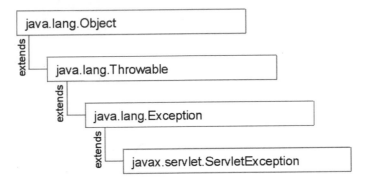

package javax.servlet;

public class ServletException

 extends java.lang.Exception

A `ServletException` is thrown to indicate a servlet error.

Constructors

ServletException

```
public ServletException()
```

This constructs a new `ServletException` object.

ServletException

```
public ServletException(String message)
```

This constructs a new `ServletException` object with the given error message.

javax.servlet
ServletInputStream

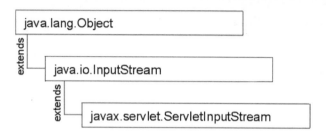

package javax.servlet;

public abstract class ServletInputStream

    extends java.io.InputStream

The `ServletInputStream` serves as an input stream for reading servlet requests and provides an efficient `readLine()` method. The `Servlet-InputStream` is retrieved from the `ServletRequest getInput-Stream()` method.

Summary

`readLine(byte[], int, int)`	Starting at the given offset, reads into the given byte array until all requested bytes have been read or a "\n" is found

Constructors

ServletInputStream

```
protected ServletInputStream()
```

This constructs a new `ServletInputStream` object. The constructor does no work.

Methods

readLine

```
public int readLine(byte b[], int offset, int length) throws
java.io.IOException
```

This reads the given length of bytes into the given byte array starting at the given offset. Bytes are read until all requested bytes have been read or a "\n" is found, in which case the "\n" is read into the byte array also. It returns the actual number of bytes read or –1 if the end of the input stream is reached.

ServletOutputStream

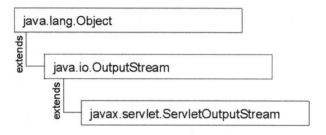

package javax.servlet;

public abstract class ServletOutputStream

    extends java.io.OutputStream

The ServletOutputStream serves as an output stream for writing servlet responses to the client. The ServletOutputStream is retrieved from the ServletResponse getOutputStream() method.

Summary

print(boolean)	Prints a Boolean value
print(char)	Prints a char value
print(double)	Prints a double value
print(float)	Prints a float value
print(int)	Prints an int value
print(long)	Prints a long value
print(String)	Prints a string value
println()	Prints a CR/LF
println(boolean)	Prints a Boolean value followed by a CR/LF

`println(char)`	Prints a char value followed by a CR/LF
`println(double)`	Prints a double value followed by a CR/LF
`println(float)`	Prints a float value followed by a CR/LF
`println(int)`	Prints an int value followed by a CR/LF
`println(long)`	Prints a long value followed by a CR/LF
`println(String)`	Prints a string value followed by a CR/LF

Constructors

ServletOutputStream

```
protected ServletOutputStream()
```

This constructs a new `ServletOutputStream` object. The constructor does no work.

Methods

print

```
public void print(boolean b) throws java.io.IOException
```

This prints the Boolean value given to the output stream.

print

```
public void print(char c) throws java.io.IOException
```

This prints the character value given to the output stream.

ServletOutputStream

print

```
public void print(double d) throws java.io.IOException
```

This prints the double value given to the output stream.

print

```
public void print(float f) throws java.io.IOException
```

This prints the float value given to the output stream.

print

```
public void print(int i) throws java.io.IOException
```

This prints the integer value given to the output stream.

print

```
public void print(long l) throws java.io.IOException
```

This prints the long value given to the output stream.

print

```
public void print(String s) throws java.io.IOException
```

This prints the string value given to the output stream.

println

```
public void println() throws java.io.IOException
```

This prints a CR/LF (carriage return and line feed) to the output stream.

println

```
public void println(boolean b) throws java.io.IOException
```

This prints the Boolean value given to the output stream, followed by a CR/LF.

println

```
public void println(char c) throws java.io.IOException
```

This prints the character value given to the output stream, followed by a CR/LF.

println

```
public void println(double d) throws java.io.IOException
```

This prints the double value given to the output stream, followed by a CR/LF.

println

```
public void println(float f) throws java.io.IOException
```

This prints the float value given to the output stream, followed by a CR/LF.

ServletOutputStream

println

```
public void println(int i) throws java.io.IOException
```

This prints the integer value given to the output stream, followed by a CR/LF.

println

```
public void println(long l) throws java.io.IOException
```

This prints the long value given to the output stream, followed by a CR/LF.

println

```
public void println(String s) throws java.io.IOException
```

This prints the string value given to the output stream, followed by a CR/LF.

javax.servlet
ServletRequest

java.servlet.ServletRequest

package javax.servlet;

public interface ServletRequest

The `ServletRequest` interface provides methods to get data from the client to the servlet for an individual service request. This interface will be implemented for a given protocol, such as HTTP (see `HttpServletRequest`).

Summary

`getAttribute(String)`	Returns the value of the given attribute field or null if the attribute does not exist
`getContentLength()`	Returns the size of the data buffer sent by the client or –1 if not known
`getContentType()`	Returns the content type of the data or null if not known
`getInputStream()`	Returns an input stream for reading the client's data buffer
`getParameter(String)`	Returns the value of the given parameter or null if the parameter does not exist (deprecated)
`getParameterNames()`	Returns an enumeration containing the names of the servlet's parameters
`getParameterValues(String)`	Returns the values of the given parameter as an array of strings or null if the parameter does not exist

`getProtocol()`	Returns the protocol and version of the request
`getReader()`	Returns a buffered reader for reading text in the request body
`getRealPath(String)`	Converts the given virtual path into a physical path
`getRemoteAddr()`	Returns the IP address of the client that sent the request
`getRemoteHost()`	Returns the host name of the client that sent the request
`getScheme()`	Returns the scheme of the URL used for the request
`getServerName()`	Returns the host name of the server that received the request
`getServerPort()`	Returns the port number on which the request was received

Methods

getAttribute

```
public abstract Object getAttribute(String name)
```

This returns the value of the given named attribute or null if the attribute does not exist. Attribute names should follow the same naming convention as package names.

getContentLength

```
public abstract int getContentLength()
```

This returns the length of the data buffer sent by the client or –1 if not known. This is analogous to the CGI CONTENT_LENGTH variable.

getContentType

```
public abstract String getContentType()
```

This returns the Internet media type of the data buffer sent by the client or null if not known. This is analogous to the CGI CONTENT_TYPE variable.

getInputStream

```
public abstract ServletInputStream getInputStream() throws
java.io.IOException
```

This returns an input stream for reading the client's request body.

getParameter

```
public abstract String getParameter(String name)
*DEPRECATED* (Use getParameterValues())
```

This returns a string containing the single value of the given parameter or null if the parameter does not exist.

getParameterNames

```
public abstract java.util.Enumeration getParameterNames()
```

This returns an enumeration of the parameter names for this request. It returns an empty enumeration if there are no parameters, or the input stream is empty.

getParameterValues

```
public abstract String[] getParameterValues(String name)
```

This returns a string array containing the values of the given parameter or null if the parameter does not exist.

getProtocol

```
public abstract String getProtocol()
```

This returns the protocol and version of the client request as a string. The format is <protocol name>/<version>. This is analogous to the CGI SERVER_PROTOCOL variable.

getReader()

```
public abstract java.io.BufferedReader getReader() throws
java.io.IOException
```

This returns a buffered reader for reading text from the request body.

getRealPath

```
public abstract String getRealPath(String path)
```

This transforms the given virtual path, applying alias rules, and returns the corresponding physical path.

getRemoteAddr

```
public abstract String getRemoteAddr()
```

This returns the IP address of the client that sent the request as a string. This is analogous to the CGI REMOTE_ADDR variable.

getRemoteHost

```
public abstract String getRemoteHost()
```

This returns the host name of the client that sent the request. If the host name cannot be determined, the IP address of the client will be returned. This is analogous to the CGI REMOTE_HOST variable.

getScheme

```
public abstract String getScheme()
```

This returns the scheme of the URL used for this request as a string—for example "HTTP," "HTTPS," or "FTP."

getServerName

```
public abstract String getServerName()
```

This returns the host name of the server that received the servlet request. If the host name cannot be determined, the IP address will be returned. This is analogous to the CGI SERVER_NAME variable.

getServerPort

```
public abstract int getServerPort()
```

This returns the port number on which the servlet request was received. This is analogous to the CGI SERVER_PORT variable.

javax.servlet
ServletResponse

java.servlet.ServletResponse

package javax.servlet;

public interface ServletResponse

The ServletResponse interface is provided so that mime data can be sent back to the client. The actual implementation will be protocol specific (see HttpServletResponse).

Summary

getCharacterEncoding()	Returns the character encoding mime type for the response body
getOutputStream()	Returns an output stream for writing response data
getWriter()	Returns a print writer for writing formatted text responses
setContentLength(int)	Sets the length of the data being returned by the response
setContentType(String)	Sets the content type for the response

Methods

getCharacterEncoding

```
public abstract String getCharacterEncoding()
```

This returns a string describing the character set encoding used for the mime request body. If no content type has been set, the character encoding is implicitly set to text/plain.

getOutputStream

```
public abstract ServletOutputStream getOutputStream() throws
java.io.IOException
```

This returns an output stream for writing response data back to the client.

getWriter

```
public abstract PrintWriter getWriter() throws java.io.IOException
```

This returns a print writer for writing formatted text responses back to the client. The content type must be set prior to calling getWriter().

setContentLength

```
public abstract void setContentLength(int length)
```

This sets the length of the content data for the response.

setContentType

```
public abstract void setContentType(String type)
```

This sets the content mime type of the response—for example, "content-type: text/plain."

java.servlet.SingleThreadModel

package javax.servlet;

public interface SingleThreadModel

Servlets that implement the empty `SingleThreadModel` interface define themselves as being single threaded. This guarantees that no two threads will execute the service method concurrently. The server guarantees this by maintaining a pool of servlet instances for each `SingleThreadModel` servlet and dispatching each service call to a free servlet.

If a servlet implements this interface it is, in essence, thread safe.

javax.servlet
UnavailableException

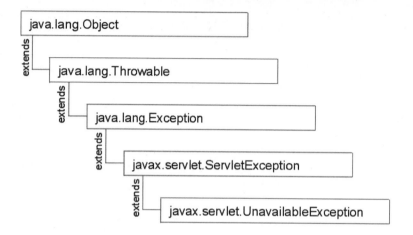

package javax.servlet;

public class UnavailableException

    extends ServletException

The UnavailableException is thrown to indicate that a given servlet is unavailable. Servlets can throw this exception at any time. There are two types of unavailability.

1. Permanent—The servlet will not accept client requests until some administrative action is taken.

2. Temporary—The servlet will not accept client requests at the given time, due to some type of systemwide problem such as insufficient memory or disk space.

Summary

getServlet()	Returns the servlet that is being reported as unavailable
getUnavailableSeconds()	Returns the amount of time the servlet estimates to be temporarily unavailable
isPermanent()	Returns true if the servlet is permanently unavailable

Constructors

UnavailableException

```
public UnavailableException(Servlet servlet, String message)
```

This constructs a new UnavailableException object with the given servlet and error message. The servlet will be reported as permanently unavailable.

UnavailableException

```
public UnavailableException(int seconds, Servlet servlet, String message)
```

This constructs a new UnavailableException object with the given servlet, error message, and the estimated number of seconds that the servlet will be temporarily unavailable. If no estimate can be made, use –1.

UnavailableException

Methods

getServlet

```
public Servlet getServlet()
```

This returns the servlet that is being reported as unavailable.

getUnavailableSeconds

```
public int getUnavailableSeconds()
```

This returns either the number of seconds the servlet has estimated to be temporarily unavailable or a negative number if not known. Note that the time will not be updated to report an elapsed time until the servlet is available.

isPermanent

```
public boolean isPermanent()
```

This returns true if the servlet is permanently unavailable.

INDEX

A

Access Control List (ACL), 23, 24–26, 27
Access control lists setup, 24–26
    Access Control List (ACL), 24–26
    principal/permissions, 24–26
    realm, 24
Access flags, class file structure, 278
Access log, 20
ACTION attribute, form tag, 86–87
Add-ons, products supporting servlets, 5
Administration. *See* Web service
    administration
Admin servlet, 29
Agent log, 20
Aliasing
    adding alias, 59
    alias pathname, 18
    file alias setup, 18
    servlet aliasing, 48–49
    servlet alias setup, 18–19
    servlet chaining by, 58–62
Apache JServ, 5
Applets
    creating for driver, 336–345
    distribution of, 291–294
    packaging of, 272
        writing, example of, 204–206
Arguments, servlets control, 28
Attribute count, class file structure, 280
Attribute table, class file structure, 280
Automating programming
    Reflection API, 235–242
    RemoteIndy example, 263–269
    RemoteMathLite example, 258–262
    template for, 242–244
    writing base code generator, 244–250
    writing the client and server, 234–235
    writing code generator, 250–257
    writing ServletGen, 242–259

B

Base code generator, automating
    programming, 244–250
Bootstrapping server, 357–358
Browsers, 10
    Java-enabled, 5
BuildUser Application, 165–170
Button input type, 90
Byte array, 156

C

Cache, bypass by browser, 174, 176
Callable statements, 124
    driver development, 335
Chaining, 54–68
    alias chaining example, 60–62
    by aliasing, 58–62
    with HTTP requests, 66–68
    and JRun, 59–60, 63
    mime chaining example, 63–66
    servlet associated with mime type, 63–65
    table filter example, 54–58
Character set tab, 14
Check box input type, 91

Classes in Java servlets
    Cookie, 364–369
    GenericServlet, 370–374
    HttpServlet, 375–379
    HttpServletRequest, 380–385
    HttpServletResponse, 386–392
    HttpSession, 393–396
    HttpSessionBindingEvent, 397–398
    HttpSessionBindingListener, 399–400
    HttpSessionContext, 401–402
    HttpUtils, 403–405
    ServletConfig, 409–410
    ServletContext, 411–414
    ServletException, 415
    ServletInputStream, 416–417
    servlet interface, 406–408
    ServletOutputStream, 418–422
    ServletRequest, 423–427
    ServletResponse, 428–430
    SingleThreadModel, 431
    UnavailableException, 432–434
Class file
    characteristics of, 272
    header, processing of, 285–286
    URL, servlets control, 28
Class file structure, 272–280
    access flags, 278
    attribute count, 280
    attribute table, 280
    constant pool, 273–278
    constant pool count, 273
    field count, 280
    field table, 280
    interface count, 279
    interface table, 280
    magic, 272
    method count, 280
    method table, 280

    minor and major version items, 272
    superclass, 279
    this class, 279
Class name, servlets control, 38
CLASSPATH, 39, 46, 170, 282
Code generator
    automating programming, 250–257
    base code generator, 244–250
    tags as directives, 243, 245
    tags processing, 249–250
Common Gateway Interface (CGI)
    CGI script directory, 14
    CGI servlet, 29
    scripts, servlet replacement for, 29
    scripts compared to servlets, 3
Common Object Request Broker
        Architecture (COBRA), 348
Connection interface, driver development,
        309–315
Connection pooling, 140–153
    benefits of, 140
    closing connection, 146
    configuration file, 141
    ConnectionObjects, 144
    ConnectionPool object, writing of,
        141–146
    finding connection, 144–146
    global pool example, 149–153
    initial pool sourcecode, 142–144
    local pool example, 147–149
    Servlet Connection, 170
Constant pool
    class file structure, 273–278
    class/interface names from, 288
    constant pool count, class file structure,
        273
    processing of, 286–287
    tag values, 273–278

Cookie class, 364–369
Cybotics Search Engine, 5

D

DatabaseMetaData, 162
   interface in driver development, 315–320
Database table
   adding user to, 174–176
   build routine, steps in, 168
   BuildUser Application, 165–170
   create routine, 168–169
   creation of, 163–170
   data types, 164–165
   SQL statement, 166–170
Data compression, driver development, 336
Data Definition Language (DDL), 163–164
Data encryption, driver development, 336
Data Manipulation Language (DML), 163
Data packet, steps in sending to server,
   190–193
Declared fields, getting list of, 241
Declared methods, getting list of, 242
Dependencies
   algorithm for finding class references,
    281
   and class file structure, 272–280
   class names, 287–289
   CreateArchive example, 289–291
   opening/reading class file, 281–284
   pitfalls related to dependency checker,
    294
   processing constant pool, 285–287
Description
   log file setup, 21
   servlets control, 27
Directory access, 15

Distribution archive, 342–343
Document root, 19
Domino Go Webserver, 5
Driver development
   applet, writing for, 336–345
   callable statements, 335
   client-side connection proxy, 311–312
   connection interface, 309–315
   and connection URL, 304, 305, 307
   DatabaseMetaData interface, 315–320
   data compression, 336
   data encryption, 336
   distribution archive, 342–343
   driver interface, 302, 304–309
   driver proxy, 305–308
   and Java Remote Method Invocation
    (RMI), 336
   lightweight driver, meaning of, 299
   limitations related to, 301
   making database connection, 345–346
   prepared statement interface, 335
   preregistering driver, 302–304
   properties of driver, 299–300
   result set interface, 324–331
   ResultSetMetaData interface, 331–335
   server configuration, 342
   server-side connection, 305–306, 313–314
   statement interface, 320–324
Dynamo Application Server, 5

E

Echo, servlet tag example, 72–75
ENCTYPE attribute, 87–88
Error log, 20
Event log, 20
Extension, mime type setup, 20

F

Field count, class file structure, 280
Field table, class file structure, 280
File alias setup, 18
    alias pathname, 18
    full pathname, 18
File input type, 91–93
File servlet, 29
Footer servlet, server-side includes
            example, 76–80
Form tag, 85–89
    ACTION attribute, 86–87
    ENCTYPE attribute, 87–88
    METHOD attribute, 88
    passing additional parameters, 88–89
    purpose of, 85
    structure of, 85

G

GenericServlet, 370–374
GET method, 88
Group name, 24
Group setup, 24
    group name, 24
    members, 24
    nonmembers, 24
    security realm, 24

H

Handler threads, 8
Header servlet, server-side includes
            example, 76–80
Hidden input type, 94

I

Host, DNS name, 19
HTML, invoking servlet with, 40, 41
HTML forms
    filling out form, 84
    form tag, 85–89
    input tag, 89–101
    compared to Java applets, 84
    placement on page, 85
    select tag, 101–103
    submitting form, 84–85
    textarea tag, 103–104
        user survey form example, 104–111
HTML refresh, Servlet Connection,
            174–176
HTTP
    basic flow of, 183–184
    servlet chaining, 66–68
    steps in servicing request, 182
    Web service, and invoking servlet, 35
    See also Tunneling
HttpServlet, 375–379
HttpServletRequest, 380–385
HttpServletResponse, 386–392
HttpSession, 393–396
HttpSessionBindingEvent, 397–398
HttpSessionBindingListener, 399–400
HttpSessionContext, 401–402
HttpUtils, 403–405
HyperText Transfer Protocol. *See* entries
            under HTTP

Image input type, 94–96
Imagemap servlet, 29
Images, 153–158
    adding to servlet, 156–157
    ImageServer servlet example, 153–156

Implemented interfaces, getting list of, 240
Input tag, 89–101
    button input type, 90
    check box input type, 91
    file input type, 91–93
    hidden input type, 94
    image input type, 94–96
    password input type, 96–97
    purpose of, 89
    radio button type, 97–98
    reset input type, 98–99
    structure of, 89
    submit button input type, 99–100
    text input type, 100–101
Interface, driver development, 302, 304–309
Interface count, class file structure, 279
Interface table, class file structure, 280
Internal servlets, 9, 28–30
    admin servlet, 29
    CGI servlet, 29
    file servlet, 29
    imagemap servlet, 29
    invoker servlet, 29
    server-side include servlet, 29–30
Internet Connection Server, 5
INTERSOLV, 117
Invoker servlet, 29
iTP WebServer, 5

J

JAR file, 272, 282
    creating new file, 288
    writing to file, 289
Java, and servlets, 3, 4

Java Database Connectivity (JDBC)
    basic flow of, 123
    bridge to Open Database Connectivity
      (ODBC), 115–118, 125–126
    connecting to database, 123–124
    connection pooling, 140–153
    development of, 114–115
    disconnecting from database, 125
    DriverManager, 123–124
    driver registration, 124
    driver types. *See* JDBC drivers
    EmployeeList servlet example, 130–139
    interoperability of, 115
    metadata, 161–163
    processing results, 125
    several pages for output, 135
    SimpleQuery example, 125–129
    and SQL, 116
    SQL statement execution, 124
Java Developer's Kit, 115
Java Remote Invocation Interface (RMI)
    activation of, 359–361
    bootstrapping server, 357–358
    client, writing with remote object,
      355–357
    execution of server, 358
    purpose of, 348–349
    remote interface definition, 350–351
    server implementation, 351–354
    servlet converted to, 361
    skeleton, 354–355
    stubs, 354–355
Java Remote Method Invocation (RMI), 336
JavaServer architecture, 8–10, 34–35
    server framework, 8–9
    server-side includes, 70–81
    service framework, 8
    servlet framework, 9–10

Java Servlets Development Kit (JSDK), 4
Java Web server, 9
  accessing server, 30
  administration of. *See* Web service
      administration
  configuring server, 39
  extensions, JRun, 44–51
  function of, 8
  management of service, 11
  port number, 30
  proxy Web service, 11
  secure Web service, 11
  services of, 11
  servlet loading, 2, 3
    starting and stopping services, 11–12
JDBC drivers
  creating driver. *See* Driver development
  Java to native API driver (Type 2),
      119–120, 298
  Java to native database protocol (Type 4),
      121–122, 298
  Java to proprietary network protocol
      driver (Type 3), 120–121, 298–300
  JDBC-ODBC bridge (Type 1), 118–119,
      298
Jigsaw HTTP Server, 5
JRun, 5, 44–51
  administration, 45–50
  and chaining, 59–60, 63
  functions of, 44–45
  Java settings, customizing, 50
  mime filters, 47
  multihoming, 49
  server/platform availability, 45
  servlet aliasing, 48–49
  servlet mappings, 46–47

K

Keep alive, 17
KonaSoft Enterprise Server, 5

L

Languages tab, 14
Live Software
  free software from, 44, 51
  Web site, 44, 45
Load now, servlets control, 28
Load remotely, servlets control, 28
Load at startup, servlets control, 28
Log file setup, 20–21
  access log, 20
  agent log, 20
  description, 21
  error log, 20
  event log, 20
  log name, 20
  log to, 21
  referrer log, 20
  which messages, 21
Log name, 20
Log to, 21

M

Magic, class file structure, 272
Manage Server and Services page, 10–12
  services on, 11
Mapping, servlet mappings, 46–47

Marshalling, 184–189
  example of, 185–190
  function of, 184–185
  serialization, 207–227
Members, 24
Memory cache, value for, 16
Metadata, 161–163
  DatabaseMetaData, 162
  ResultSetMetaData, 163
METHOD attribute, 88
  GET method, 88
  POST method, 88
Method count, class file structure, 280
Method table, class file structure, 280
Mime filters, JRun, 47
Mime type setup, 20
  extension, 20
  type/subtype, 20
Monitor control, 21–22
  resource usage screen, 22
Multihoming, JRun, 49
MULTIPLE attribute, select tag, 102

N

NAME attribute, select tag, 102
NetForge Web Server, 5
Network setup, 13
  port, 13
    provide service on, 13
Nonmembers, 24

O

ObjectInputStream, 208–213
ObjectOutputStream, 208–213
Object Request Broker (ORB), 349
ObjectStreamEcho, servlet, 212–213
Open Database Connectivity (ODBC), 114
  bridge to Java Database Connectivity
    (JDBC), 115–118, 125–126
  JDBC-ODBC bridge driver, 118–119
Options tab, 14–15

P

Password input type, 96–97
Pathname
  alias, 18
  full pathname, 18
Permissions, 24–26
  file and folder permissions, 26
  listing of, 26
  servlet permissions, 26
Ports
  defining for Web service, 13
  Java Web server installed on, 30
  port 6060, Web proxy installed on, 11
  port 7070, SHTTP installed on, 11
  port 8080, HTTP protocol installed on,
    11, 13
POST method, 88
Prefix mappings, 46–47
Prepared statement, 124
  interface in driver development, 335
Principal, 24
Proxy Web service, 11

R

Radio button type, 97–98
Realm
  access control lists setup, 24
  groups setup, 24
  lists setup, 24
  resources setup, 26
  security realm, 24
  users setup, 23
Referrer log, 20
Reflection API, 235–242
  function of, 235
  reflection methods, listing of, 236
  as security violation, 237
  ShowClass example, 237–242
Remote invocation. *See* Java Remote
    Invocation Interface (RMI)
Reset input type, 98–99
Resources setup, 26–27
  Access Control List (ACL), 27
  realm, 26
  resource, 26
  scheme, 27
  type, 27
Resource usage screen, 22
Result set interface, driver development,
    324–331
ResultSetMetaData, 163
  interface in driver development, 331–335
Rmiregistry, 354, 357, 360
Root directory, 14
  JRun, 46
ROWID, 139
Row identifier, 139

S

Scheme, resources setup, 27
Secure Web service, 11
Security
  security check, 15
  security control, 23
  security manager, for JRun, 50
  security realm, 23, 24
  and servlets, 2
SELECTED attribute, 102
Select tag, 101–103
  function of, 101
  MULTIPLE attribute, 102
  NAME attribute, 102
  SELECTED attribute, 102
  SIZE attribute, 102
  structure of, 101
Serialization, 207–227
  compared to marshaling, 211–212
  ObjectOutputStream/
      ObjectInputStream, 208–213
  ObjectStreamEcho servlet, 212–213
  pitfalls related to, 208
  purpose of, 207–208
  RemoteIndy tunneling example, 216–227
  TestObjectStream application, 209–211
  tunnel client implementation, 213–215
  tunnel server implementation, 215–216
Server framework, JavaServer architecture,
    8–9
Servers
  products supporting servlets, 5
  as virtual machine, 8–9
  See also Java Web server
Server-side includes, 70–81
  Echo servlet tag example, 72–75
  functions of, 70–71

header and footer example, 76–80
    servlet, 29–30, 71
    servlet tag syntax, 71
Server socket, 8
Service
    definition of, 8
    server socket, 8
Service framework, JavaServer
        architecture, 8
Service tuning setup, 15–17
    capacity, 16
    keep alive, 17
    maximum, 16
    memory cache, 16
    minimum, 16
    timeout, 17
Servicing request, Servlet Connection,
        176–178
Servlet aliasing, 48–49
    function of, 48
Servlet alias setup, 18–19
    alias, 18
    servlet invoked, 18–19
Servlet CGI Development Kit, 5
ServletConfig, 409–410
Servlet Connection
    connection pooling, 170
    database creation, 161–163
    database use, 174
    generic table creation, 163–170
    HTML refresh, 174–176
    login page, 160, 172–174
    servicing request, 176–178
    session tracking, 170–172
    submission of form to server, 160
ServletContext, 411–414

Servlet creation
    invoking with HTML, 40, 41
    properties servlet code listing, 37–39
    server configuration, 39
    writing servlet, 36
ServletException, 415
ServletExec, 5
Servlet Express, 5
ServletGen
    automatic generation example, 242–259
    writing of, 242–259
ServletInputStream, 416–417
Servlet interface, 406–408
Servlet mappings, 46–47
    prefix mappings, 46–47
    suffix mappings, 47
ServletOutputStream, 418–422
ServletRequest, 423–427
ServletResponse, 428–430
Servlets, 4
    actions of, 2
    add-ons supporting servlets, 5
    advantages of, 3–4
    automation of programming. See
        Automating programming
    basic flow within, 2–3, 34–36
    chaining, 54–68
    characteristics of, 3–4
    classes. See Classes in Java servlets
    compared to Common Gateway
        Interface (CGI) scripts, 3
    development kit for, 4
    framework of, 9–10
    functions of, 2, 9
    internal servlets, 9, 28–30
    and Java, 3, 4
    running of, 4–5

Servlets *(cont.)*
 and security, 2
 server products supporting servlets, 5
 servlet chains, 15
 servlet invoked, 18–19
 writing. *See* Servlet creation
Servlets control, 27–28
 arguments, 28
 class file URL, 28
 class name, 38
 description, 27
 load now, 28
 load remotely, 28
 load at startup, 28
 name, 27
Servlet tag
 Echo servlet tag example, 72–75
 syntax, 71
Session tracking
 Servlet Connection, 170–172
 session tracking setup, 15
Setup control, 12
.shtml file, 74–75
SingleThreadModel, 431
Site setup, 14–15
 CGI script directory, 14
 document root directory, 14
 options setting page, 14–15
 welcome files, 14
SIZE attribute, 102
Skeleton, 354–355
 function of, 354
 generation of, 355
Socket, server, 8
SQL
 database table creation, 166–170
 and Java Database Connectivity (JDBC),
  116, 124–125
 statement objects, 124

SQLHelper, 165–168
SQLServlet. *See* Driver development
Statement interface, driver development,
 320–324
Statement objects, 124
Stubs, 354–355
 function of, 354
 generation of, 355
Submit button input type, 99–100
Suffix mappings, 47
Superclasses
 class file structure, 279
 getting list of, 239

T

Tags
 code generator tags, 243, 245
 constant pool tag values, 273–278
 tags processing, 249–250
Templates, automating programming,
 242–244
Tengah Application Server, 5
TestObjectStream, 209–211
Textarea tag, 103–104
 function of, 103
 structure of, 103
This class, class file structure, 279
Timeout, 17
Tunnel client, for serialization, 213–215
Tunneling
 applet, writing of, 204–206
 base tunnel client class, 190–193
 base tunnel servlet class, 195–197
 call on client example, 231–232
 client proxy, writing of, 200–202
 lite tunnel client, 194–195
 lite tunnel server, 197–198

RemoteIndy, serialization example,
    216–227
RemoteMathLite example, 199–207
server implementation example, 233–234
server interface, writing of, 199
server object, writing of, 200
server stub, writing of, 202–203
URL, connecting with, 193
Tunnel server, for serialization, 213–215

U

UnavailableException, 432–434
Uniform Resource Indicator (URI), 138
Uniform Resource Locator (URL), 170
    class file URL, 28
    driver connection, 304, 305, 307
    JDBC connection with, 123
    rmiregistry, 354
    tunneling and connection, 193
Users setup, 23
    security realm, 23

V

Virtual host setup, 19
    document root field, 19
    host field, 19
    multiple host names, 19

W

Web service administration, 12–27
    access control lists setup, 24–26
    file alias setup, 18
    groups setup, 24

installation port, 10
JRun, 45–50
log file setup, 20–21
mime type setup, 20
monitor control, 21–22
network setup, 13
resources setup, 26–27
security control, 23
service tuning setup, 15–17
servlet alias setup, 18–19
servlets control, 27–28
session tracking setup, 15
setup control, 12
site setup, 14–15
user name/password, 10
users setup, 23
virtual host setup, 19
WebSite Professional, 5
Welcome files, 14
Which messages, log file setup, 21
Writing the client, repetition of steps in,
    230–232
Writing the server, repetition of steps in,
    232–234

X

X/Open CLI, 114, 115

Z

ZIP file, 272, 282
    creating new file, 288
    writing to file, 289

ABOUT THE AUTHOR

Karl Moss is a senior member of the Research and Development team at SAS Institute, where he is working with distributed object technologies. In addition, Karl is heavily involved with database access methodologies and was instrumental in the development of the JDBC specification. Before joining SAS Institute, Karl was part of the Data Direct team at INTERSOLV, where he was the sole developer of the JDBC-ODBC Bridge, which now ships with the JDK. Karl is also the co-author of *Java Database Programming with JDBC* (Coriolis). You may contact him via email at karlmoss@mindspring.com.

SOFTWARE AND INFORMATION LICENSE

The software and information on this diskette (collectively referred to as the "Product") are the property of The McGraw-Hill Companies, Inc. ("McGraw-Hill") and are protected by both United States copyright law and international copyright treaty provision. You must treat this Product just like a book, except that you may copy it into a computer to be used and you may make archival copies of the Products for the sole purpose of backing up our software and protecting your investment from loss.

By saying "just like a book," McGraw-Hill means, for example, that the Product may be used by any number of people and may be freely moved from one computer location to another, so long as there is no possibility of the Product (or any part of the Product) being used at one location or on one computer while it is being used at another. Just as a book cannot be read by two different people in two different places at the same time, neither can the Product be used by two different people in two different places at the same time (unless, of course, McGraw-Hill's rights are being violated).

McGraw-Hill reserves the right to alter or modify the contents of the Product at any time.

This agreement is effective until terminated. The Agreement will terminate automatically without notice if you fail to comply with any provisions of this Agreement. In the event of termination by reason of your breach, you will destroy or erase all copies of the Product installed on any computer system or made for backup purposes and shall expunge the Product from your data storage facilities.

LIMITED WARRANTY

McGraw-Hill warrants the physical diskette(s) enclosed herein to be free of defects in materials and workmanship for a period of sixty days from the purchase date. If McGraw-Hill receives written notification within the warranty period of defects in materials or workmanship, and such notification is determined by McGraw-Hill to be correct, McGraw-Hill will replace the defective diskette(s). Send request to:

Customer Service
McGraw-Hill
Gahanna Industrial Park
860 Taylor Station Road
Blacklick, OH 43004-9615

The entire and exclusive liability and remedy for breach of this Limited Warranty shall be limited to replacement of defective diskette(s) and shall not include or extend to any claim for or right to cover any other damages, including but not limited to, loss of profit, data, or use of the software, or special, incidental, or consequential damages or other similar claims, even if McGraw-Hill has been specifically advised as to the possibility of such damages. In no event will McGraw-Hill's liability for any damages to you or any other person ever exceed the lower of suggested list price or actual price paid for the license to use the Product, regardless of any form of the claim.

THE McGRAW-HILL COMPANIES, INC. SPECIFICALLY DISCLAIMS ALL OTHER WARRANTIES, EXPRESS OR IMPLIED, INCLUDING BUT NOT LIMITED TO, ANY IMPLIED WARRANTY OF MERCHANTABILITY OR FITNESS FOR A PARTICULAR PURPOSE. Specifically, McGraw-Hill makes no representation or warranty that the Product is fit for any particular purpose and any implied warranty of merchantability is limited to the sixty day duration of the Limited Warranty covering the physical diskette(s) only (and not the software or in-formation) and is otherwise expressly and specifically disclaimed.

This Limited Warranty gives you specific legal rights; you may have others which may vary from state to state. Some states do not allow the exclusion of incidental or consequential damages, or the limitation on how long an implied warranty lasts, so some of the above may not apply to you.

This Agreement constitutes the entire agreement between the parties relating to use of the Product. The terms of any purchase order shall have no effect on the terms of this Agreement. Failure of McGraw-Hill to insist at any time on strict compliance with this Agreement shall not constitute a waiver of any rights under this Agreement. This Agreement shall be construed and governed in accordance with the laws of New York. If any provision of this Agreement is held to be contrary to law, that provision will be enforced to the maximum extent permissible and the remaining provisions will remain in force and effect.